BASTARDS OF UTOPIA

BASTARDS

LIVING RADICAL POLITICS AFTER SOCIALISM

OF UTOPIA

MAPLE RAZSA

INDIANA UNIVERSITY PRESS   BLOOMINGTON & INDIANAPOLIS

This book is a publication of

Indiana University Press
Office of Scholarly Publishing
Herman B Wells Library 350
1320 East 10th Street
Bloomington, Indiana 47405 USA

iupress.indiana.edu

Library of Congress Cataloging-in-Publication Data

Razsa, Maple.
    Bastards of utopia : living radical politics after socialism / Maple Razsa.
    pages cm. — (Global research studies)
    Includes bibliographical references and index.
    ISBN 978-0-253-01583-9 (cloth : alk. paper) — ISBN 978-0-253-01586-0
(pbk. : alk. paper) — ISBN 978-0-253-01588-4 (ebook) 1. Radicalism—Croatia.
2. Youth—Political activity—Croatia. 3. Youth—Croatia—Attitudes. 4. Anti-
globalization movement—Croatia. 5. Occupy movement—Croatia. 6. Postcommunism—Croatia. 7. Croatia—Politics and government—1990– I. Title.
    HN638.Z9R373 2015
    303.48'4094972—dc23

                                                                2014044169

1 2 3 4 5   20 19 18 17 16 15

Aleksandar "Aco" Todorović (1955–2014)
Founding president of the Association of Erased Citizens of Slovenia

CONTENTS

ACKNOWLEDGMENTS

Spending years with activists who embraced "mutual aid," "copyleft," and "commoning" as core political principles—principles to be put into practice in everyday life whenever possible—made me acutely aware that I have relied on the work of others at every stage of this project. This book certainly could not have been written without the activists I call "Rimi," "Pero," and "Jadranka," or the main "characters" of the feature documentary, Fistra, Dado, and Jelena. Their creativity and commitment mark every page that follows. They shared their lives and activism with me, deeply influenced my analysis with their own, and fundamentally changed what I think of as a life well lived. While these activists bore the brunt of my constant presence and relentless questions, there were many activists in Croatia, Slovenia, and beyond who contributed to this research. They patiently and impatiently corrected my misconceptions. They demonstrated to me time and again that their stories of creative struggle could be a vital resource with which to confront the political crises of our era.

Mindful of my collaborators' safety, not least the constant fear of police surveillance and intervention that marred their lives, I will resist the strong urge to acknowledge the individual activists who have given me so much over the years. I offer instead a partial list of the initiatives, organizations, networks, and movements around which my fieldwork was organized: Abolishing the Borders from Below, the Anarcho-Syndicalist Initiative of Serbia, Antifašistička akcija, Antiratna kampanja Hrvatske, Arkzin, the Belgrade Circle, Balkan Anarchist Bookfair, the DHP Collective, the Association of the Erased, Časopis za kritiko znanosti, Disobedienti, Dosta je ratova!, Dost je!, Fade in, Gmajna, Hrana a ne oružje, IndyMedia Croatia, Invisible Workers of the World, Metelkova, Multimedijalni institut, Occupy Slovenia/15o, People's Global Action, Reciklirano imanje, Rijeka Anarchist Initiative, Social Center Rog, Što čitaš?, Što gledaš?, Take it or Leave it, Tovarna Rog, Tute Bianche, Urad za intervencijo, the Wasp's Nest Collective, Ya Basta!, Zagrebački anarhistički pokret, Zelena akcija, and many others.

There are a few names from "the region" that need not remain shrouded in anonymity and whose contributions to my research—and the richness of my life—I acknowledge with pleasure. In Croatia this includes Igor Bezinović, Boris Buden, Vlatka Blaguš, Teodor Celakoski, Vesna Janković, Hrvoje Jurić, Iva Kraljević, Marcell Mars, Tomislav Medak, Robert Perišić, Dražen Šimleša, Oliver Sertić, and Marko Strpić. During the period of my primary fieldwork in Zagreb, I enjoyed affiliation with the Institute for Ethnology and Folklore. The scholars at IEF were warm hosts throughout, providing assistance, camaraderie, insight, and, on numerous occasions, excessive amounts of regional cuisine. Renata Jambrešić Kirin, who was an informal mentor, helped in ways too numerous too count.

In Slovenia, where the line between friends, colleagues, and comrades is especially blurry, I must mention David Brown, Metod Dolinšek (who is to blame for everything, but will never accept responsibility for anything), Vito Flaker, Aigul Hakimova, Gašper Kralj, Peter Medica, Sara Pistotnik, Armin Salihović, and Darij Zadnikar. Barbara Beznec and Andrej Kurnik, both together and individually, are the embodiment of what it means to make revolutionary struggle a joy and pleasure. While they pursue radical change with all their vitality, they never treat it as a burden to be carried with a sense of guilty obligation. Almost every line in this book is tinged with our discussions over the past dozen years.

This book, as well as the film of the same title, began with my graduate training in the Department of Anthropology at Harvard University. I enjoyed the support and friendship of many across the institution, including mentors, fellow students, and fellow travellers. A very partial list of those who helped keep Harvard's malevolent forces at bay during my years in Cambridge and Somerville: Aaron Bartley, Naor Ben-Yehoyada, Ted Bestor, Elaine Bernard, Eric Beverly, Curtis Brown, Manduhai Buyandelgeriyn, Melissa Caldwell, Steve Caton, Matt Daniels, Ann Falicov, Brett Gustafson, Tracey Heatherington, Yuson Jung, Smita Lahiri, Lilith Mahmud, Thomas Malaby, Benjamin McKean, Vasiliki Neofotistos, Claudio Sopranzetti, Sue Hilditch, Matthew Skomarovsky, Noelle Stout, Lindsay Smith, Ajantha Subramanian, and Kay Warren. Diana Allan and Jessica Mulligan were thoughtful and giving readers of the manuscript-in-progress—and wonderful friends and confidantes. I thank the members of my committee, Mary Steedly and Lucien Taylor. As Director of the Film Study Center, Lucien provided essential moral and material support during the lengthy process of producing the documentary film version of *Bastards of Utopia*. While writing, I enjoyed a year of support from the

Hauser Center for the Nonprofit Organization, at the Kennedy School of Government, and the writerly companionship of Warigia Bowman, Peter Dobkin Hall, Prabha Kotiswaran, Moria Paz, and, in particular, Jonathan Laurence who, among other shared adventures, fled headlong from the Carabinieri through the streets of Genoa with me in 2001.

My greatest scholarly debt is to my advisor and mentor, Michael Herzfeld. Despite considerable efforts on my part, I was unable to find any limits to his support, guidance, and generosity. This is not empty phrasing. Michael held his classes through a megaphone outside Massachusetts Hall in solidarity when I was inside, occupying the president's office as part of a sit-in for living wages for Harvard's cooks and janitors. He was my advocate at the disciplinary hearing that followed. He sheltered (and, of course, fed) me in Rome when I fled Genoa, deeply shaken by the police assault on the G8 protests there. He offered nothing but support as I struggled to balance my commitments to political activism, filmmaking, and the ethnographic tradition. These are not debts that can be repaid; they are gifts.

As will soon be clear, this book cannot be disentangled from the feature and interactive documentaries, also titled *Bastards of Utopia*, which were produced during the same fieldwork on which this book is based. The films, in turn, cannot be disentangled from my years of filmmaking collaboration with Pacho Velez. I thank him for persevering in the face of all the barriers we encountered making *Bastards*. Sever Hall's video editing suites swallowed more of our lives than either of us probably cares to recall. There are too many others to thank for their contributions to the film, but I will try to name some who should not go unnamed: Ernst Karel, Jose Klein, Irene Lusztig, Ross McElwee, Robb Moss, Richard Porton, Benjamina Dolinšek Razsa, and James Razsa.

The interactive—or remixable—version of the documentary was made in close collaboration with a number of talented student research assistants at Colby College, including Scott Wentzell, Milton Guillén, David Murphy and, most especially, Molly Bennett, who, among her many talents, possessed a poet's ear for the telling phrase in my collaborators' banter. Karen Santospago—even when clutching a newborn in one arm—knew which design tweaks were needed to make the documentary intuitive and truly remixable.

Ongoing exchanges with social movement scholar-activists affirmed the importance of this work and helped me hone my arguments. They include Daniel Goldstein, David Graeber, Andrej Grubačić, Ghassan Hage, Michael Hardt, Angelique Haugerud, Brian Holmes, and Catherine Lutz. They also include my four superb (once) anonymous reviewers for Indiana University Press, Luis Fernandez, Jessica Greenberg, Marianne Maeckelbergh, and Jeff Juris. Jeff went above and beyond, in this and many different roles, helping me to navigate the volatile intersection of publishing and activism. Many thanks.

I benefited from two longer reprieves from teaching that allowed me to complete first the film and then the manuscript. I spent as wonderful a year at Amherst College as one can have studying violence and editing *Bastards*. My interlocutors there included Austin Sarat, Mark Doyle, Thomas Dumm, Amy Huber, Dale Hudson, Doreen Lee, Sheetal Majithia, and Leo Zaibert. Chris Dole was a true friend then, and ever since. My retreat to Stockholm University's Department of Social Anthropology for a year allowed me to dedicate the time I needed to writing and make the crucial breakthrough in preparing this manuscript. I learned much from conversations with Gudrun Dahl, Ulf Hannerz, Eva-Maria Hardtmann, Hege Høyer Leivestad, Mark Graham, Beppe Karlsson, Shahram Khosravi, Fernanda Soto, Staffan Löfving, Karin Norman, Erik Nilsson, Juan Velasquez, and Helena Wulff. It was Johanna Gullberg and Johan Lindquist who made the year in Stockholm a pleasure for Benjamina, Milos, and me. Johan has probably made more improvements to this manuscript than anyone else—among his many other acts of friendship.

I was fortunate to carry out this research during a period marked by innovative scholarship on the former Yugoslavia. My analysis of the region was influenced greatly by conversations with Pamela Ballinger, Johanna Bockman, Tone Bringa, Keith Brown, Ellen Bursać, Ana Dević, Chip Gagnon, Eric Gordy, Jessica Greenburg, Bob Hayden, Elissa Helms, Azra Hromadžić, Stef Jansen, Nicole Lindstrom, Ivana Maček, Vjeran Pavlaković, Tanja Petrović, Sabrina Ramet, Paul Stubbs, and Maria Todorova. Drew Gilbert was, as in all things, thoughtful and generous in his reading of my work-in-progress. Dušan Bjelić has left a deep impression on my life, pushing me to conduct research on the Belgrade Circle when I had sworn I would never return to the former Yugoslavia—then pushing me to return to the academy when I felt only slightly more positive about it than war-torn Croatia. My life would be very different, and much worse, without you, Dušan.

I have been very fortunate to find a home at Colby College. The institution has been endlessly supportive of my teaching and research, not least through its capacious travel and research funding. I am sincerely grateful for the flexibility of the college and my colleagues in permitting me three years of leave, including a pre-tenure sabbatical, to complete this book and begin several new research projects. It is my colleagues who make Colby an exceptional scholarly and personal home. There are many anthropology departments at far larger research universities where I would not find interlocuotors like Jeff Anderson, Catherine Besteman, Chandra Bhimull, Mary Beth Mills, David Strohl, and Winifred Tate. The mentorship of Catherine and Mary Beth, as well as my Global Studies colleagues Patrice Franko and Jen Yoder, has gone far beyond what I might have reasonably expected.

I appreciate the determination, thoughtfulness, and sincerity of so many of my students at Colby, especially those in my senior seminars who read earlier versions of these ideas. They pressed me to write in an accessible manner, focusing on the most important social and political stakes of the worlds I was studying. Of particular note were two outstanding research assistants, Amila Emšo and Rachel Gleicher, who worked with me for years on this research and writing. Discussions with other colleagues, such as Lisa Arellano, James Barrett, Ben Fallaw, Peter and Natalie Harris, Walter Hatch, Carleen Mandolfo, Betty Sasaki, Cyrus Shahan, and Julie de Sherbinin, among others, enriched this text and my life in Waterville.

I have been very fortunate to have generous financial support for this project over the years. The International Research and Exchanges Board, with funds provided by the United States Department of State through the Title VIII Program, made possible stints of fieldwork in 2002–2003 and 2011–2012. During graduate study I received funding from the Foreign Language and Area Studies Fellowship, the Truman Scholarship, as well as at Harvard University's Minda de Gunzburg Center for European Studies, the Hauser Center for Nonprofit Organizations, the Davis Center for Russian and Eurasian Studies, the Kokkalis Program for Southeastern Europe, the Weatherhead Center for International Affairs, the Film Study Center, and, most especially, the Department of Anthropology. The Copeland Fellowship at Amherst College and Stockholm University's International Research Collaboration Fellowship supported writing after graduate school. At Colby I have received multiple Interdisciplinary Studies Division Faculty Research Grants for fieldwork and equipment; a Goldfarb Center Visiting Fellowship that allowed Andrej Kurnik to visit campus to further our collaboration; and a pivotal pre-tenure sabbatical. I will always be grateful for this support.

At Indiana University Press, I thank Rebecca Tolen for her guidance in completing this manuscript, Lindsey Alexander for her diligence in correcting many errors and smoothing many rough-hewn passages, and Darja Malcolm-Clarke.

Portions of Chapter 1 and Chapter 3 were published previously as "Beyond 'Riot Porn': Protest Video and the Production of Unruly Political Subjects," *Ethnos: Journal of Anthropology*. Chapter 5 was published previously as "The Occupy Movement in Žižek's hometown: Direct Democracy and a Politics of Becoming" (co-authored with Andrej Kurnik), *American Ethnologist*, Volume 39 Number 2 (May 2012) pp. 238–258. Thanks again to Angelique Haugerud.

Researching and writing this book has required personal sacrifices that have necessarily also affected those closest to me. My friends, especially Chris Colin, Amy Standen, and Jose and Rosa Klein, have been supportive throughout. My brother James read every chapter and asked challenging questions that improved each one markedly. My parents, if always a little skeptical of the apparent scam I was running with a career in the academy, were always encouraging. I am eternally grateful to them for so many things. Here it is appropriate to remember that they accepted and even encouraged my own rebellious and antiauthoritarian tendencies from a young age. This was by no means a painless approach to parenting. Milos Val, my three-year-old son, will be disappointed that Indiana University Press, though generous, did not allow more illustrations. *Bastards of Utopia* is not what he had in mind, I imagine, when he said, with pride, that his dad was writing a book. In any case, I am deeply thankful that he reminds me every day that we humans have deeply rooted proclivities for collaboration and empathy—but that we are also staggeringly open-ended, capable of being many different kinds of people. How can I possibly thank my partner Benjamina? From our first months living together on the Square of the Victims of Fascism, through smuggling videocassettes to her out the rear window of a squatted factory surrounded by riot police, to those long years when it seemed this book would never be written, she was with me through every stage. Benjamina and I are woven together throughout this book and across every aspect of our common life. I would not want it any other way.

This book is dedicated to all the rebellious and unruly subjects who have resisted the imposition of "transition" in the former Yugoslavia, especially Aleksandar "Aco" Todorović (1955–2014). The founding president of the Association of Erased Citizens of Slovenia, Aco never compromised with authority—and he paid a bitter personal price. *Slava padlim borcem!*

GUIDE TO VIEWING
COMPANION VIDEO ONLINE

The book you hold in your hands forms one panel in a broader *Bastards of Utopia* triptych. In addition to this written ethnography, there are two documentary film projects: a traditional feature documentary and an online interactive documentary. Instructions on how to purchase the feature documentary are available at www.bastardsindex.com. The interactive, or "remixable," version of the film—a new form that some have described as a choose-your-own documentary—is tightly integrated with this book and is available free of charge online. The remixable version includes scenes from the feature film, videos shot by local activists, and additional scenes from the two hundred hours of footage my co-director and I shot in the field. Many episodes in the book are direct descriptions of, or are closely related to, scenes in the remixable documentary. Relevant videos are referenced in the book by their title in parentheses, such as (watch "Down with Fortress Europe"). You can access a full list of these videos at www.bastardsindex.com. Simply scroll through the list or use your browser's search function to find the specific video title you would like to watch. This book can stand alone without reference to the parallel video ethnographies, but text and video complement each other and make possible a richness and complexity of representation that remains largely unexplored within anthropology.

BASTARDS OF UTOPIA

INTRODUCTION

In May of 2003 an unruly "bicycle caravan" snarled midday traffic in Zagreb. Before police could respond to the unannounced protest, a few masked activists scarred the façade of the Ministry of Foreign Affairs with antiwar graffiti. Numbering no more than forty, the caravan was the latest in a series of actions protesting Croatia's support for the ongoing U.S.-led invasion of Iraq. Official Croatian support allowed U.S. Defense Secretary Donald Rumsfeld to include Croatia in both the "Coalition of the Willing" and "New Europe"— those compliant once-socialist states he contrasted favorably with the "Old Europe" of (antiwar) France and Germany. Before the caravan could reach the U.S. Embassy, armored Range Rovers blocked its forward progress. Activists bunched together, ringing their bikes to form a flimsy defensive barrier. As a plainclothes officer pointed out whom to arrest, a dozen police in riot gear waded into the small crowd. Soon bulky "RoboCops" were dragging protesters toward a prisoner van. Pero—one of my most important collaborators—was detained (watch "Down with Fortress Europe").

Shortly after his release, I spoke with Pero at his jam-packed apartment. He sat among stacks of silk-screened T-shirts ("No War Between Nations, No Peace Between Classes") and large rolls of "Enough Wars!" campaign posters that read, "We've been through war and we wouldn't wish it on anyone else." Pero reported, "They knew almost everything about me." During his interrogation, police confronted him with a bulging security dossier. They knew Pero was affiliated with the Antifascist Front, the Zagreb Anarchist

Movement, and Food Not Bombs. They knew he played bass in the anarcho-punk band AK47. They even knew he was sleeping with Vanja. At this, Pero smiled slyly and noted, "That is not current information, however, and reflects badly on the capabilities of the state security apparatus." Furthermore, despite all the intelligence gathering, he concluded, "They did not understand anything about my politics." The detective just kept demanding: "What political party are you affiliated with? Who are your leaders? How many of you are Serbs? Which embassy is funding your activities?" "It was," Pero said, "like he thought I was one of those fucking NGO-niks!"

In other words, though Pero is a declared anarchist, the police did not seem to understand that their questions were utterly at odds with the way that he and his fellow activists conceived of their politics: informal, antiauthoritarian, antinationalist, and self-organized. The misguided interrogation reflects more than a police force poorly trained in radical political theory. The fundamental gap between Pero's politics and the police's understanding of that politics highlights the emergence of an activism in the former Yugoslavia with aspirations and practices starkly different from those familiar to the detective. Their radical[1] political commitments made these activists the unanticipated—and unwanted—offspring of the preceding socialist and contemporary neoliberal-nationalist eras.

This narrative ethnography—and the interactive video archive that accompanies it, including scenes like Pero's arrest—embodies the experiences and political imagination of this generation of radical activists in the former Yugoslavia. Following individual participants from the dramatic rise and eclipse of transnational globalization protests in the early 2000s through the Occupy Movement of 2011, the book asks what it means to be a leftist after socialism. In a territory one activist described as the "ground zero of leftism's defeat," activists' responses to this question articulated fundamental critiques of the transition from socialism to market-oriented liberal democracy, including the ambivalent role of NGOs in this transition. This book is also an ethnography of postsocialism in a wider sense, one not limited to "New Europe." The collapse of state socialism, which oriented much of the international left during the twentieth century, precipitated a crisis of radical politics globally. Around the world new movements struggled to fundamentally reimagine radical politics. My collaborators' response was to shun utopian ends and centralized authority of any kind. Instead, they embraced forms of direct action that modeled change "here and now"; experimented with new forms of direct democracy; and devoted much of their energy to developing individual and collective subjects with radical social and political desires. Just a few years before Pero's arrest, I would have been as puzzled as his interrogator to encounter radical activists—especially ones highly critical of NGOs—in what was Yugoslavia. How had activists broken with the dominant rightist politics I had come to expect from the region? How had they developed radical left political sensibilities and desires in such a territory?

The End of Socialism and the Formation of New National States

To explain why I pose these particular questions, and why I look for answers in the specific places I do, I must return to late July 1990 and my arrival in the central Serbian industrial town of Svetozarevo, where I was to spend a year as a high-school exchange student. A relatively modest provincial city of forty thousand, Svetozarevo was best known for its heavy cable factory.[2]

In stubborn reaction to the anti-communism of my U.S. public education, I went to Yugoslavia because I was captivated by socialism. I was convinced—certain in my thin knowledge of Yugoslavia—that the country's relative personal freedom, "socialism with a human face," and "worker self-management," made it preferable to the Soviet satellite states of the Warsaw Pact. I learned my first phrases of what was still, just barely, the unified Serbo-Croatian language—not yet divided into Serbian and Croatian and Bosnian and Montenegrin—on the final leg of the journey, flying from Prague to Belgrade. At age 18, I knew just enough to hope I was going to a socialist utopia.

So I was caught off guard when, shortly after I arrived, images began to flicker across the family television screen of armed Serbs setting up roadblocks and seizing control of rural sections of Croatia, one of the six federal republics that constituted the Socialist Federal Republic of Yugoslavia. Nor did I know how to respond when my host father explained that Serbs were victims of a vast anti-Serbian conspiracy within Yugoslavia. Only when I attended a November rally in the town center, organized by Vuk Drašković's Serbian Movement of Renewal (SPO), did this growing conflict begin to seem like more than a strange abstraction, more than images from somewhere far away.

My classmates from gymnasium skipped school en masse to attend. They translated the promises to defend ethnic Serbs in Croatia to me. They translated the chants: "Vuk: bring the salad, there will be meat—we'll slaughter the Croats!" (*Vuče, daj salate—klaćemo hrvate!*). Some in the crowd waved knives overhead.[3] The massacres did not begin, however, until spring. By the time

I boarded a plane for Frankfurt on July 5, 1991, the country I had grown to love—and, if I am honest, also to hate—was no more. As I flew from Belgrade, fighting was at its peak in the northwestern republic of Slovenia. That first ten-day war, the least destructive of the armed conflicts that marked Yugoslavia's dissolution, was almost over. Croatia, Bosnia, and then Kosovo would follow. More than one hundred thousand would be killed. Millions would be driven from their homes.

Since that year, I have spent a good part of my life trying to grasp what happened to Yugoslavia. I have wondered how I, and others around me, ought to have responded to the crisis. Initially this involved collaboration and research, both in Yugoslavia and abroad, with what is usually called civil society. In 1992, I volunteered with a support and mutual aid network for young conscientious objectors from Yugoslavia who were living illegally in Amsterdam. In 1993, I worked with Veterans for Peace—an antimilitarist organization of U.S. veterans—on a program to evacuate injured Bosnian children to Portland, Maine. The hope was to highlight the human cost of the war for Americans who otherwise experienced the war as a set of images from somewhere far away.

During 1995, I collaborated with and researched the Belgrade Circle, an association of antinationalist intellectuals in Serbia, who, at the height of the Serbian siege of Sarajevo, openly opposed Serbian aggression. Unable to return to Serbia because of international sanctions, in 1996 I headed to Zagreb, Croatia, where I have continued to conduct much of my research ever since. The war had ended only a few months earlier, and the Anti-War Campaign of Croatia was supporting minority Serbs' return to the rural homes from which they had been driven only a year earlier. Throughout these years, I was consistently struck by the courage of those Serbs and Croats who resisted the overwhelmingly dominant logic of ethnic war. They were a small minority swimming against a riptide of nationalist exclusion, sometimes at great personal cost. For the founders and staff of these human-rights and peace organizations—what were collectively known as "civil society," or sometimes more modestly as the "civil scene" (*civilna scena*)—NGOs were the embodiment of all that was hopeful in their societies' politics.

Like many left-leaning ex-Yugoslavs, however, I was dogged by a nagging sense of ineffectiveness during those years. The problem was not only that antiwar initiatives were too weak to prevent the unfolding tragedy. Only the most delusional optimists in the region believed—once the wars had begun in earnest—that they could do much more than set a counterexample. Most felt they could only challenge the widespread belief that *all* Serbs, *all* Croats, or *all* Bosniaks were advocates of war and intolerance. The sense of inadequacy was of a different order. My misgiving was that dissidents often shared fundamental assumptions with the political forces they criticized, even shared some of the key beliefs underpinning the ethnic conflict against which they were deployed.

First, while some dissidents developed unflinching critiques of the dominant politics of nationalist hatred—despite being treated as traitors in their societies' mainstream media—they did not typically challenge the underlying conception of "the people" and "the nation" on whose behalf the nationalists claimed to act. Ironically, critics of nationalism sometimes asserted that the nationalists had betrayed the nation's true interests. In this and other ways, they reinforced the idea that there *were* national interests. Indeed, at times, antinationalists seemed to be an alternative national elite waiting in the wings for their opportunity to rule (Razsa 1996).

Second, most opponents of extreme nationalism, war, and ethnic violence believed that these phenomena were retrograde, primitive, rural, and "Balkan." What was needed, most agreed, was to "return" Croatia to its rightful path toward Europeanization. They blamed the nationalists for their country's isolation from the West. Ironically, most critics shared with most nationalists the sense that their country was, or at least should be, European. Nationalists, for their part, often saw their states as bulwarks against the East, the last wall of defense against a Muslim—or a Muslim and Orthodox—East. In the classic formulation they were *Antemurale Christianitatis*, the protective walls of Christian Europe against the barbarians. I was troubled by how even critics' formulations reinforced the hierarchies implicit in this central opposition between Europe and the Balkans, the very hierarchies around which much of the violence was organized (Todorova 1997; Razsa 1997a, 1997b; Bjelić and Savić 2002; Razsa and Lindstrom 2004).

Anthropologists have long viewed such hierarchies with considerable skepticism (Douglas 1966; Fabian 1983). And with each return to the former Yugoslavia, I was less convinced by explanations of the crisis that drew on a series of related oppositions: Europe/Balkan, West/East, urban/rural, and civilized/primitive. I was becoming increasingly discomfited by Western analyses of the violent dissolution of Yugoslavia as rooted in the innate ethnic hatreds of the Balkans (Kaplan 1993) or their underlying civilizational antagonism (Huntington 1996). Not only was the inherent discrimination of the Europe/Balkan formulations objectionable; such interpretations obscured what was actually taking place in the former Yugoslavia. Rather than attributing it to a Balkan tendency, I was coming to believe that the violence might be better understood as the region's ultimate Europeanization (Žižek 1994:13; Todorova 1996; Razsa 1997a; Hayden 2000; Razsa and Lindstrom 2004). "Ethnic cleansing" was finally and definitively dismantling the multinational, multiconfessional tapestry of Yugoslavia's ethnic inheritance from the Habsburg and the Ottoman empires. Both the federation of republics and the ethnic diversity within each of those republics were being razed in favor of state projects, each with a sovereign nation/people (*narod*) at its center. This was not then the inherent chaos of the Balkans but the supremely modern political logic of the ethnically defined nation-state—a violence that owed more to Herder and Hegel than ancient tribalism (Hayden 2000).

Finally, while I was not nostalgic for Yugoslavia's socialism—any promise that system had offered was thoroughly hollowed out by the time I came to Yugoslavia in 1990[4]—I nonetheless felt a loss associated with the country's dissolution. My nostalgia was not only for the relative ethnic peace of socialist Yugoslavia, though one could not help but view that aspect of Yugoslavia wistfully during the wars of the 1990s. I also felt the loss of the utopian hope that had underwritten the Yugoslav project. From the vantage point of the 1990s and 2000s, it was hard to conceive of a period when some Yugoslavs had imagined themselves masters of their own fate, agents who could remake the world in new, more just ways. But indeed, despite their peripheral Balkan status and largely rural population, Yugoslavs organized the most successful World War II antifascist resistance movement, founded a multinational state despite interethnic bloodletting fomented by Western powers, forged an independent socialist state after breaking with Stalin at the height of his power, and developed a unique worker self-managed economy. In short, I was not specifically nostalgic for the object of Yugoslav socialists' political hopes—the socialist state and economy—but for political hope itself.[5]

In the polarized conditions of 1990s former Yugoslavia, one had starkly and aggressively opposed choices. These choices, however, were highly circumscribed and did not admit to much political hope. One could align oneself with the populist-nationalist party in power or with the marginalized and vilified moderate parties and NGOs that sought to promote the politics and values of Western liberal democracy. Even leaving aside for a moment the constraints imposed by ethnic conflict, the global conditions in which these new states achieved independence curtailed political aspirations. This was not the post-World War II era of newly independent former colonies dreaming of fashioning their own unique paths to modernization and development, the period when Yugoslavia's first president, Josip Broz Tito, founded that central institution of anticolonialism, the Non-Aligned Movement, together with India's first prime minister, Jawaharlal Nehru; Indonesia's first president, Sukarno; Egypt's second president, Gamal Abdel Nasser; and Ghana's first president, Kwame Nkrumah. By the 1990s, socialism was dead, the end of its history declared (Fukuyama 1992). Indeed, perhaps nowhere else on earth was the triumphalism of neoliberalism's market orthodoxy more strident than in Eastern Europe (Eyal 2003). The horizons of political possibility were, therefore, extremely narrow. Those who opposed the wars of Yugoslav succession, insofar as they could muster any hope at all, aspired to approximate the liberal democracies, "rule of law," and market economies of the West.

A New Radical Leftism

These preoccupations—the role of national sovereignty in the dismantling of Yugoslavia, the loss of political hope, the dominance of a single neoliberal model in the postsocialist world—were still very much on my mind when I returned to Croatia in 2001. I wanted to make a film about how contemporary Croats remembered—and, as was more often the case, forgot—the WWII Partisans. The Partisans' antifascist resistance—in many ways the most successful in occupied Europe—had functioned as socialist Yugoslavia's foundational source of legitimacy. I believed, therefore, that current attitudes toward them would provide rich material for understanding how people made sense of both the preceding socialist state order as well as the current nationalist-liberal one.

By late July, I had completed most of the shooting for a documentary film on the Partisans (Razsa 2001)[6] and was immersing myself in archival footage, including the legendary Partisan epics that were the preeminent productions of Yugoslav cinema. When two Croatian friends, left-leaning but never particularly politically active, invited me to what they promised would be an interesting event—a "Noborder Camp"—I was wary of being diverted from my Partisan research. I eventually acquiesced because the camp was only a two-hour drive away, near the intersection of the Hungarian, Slovene, and Croatian borders. I did not know that this camp would serve as a staging ground for the imminent protests against the G8 in Genoa. Nor did I know that I would meet the Slovene and Croatian activists—including Pero—whose deeds, words, and friendship would inspire my research, filmmaking, and activism for the next dozen years. Gathered with a motley assembly in a decrepit socialist-era campground for three days, I found myself surrounded by members of Ya Basta!, an Italian Zapatista support group turned union for the unemployed, an Austrian street theater caravan, a Slovene anarcho-syndicalist union, and Croatian antifascist youth. There were workshops on "migrant rights," "a Europe without borders," and "resistance to neoliberal global capitalism." Activists collaborated in border protests, public education and outreach, civil disobedience training, and theatrical performances outside a detention center for migrants arrested trying to cross into the European Union.

. At the end of this long weekend, I traveled on to Italy with new Croatian acquaintances in their wheezing Yugo—the much maligned Yugoslav automobile export. In Trieste we embarked on the "G8 Express," transporting protesters to the Genoa summit where political leaders from the world's most developed economies were gathering. As the train zigzagged across northern Italy—Monfalcone, Venice, Padua, Milan, Bologna—we stopped to pick up new bands of protesters at each station, many equipped with helmets, homemade armor, and Plexiglas shields. When the Carabinieri, Italy's paramilitary police force, blocked these reinforcements, the train would empty and occupants would sit down on the tracks—effectively closing all lines into the city in which we found ourselves at that moment. The Italians did not return to the G8 Express until their comrades were released and we were permitted to continue on our way. On the train I met dozens of ex-Yugoslavs, a few Serbs, but mostly Croats and Slovenes. A few seemed, like me, stunned by the open, festive, yet confrontational militancy of our Italian hosts, most of whom identified with the Italian tradition of autonomist communism that was hostile to party discipline. But many ex-Yugoslavs squeezed their way through the standing-room-only train, catching up with old friends, sharing stories from recent anticapitalist demonstrations, and debating the relative strengths of the militant tactics of the Black Bloc, more commonly associated with anarchists, and Tutte Bianche (White Overalls), more commonly associated with autonomous Marxists. For the next three days, these travelers would participate in the largest and most militant European protests in a generation. Hundreds of protesters would be beaten and hospitalized. One young Italian—

who, I could not keep myself from thinking, was similar to Pero in many ways—was shot in the head and killed by the Carabinieri.[7] Suddenly the left was tumultuously, disruptively alive (watch "Genova Libera").

Global Postsocialism

For this new generation of activists from the northwest of ex-Yugoslavia, activists of Pero's generation, coming of age in the midst of these militant European protests against neoliberal globalization, civil society had very different associations than it did for those involved in the 1990s antiwar and human-rights organizations. This younger generation saw in NGOs professionalization rather than voluntary initiative; compromising dependence on foreign funding rather than autonomous self-organization; and ritualized, polite expressions of dissent rather than creative direct action. By carefully tracing shifting attitudes toward, and struggles around, civil society, *Bastards of Utopia* offers a critical new understanding of the vicissitudes of postsocialist democratization. While many scholars—like those from the civil scenes in Zagreb and Ljubljana—hail civil society as a prerequisite for any successful transition to democracy (Almond and Verba 1989; Putnam et al. 1993), few scholars have addressed the implicit and explicit critiques emerging from what one young activist termed the "uncivil society" of radical politics: unruly, impolitic, and fundamentally skeptical of regimes of state and national citizenship. As an ethnography of grassroots activism, *Bastards of Utopia* contributes to the critical scholarly reassessment of the Western promotion of "democratization" (Rivkin-Fish 2008; Caldwell 2012; Hemment 2012) and the larger postsocialist "transition" informed by my collaborators' radical political imaginations. Indeed, activists' practices and political sensibilities—including their oft-repeated (and fundamentally anthropological) slogan "Another World is Possible"—were a refutation of the teleological assumptions that structured first socialism, and then the transition from socialism to market democracies (Verdery and Burawoy 1999; Brandtstädter 2007). They were also expressions of fundamental political hope that would have been unimaginable a few years earlier.

This study is also an ethnography of postsocialism in a broader sense, one not limited to those territories once governed by socialist regimes. After all, there were global repercussions when Eastern Europeans dismantled capitalism's primary rival after 1989: the triumphal dominance of "free market capitalism" and a single neoliberal model of development. The political left lost the utopian telos that had oriented it for much of the twentieth century, precipitating a profound crisis of the political imagination (Holloway 2002). This book explores my collaborators' response to this crisis, seen in their experimental efforts to confront local neoliberalization, affirm a distinct vision of social justice, and also reckon critically with the painful revolutionary legacy of state socialism. The struggles of activists in Croatia and Slovenia, the former Yugoslav republics where I conducted most of my fieldwork, were echoed elsewhere—in Mexico (Nash 2001; Holloway 2002), South Africa (Gibson 2006), North America (Graeber 2009), and Western Europe (Juris 2008; Maeckelbergh 2009)—by those movements that were often glossed as the "anti-globalization movement" in the North American press (Friedman 1999). Insofar as globalization stands in for the inevitability of a global market economy (Trouillot 2003) or the rise of global corporate power (Korten 2001), this is not a misnomer. This is the hegemonic notion of globalization, associated with a specific political project—the Washington Consensus promoted by the International Monetary Fund (IMF), World Bank, and U.S. Treasury—which included the promotion of privatization, trade liberalization, deregulation, export-oriented production, and reductions in social expenditures (Williamson 1989).

There are, however, a "plurality of globals that emerge and come to rest in different guises, locales, and performances," (Kahn 2014:14) and the movements with which I collaborated were themselves thoroughly transnational, richly linked to one another across borders. My collaborators traveled to London, Porto Alegre, Chiapas, Barcelona, and more recently Tunis, to participate in and learn from contemporaneous movements. Activists insisted on describing their efforts as "globalization from below," "grassroots globalization," or "alterglobalization."[8] They were, in other words, fundamentally transnational and antinationalist, to a degree I had not observed among the NGOs of the 1990s. So while Khasnabish, not incorrectly, objects to the claimed universality of "global movements," insisting instead that these movements are more accurately described as transnational rather than truly global (2013)—what, after all, is fully global?—I opt to call this the "alterglobalization movement" here. This term acknowledges that there are multiple and conflicting globalizations as well as a subjective aspiration within these movements to transcend national limits, both geographically and ideologically. As I explore in the next chapter, one of the reasons Zagreb activists were drawn to the alterglobalization movement was that it offered them a path beyond what one activist described as the "nationalist claustrophobia" they experienced in Croatia.

Nonetheless, despite the numerous interconnections and parallels among movements, there is a particular urgency—and poetic justice—to listening for local responses to the question of what it means to be a leftist after socialism in a territory that actually experienced state socialism, a socialism that was dismantled with a singular fury in Yugoslavia. Pero's generation of radical activists answered this question by disavowing state power and adopting anti-authoritarian organizational forms. They shifted away from an emphasis on a future utopia and toward a commitment to forms of practice, away from ends and toward means. In particular they embraced direct action, understood as an intervention against existing conditions in a way that prefigures an alternative (cf. Graeber 2002:62). This prefigurative politics often focused on experiments in direct democracy, a trend that only intensified with the recent Occupy encampments (Razsa and Kurnik 2012; Juris and Razsa 2012).

How, one wonders, did this new generation of activists—most only a few years younger than those I met in the peace movement of the 1990s—develop such different political sensibilities? How did they cultivate radical political hopes in the infertile soil of postsocialist and postwar Yugoslavia? Their radical sensibilities were not simply a logical consequence of subscribing to radical ideologies, nor were they the accidental byproducts of activist experience. The cultivation of radical subjects, who not only questioned dominant political trends but also had strong desires to challenge them—who were willing, as Pero was, to face arrest and police beatings—was central to activist politics. In part this emphasis on cultivating radical desires followed from activists' understanding of the political, which they viewed, like many contemporary anthropologists, as permeating every aspect of lived experience rather than remaining a discrete sphere of electoral politics or "affairs of state." Many of my conclusions emerge from the interaction between my anthropological sense of the political and their activist sense of the same. Their commitment to direct action extended beyond confrontations with public authorities, such as those around the bicycle caravan, into the politicization of daily life. Beyond affirming the feminist insight that the personal is political, activist practices implied a subjective turn, in which they sought to intervene in their self-understandings and in the constitution of their very desires (Razsa and Kurnik 2012; Razsa 2012b). The subjective turn embodies what critical theorists Hardt and Negri describe as a counterpower, the alternative production of subjectivity, which not only resists power but also seeks autonomy from it (2009:57).

Put another way, if the Marxist and anticolonial movements of the twentieth century centered on seizing the state—and with it the means of production—my collaborators struggled to seize the means of producing themselves as subjects. Activists' appropriation of technologies and practices of subjectivation is perhaps seen more clearly in a concrete example, such as their use of digital video, in particular their engagement with the footage of physical confrontations with the police they sometimes called "riot porn." In most videos associated with human-rights campaigns, suffering bodies are represented as innocent victims (McLagan 2005). In riot porn, by contrast, activists sought out, watched repeatedly, valorized, and emulated images of insubordinate bodies confronting state violence. In fact, activists in Zagreb watched a series of such videos the morning before they set out on the bicycle caravan that led to Pero's arrest. Whereas biopower, as Foucault formulated it, produces docile bodies (1977), activists explicitly sought to produce unruly bodies, bodies prepared, even desirous, of confrontations like those generated by the bicycle caravan.[9]

Video and *Bastards of Utopia*

Video is more than an empirical and analytical thread woven through this book. I have used the technology to transform my methods, to embed my fieldwork in activist struggles, and to represent my research findings, thus opening a number of productive reciprocities between scholarship and political engagement. *Occupation,* a documentary I produced about a three-week sit-in for living wages for service workers at Harvard University (Razsa and Velez 2002), helped convince activists I could be trusted to participate in and document their activities. And while there was little interest in my ethnographic writing project, filming protests transformed my presence for many of my collaborators into a constructive (and comprehensible) part of activist life. In fact, activists soon demanded that I record most actions—as they did during the bicycle caravan (see figure 0.1). Video, therefore, played a crucial role in my incorporation into daily life and became central to my methodology, as I shot extensive video "field notes." More than a mnemonic device, as images are sometimes reductively understood in anthropology, video profoundly influenced my perception and thinking. Watching and discussing video footage with participants and others proved a revealing way of eliciting reflections on what actions meant locally and transnationally (cf. Cowan

Figure 0.1. The author records as police arrest activists at a Zagreb demonstration against the U.S.-led invasion of Iraq. Zagreb, May 2003.
Photo by Markos.

1990; Herzfeld 2004:92–93).[10] After the bicycle caravan, for example, activists gathered to watch and rewatch—and discuss at length—my footage, asking how the protest appeared to nonparticipants and how they might be more effective in the future.[11] Video is as important to the representation of my fieldwork as written ethnography. Drawing on two hundred hours of video shot over seven years, I codirected and edited *Bastards of Utopia* (Razsa and Velez 2010), about everyday life and radical politics in Zagreb. More subtly, working in video encouraged me to be attentive to forms of observation I might have otherwise neglected. Often, anthropologists listen for the discursive—for our informants' words—to the detriment of our other senses (Taylor 1996).

Working in a visual medium attuned me to dimensions of social life not expressed in language, such as gestures and space, as well as the sensory, affective, and embodied aspects of protest—the very dimensions of activists' video practice, for example, that were crucial in cultivating embodied desires. The conclusions I reach here are deeply indebted to this submersion in visual methods, my own and my collaborators' alike, and indicate that video can transform the sensoria of ethnographers as well as activists. Finally, these video methodologies, and the presence of my own camera, along with those of activists, indicate how my own knowledge production came to be woven into the fabric of activist struggle, reflection, and political articulation. As such, my fieldwork is one example of what has been called "militant research" (Colectivo Situaciones 2003) or "militant ethnography" (Juris 2008), in which the researcher both seeks to study as well as contribute to social struggles. In any case, any knowledge produced by my research emerges from this participation in activist struggles and in dialogue with movement knowledge production.

The integration of text with video also made possible unexpected and distinctive scholarly insights. First, due to my collaboration with filmmaker Pacho Velez, I am present as a "character" in many scenes in the documentary. This means fieldwork itself is opened to observation, an especially compelling and rarely explored form of reflexivity that allows the reader-viewer to consider my ethnographic methods and the specific ethical dilemmas of my fieldwork.[12] Second, anthropologists have produced only a handful of ethnographies and films based on common fieldwork. Especially rare are pairings of a companion book and film organized around the same themes, events, and characters. This means that readers of this ethnography have the opportunity to explore the distinct representational potential and limits of text and video as media.

Working in film also comes with risks, however. The three activists at the center of the feature film *Bastards of Utopia*—Dado, Fistra, and Jelena—obviously had to relinquish anonymity when they agreed to collaborate with Pacho and me to make the documentary because their faces appear and their names are heard throughout the footage (watch "Opening"). They did not make this decision lightly—and there were scenes that were not included in the final cut because they exposed activists to risk of arrest or right-wing vigilante attack. In the interest of protecting those aspects of their lives that Dado, Fistra, and Jelena did not want exposed, while also striving to bring the film and book into close alignment, I have crafted three composite characters, Pero, Rimi, and Jadranka. They share many characteristics with Dado, Fistra, and Jelena respectively, but they also have characteristics and experiences that are drawn from the lives of other activists in the Zagreb scene. In other words, as Dado put it when I discussed this representational strategy: "As long as a cop or a skinhead reading it knows that Pero isn't me, that I didn't do all the stuff you say he does, then it sounds good to me."

An Ethnography of Anarchists

My intensive collaboration with the cluster of Zagreb activists who partici-pated in the making of the film, especially the three main "characters," left a deep impression on my research, even on my world view. Despite the suspi-cion generated by the close police surveillance activists faced, we formed close relationships, and when I returned home to the United States I continued to watch and rewatch the footage of the time I spent with them. In the course of years of editing, I watched some scenes hundreds of times, coming to know every gesture, every phrase, every moment of silence, by heart. So it is not sur-prising that these activists came to figure so prominently in this book. Their prominence is more than a coincidental byproduct of the film, however. Over the course of my fieldwork, these activists influenced the kinds of questions I was asking and therefore the knowledge I generated—and they helped to re-solve an inescapable methodological problem inherent to studying alterglo-balization movements. During my years in the field, I worked with a broad range of activist networks in the northwest of the former Yugoslavia, espe-cially in the activist hubs of Zagreb, Croatia, and Ljubljana, Slovenia. These militant factions, video collectives, NGOs, alternative publishing projects, subcultural scenes, citizens' initiatives, and protest movements were all, in distinctive ways, involved with transnational networking and collaboration. The range and intensity of these flows—that is the networked character of the "movement of movements"—meant that any given activist in Zagreb or Lju-bljana was only one or two degrees of separation from a staggering array of other initiatives. It was this rich connectivity that posed a methodological challenge: Where did the movement begin and end? There was no discern-able center within this nearly boundless web of interconnections. Even within Zagreb, for example, the movement had no definable edge, fading off by de-grees into other domains: free-software development, critical art practice, punk music subculture, new age spiritualties, and, yes, even NGO initiatives.

Other ethnographers of alterglobalization have grappled with the diffi-culty of defining a discrete object of study within geographically dispersed, dynamic, and decentralized networks, and each has developed specific methods appropriate to his or her theoretical, ethnographic, and political concerns. In *Networking Futures*, Juris (2008) approaches this self-consciously globalizing movement from the locally grounded perspective of the activist networks in Barcelona—perennially a key node in the movement. Resisting the tendency to fetishize the network as essentially positive or reify it as an already existing object, Juris's ethnography is a description of the concrete practices "through which decentered networking logics are produced, re-produced, and transformed within particular social, cultural and political contexts" (2008:11). In *The Will of the Many*, Marianne Maeckelbergh also focuses on practices—directly democratic decision-making in her research—but rather than choosing to ground her ethnography in a single location, she follows the practices themselves, crafting a fundamentally transnational field site across movement convergences where these political practices are en-acted, such as counter-summits (2009). While questions of transnational net-working and direct democracy are important to any account of contemporary radicalism, the questions I address are different in emphasis. Namely, how did activists develop radical views, disobedient desires, and unruly sensibilities in a territory dominated by nationalist and right-wing politics? How have ac-tivists rethought what it means to be a leftist after socialism? What enabled the imagining of new political possibilities and the creation of subjects pre-pared to pursue those possibilities? To answer these questions—and to have a strategy to sharpen my attention in the vast complex of interwoven webs of movement activity—I focus closely on the experiences of my key collabo-rators. To be sure, I draw on the spectrum of other activists and movements I encountered during forty-two months of fieldwork in the northwest of the former Yugoslavia between 1996 and 2011 to contextualize the Zagreb scene. My parallel fieldwork in Ljubljana, Slovenia, especially with the activists who organized the Noborder Camps, was an especially important counterpoint to what was happening in Croatia. Primarily, however, I trace the intercon-nections throughout the region by following my Zagreb collaborators as they travel to protests, conferences, and trainings. In addition to Genoa and the Noborder Camps, a number of transnational opportunities presented them-selves during fieldwork: the European Social Forum in Florence, where rep-resentatives from social movements, leftist parties, and NGOs met to discuss continent-wide priorities; the founding congress of the Anarcho-Syndical-ist Initiative of Serbia, which drew activists from throughout the former Yu-goslavia; Eastern European protests in Prague against NATO expansion; and demonstrations against the European Union in Thessaloniki, Greece (watch "War and Sabotage"). I also followed the currents of the movement as they in-tersected with my collaborators' lives in Zagreb as speaking tours they orga-nized or attended; fanzines they read; calls to action they made and heeded; independent videos they watched, screened, and made; visiting activists they hosted; traveling punk bands they promoted; and digital communications they read and wrote. In other words, their subjective experiences are not only a central focus, they also help to form the methodological limit of my research, a means with which to chalk off a segment of the otherwise immeasurable fabric of the alterglobalization movement.

The activists of the "Zagreb scene"—including homeless teens, anarchist punks in their twenties, and activist-researchers in their thirties, forties, and fifties—mostly described themselves as antiauthoritarian leftists of one stripe or another. The Slovenes with whom I worked were largely inspired by the militant legacy and theoretical innovation of *Operaismo* (or Workerism), the autonomous and nonparty Marxist movement that was especially strong in 1970s Italy and was revitalized in the late 1990s and early 2000s. In Croatia, on the contrary, the dissolution of the Socialist Federal Republic of Yugoslavia in the early 1990s was much more violent and the anticommunism more pronounced—any affiliation with Marxism was stigmatized. While anarchism has come to have a powerful grip on the leftist imagination since the end of the Cold War, even usurping the place that Marxism held for the radicals of the 1960s (Epstein 2001; Graeber 2002), it was nonetheless unusual that nearly all of Zagreb's radicals drew on the anarchist tradition (Razsa 2008). As much of this book focuses on the practices of self-declared anarchists like Pero, and because anarchists are among the most misunderstood and vilified of political actors, it is worth dwelling for a moment on what anarchism meant to my collaborators and how it is related to the ideas that animate this book.

Rendering anarchist politics intelligible is complicated by a number of factors, not least a tradition of dismissive scholarship, perhaps even, as some have argued, an inherent antipathy between academic and anarchist practice (Graeber 2004:66). Historical research on anarchist movements, for example in Republican Spain, which many see as the apex of twentieth-century anarchist politics, is symptomatic and echoes many contemporary misreadings of anarchism. Key historians represented Spanish anarchism as highly moralistic in character, even as reflecting a millenarian fanaticism that owed much to the Catholic faith it condemned (Brenan 1950). Similarly, in *Primitive Rebels,* Eric Hobsbawm argues that anarchism was "a form of peasant movement almost incapable of effective adaptation to modern conditions," a rejection of the "evil world" and an embodiment of the "primitivism" and "ritualism" typical of social movements lacking modern forms of party organization and discipline (quoted in Maddox 1995:127). Many who dismiss contemporary anarchism do so in a style that echoes the attitudes of scholars of early anarchism, while also drawing on the rhetoric of market triumphalism. They see anarchists as Luddites and flat-earthers who resist an inevitable economic global order (Friedman 1999:A26). These dismissals of anarchism, I contend, are in part the product of a persistent developmentalism, especially the notion that the state is the ultimate instantiation of modernity and reason (Herzfeld 1987:11–12).[13]

If one can speak of an anarchist movement in Croatia, it consists of perhaps five hundred activists, the majority, though by no means all, of whom are based in Zagreb.[14] There were no formal anarchist organizations—no membership rolls, no registration with the state Office of Associations, none of the foreign, religious, or state funding that sustains the Croatian nongovernmental sector.[15] What did exist was a variety of informal groups, projects, and initiatives that worked on a range of issues: antifascist, anticapitalist, antimilitarist, ecological, feminist, peace, and mutual assistance.

Anarchists in Zagreb would, if asked directly, articulate a utopian vision of anarchism that approximated a dictionary definition. They would describe anarchism as the "abolition of all government and the organization of society on a voluntary, cooperative basis without recourse to force or compulsion" (*Oxford American Dictionary* 2005). Dražen, a Zagreb-based anarchist in his late twenties, contrasted his politics with Marxism, insisting that anarchism was not an ideology for him the way that "Marxism was for most communists."[16] Indeed, as he expressed it in an essay on anarchist politics,

> anarchism as such is not so important to me. Horizontal organization, solidarity, mutual aid, love of freedom for all individuals who respect the freedom of others, tolerance, self-initiative, and other aspects of anarchism . . . present, in fact, a method, a method of everyday behavior and living that I try, more or less successfully, to share with those around me (Šimleša 2005:6).

The focus, with few exceptions, was not then on an eventual utopian telos or on a revolutionary rupture but on a process of riddling the contemporary world with alternative practices.

Politics as practice and process was conceived of as *direktna akcija* (direct action; see figure 0.2). For Zagreb's anarchists, direct action could be stealing the flag from the headquarters of the neofascist Croatian Party of Rights at three in the morning or it could be feeding the homeless with collectively gathered and prepared food (watch "Food Not Bombs"). Again, direct action can be defined as a rejection of a politics that appeals to governments to

Figure 0.2. Patches such as "*Direktna Akcija*" (Direct Action) were popular within the anarcho-punk scene and were often sewn onto the clothing of Zagreb activists.

modify their behavior, in favor of physical intervention against state power in a form that prefigures an alternative (Graeber 2002:62).

Notwithstanding the academic antagonism toward anarchism, one could describe at some length the shared features of anthropology and anarchism. Both emerged in their modern form in opposition to the social Darwinism of the late nineteenth and early twentieth centuries (Kropotkin 1902; Boas 1911). More recently, there have been proposals for the conjoining of anarchism and anthropology (Orgel 2001; Graeber 2004). Indeed, as Graeber points out, anthropologists have long studied tribal societies that maintained order outside the state and could, therefore, be useful in demonstrating the sheer range of human possibilities (2004:16). It is for this reason that anarchists have often "prospected" in the ethnographic record for models of nonstate self-governance and egalitarian social relations (Robinson and Tormey 2012).

For the purposes of this book, two common features of anarchism and anthropology are significant. First, anarchists proved to be particularly compelling collocutors in thinking ethnographically about both neoliberalism and the forms of resistance it engenders. Like anthropologists, anarchists understand the political not as a separate sphere, but as permeating every aspect of social life. In this spirit, I am attentive in this book to activists' efforts to remake daily life through squatting (watch "Jelena's Mess"), scavenging (watch "Perfectly Good Cheese"), graffiti (watch "Honk for Police"), self-education, and the organization of an "autonomous" social and cultural existence. Indeed, more than simply a politicization of everyday life, it is this understanding of power that animates those forms of activism that constitute what I am describing as a subjective turn, in which one of activists' goals is the production of new political subjectivities and new ways of life (Hardt and Negri 2000; 2004).

Second, anthropology and anarchism are dedicated to forms of practice that provide an important corrective to the political and scholarly tendency to treat theory or ideology as somehow more original or transcendent than ordinary practice. *Fieldwork* in anthropology and *direct action* in contemporary radical politics "enforce a dialectic of theory and practice" that sheds light on of the "frail provisionality" of theory and ideology (Herzfeld 1987:x). In short, both anarchism and anthropology, at their best, apprehend social life in an antiessentialist and processual manner, grounding this understanding in the everyday rather than in theoretical/ideological abstraction—another reason for bringing these two traditions into dialogue. That said, anarchists are as vulnerable to the temptations of moral absolutism, reification, and fundamentalism as anthropologists are to their scientific analogues—positivism, empiricism, and scientism. Just as anthropology's effort to overcome ethnocentrism is never complete, anarchism struggles with its own essentialisms, for example, vanguardism and reified conceptions of the state as a mortal enemy. This persistence of essentialism is not a reason to dismiss anarchists as hypocrites any more than it is to dismiss anthropologists. It is rather an opportunity to recognize that anarchism is a human endeavor, embedded in social life, and ripe for ethnographic study and analysis. In the course of my

Figure 0.3. The press made wide use of video recordings that activists shared with them of Pero's arrest, including this series of images and quotations. The excerpt at the center of the article reads: "In the recording it is clear that the police behaved brutally to the protesters as they screamed: This is Croatia!" *Jutarnji list,* May 11, 2003.

fieldwork it also became clear that the anarchist tradition demands critical reflection about anthropological knowledge production.

From Critique to an Affirmation of Alternatives

I have chosen to emphasize rather than conceal the ways my research was conducted within the growing tradition of activist anthropology (Hale 2006; Goldstein 2012, Low and Merry 2010) and militant research (Sukaitis et al. 2007; Juris 2008; Colectivos Situaciones 2009). The synergizing—even dovetailing—of research and activism was clearest during my fieldwork. After all, participating in the daily life of the community we study—in my case, learning about activist life by squatting, meeting, graffiti-writing, scavenging, protesting, and debating—fits squarely within the anthropological tradition of participant observation. Regardless of any synergies, committed participation was a precondition of access to daily life; activists would not have tolerated a nominally objective observer who constantly filmed and questioned them during a period of intense police surveillance and criminalization.

Again, I do not want to hide behind these primarily research-centered arguments: I also tried to find ways for my research to contribute to the struggles I studied. This reciprocity is perhaps most easily seen in activist appropriations of my video recordings. For example, my recordings of Pero's arrest were used extensively by activists, including as evidence against the official on the scene who ordered police intervention. Activists circulated my recordings to key media outlets, highlighting footage that directly contradicted the official's statements to the press about the arrests (see figure 0.3). He was eventually forced to resign when he was proven to have lied to journalists about his role.

The relationship between activism and other aspects of my research, especially academic publishing—including this book—is more ambivalent. Scholarly writing typically rests on individual expertise and authorship, which sit uneasily with activist commitments to antiauthoritarianism and democratic participation, and some would even argue scholarly writing constitutes the privatization of collectively generated knowledge. That academics write predominately for specialized journals and presses—the primary basis for the individual author's professional advancement (cf. Juris and Khasnabish 2013:27–28)—further limits contributions to activist struggles. For these reasons and others, riffing on the classic anarchist slogan of "No Gods, No Masters," the CrimethInc. Collective penned the essay, "No Gods, No Masters Degrees" (2007). Cognizant of these tensions between militant research and scholarly publishing, I have adopted a number of strategies to try to bring the research and representation of my scholarship into a more coherent political alignment. I produced the film, in part, to be sure my research was accessible to a wider audience—and activists have made use of the film in a range of settings.

With an eye to making this book politically relevant—despite my collaborators' complete lack of interest in my publishing plans—I have watched for opportunities to contribute to the tradition of critical anthropological writing on neoliberalism (Comaroff and Comaroff 2000; Ferguson 2006; Ong 2006). Specifically, I draw on activists' interventions in daily life, building on their resistance to develop a locally grounded—though also transnational—critique of what Claus Offe (1991) has termed the "triple transition" of Eastern Europe from state socialism. This includes the formation of new national states from what had been multinational federations, the transition to a market economy, and the transition to democracy.

In chapter 1, "Grassroots Globalization in National Soil," I document how my collaborators embraced anarchist politics following the widespread violence of Croatia's "War of Independence" and in response to the far-right nationalist and neofascist politics that accompanied Croatian state formation. Many of my closest interlocutors, like Rimi and Pero, narrated their politicization, especially their antinationalism, as a direct response to the violence of Croatia's secession from Yugoslavia. They told of Serbian friends hounded from school and older brothers returning from the front lines with chilling stories of atrocities. Some even insisted that their commitment to anarchism—their investment in a politics of organizing beyond and against state authority—derived from these early lessons about the violent nature of the state. They developed an antinationalist subculture in an effort to resist incorporation into the body politic of the nation-state, speaking an ethnically mixed dialect, marking public spaces with alternative meanings, fighting fascist youth, and staging antinationalist rituals.

In a similar spirit of critical anthropology of transition, I turn in chapter 2, "Uncivil Society: NGOs, the Invasion of Iraq, and the Limits of Peaceful Protest," to how Zagreb's anarchists confront "democratization" in postsocialist Croatia. I focus on the local protest campaign sparked by the U.S.-led invasion of Iraq, which was part of the largest international peace movement in history. Particularly revealing were the struggles for control of the Enough Wars! campaign, waged between the radical younger generation and those who came of age politically within the human-rights and peace organizations founded in the 1990s, many of which still received much of their funding from the U.S. These struggles evince much about the nature of civil society's role in democratization and why younger activists were alienated from it. In contrast to the formal institutions of civil society, which are often seen by scholars of democratization as the vital tissue of a democratic culture—and the precondition for successful democratic transition—I explore the contribution to be gleaned from the uncivil society of the younger generation, who are unruly, impolitic, and fundamentally skeptical of regimes of state and national citizenship.

In chapter 4, "'Struggling for What is Not Yet': The Right to the City in Zagreb," I narrate activists' efforts to establish a "Free Store" in a former factory—one of their most direct confrontations with the third of the transitions: marketization and privatization. Returning from major transnational protests with the desire to do more local organizing, a few dozen activists, operating under the name "The Network of Social Solidarity," broke into and occupied, or "squatted," an abandoned factory. They proceeded to clean and renovate the space before opening the Free Store and community center. As the international grocery chain next door made plans to tear down the complex to make room for additional parking, activists saw the space as an ideal one in which to intervene against the commercialization of the urban landscape around them.

While critical insights about neoliberalism generated by activist engagements are central to this book, I have nonetheless come to see critique as having distinct political and theoretical limitations. These limitations have come more sharply into focus in the light of the prolonged global financial crisis, especially with the whole new wave of popular mobilizations it has sparked beginning with the Arab Spring, then continuing with Wisconsin and the Occupy Movement in North America, the antiausterity movement in Europe, and numerous other "global uprisings" from Chile to Israel (Juris and Razsa 2012). The existing order has been challenged in ways not seen since 1968, or even 1848 (Mason 2013). Skepticism of neoliberalism—even capitalism itself—has become widespread, especially across Southern and Eastern Europe, where the crisis has been particularly acute. The crisis of neoliberalism's legitimacy has not, however, ended the crisis of the political imagination I experienced after Yugoslav socialism's collapse: it remains very difficult to imagine an alternative to the present political and economic order. In this context, further critique is inadequate; indeed it may only confirm neoliberalism as the primary frame of reference (Razsa 2013). What is needed instead is the affirmation of alternatives. Throughout this book, I find ways to move beyond what James Ferguson has called a politics of "the antis" (2010:166), a politics which only denounces: antiglobalization, anticolonialism, and antineoliberalism (cf. Rethmann 2013). I tease out the implicit political, social, and economic alternatives embedded in my collaborators' practices. I describe the ways they craft themselves and others as political subjects committed to pursuing these alternatives.

In this affirmative spirit, I not only emphasize the ways that my collaborators, for example, refused the nationalist culture that predominated for years after the war but also show the ways they actively participated in the production of an alternative transnational community. They collaborated in a whole web of initiatives that transcended national borders, not least by borrowing tactics developed elsewhere. Rather than only reject "national culture," activists affirmed a do-it-yourself (DIY) culture. This reflected an understanding of culture as a participatory field of struggle, of culture as a domain for making meaning—and new political subjects. Similarly, my collaborators in Croatia and Slovenia rejected the touchstones of liberal democratization—electoral politics and civil society—and instead struggled to enact direct forms of democracy in the antiwar campaign and in almost every initiative they undertook. Activists not only rejected private property, the central concept of neoliberal transition, they also modeled an alternative form of property by squatting a former factory and transforming it into a social center. In addition to democratic collective management, the Free Store became, for however brief a time, "a common." It was repurposed to serve a social good and reorganized around exchange based on mutual aid rather than profit. It sought the support of the wider neighborhood and city for its defense rather than relying on a legal title, and was open to all who saw its mission as an important one for Zagreb.

As I discuss in chapter 3, "'Feeling the State on Your Own Skin:' Subjective Experiences of Militant Protest," even the most oppositional of practices—the countersummit—prefigured other possible political futures and other social relationships. I describe the experiences of activists participating in large confrontational protests—the most visible public manifestations of the alterglobalization movement—with special attention to the ways that violent encounters with the state affected their interpersonal relations and senses of self. I trace the paths of Jadranka, Pero, and Rimi as they traveled to mass protests against the European Union in Thessaloniki, Greece. I argue that the most physical confrontations were expected by activists, and at times even relished because they confirmed anarchist beliefs in the violent nature of the state. At the moment when the instruments of state violence were turned on protesters—tear gas, rubber bullets, helicopters, and armored vehicles—the state became most palpable; protesters felt the state on their own skin. Experiences of a global movement were also at their most visceral, what one activist called "love at the barricades." These experiences, which generate profound subjective transformation, may have been one of the most overlooked and significant consequences of participating in such collective struggles.

To be clear, a turn to the affirmative does not imply that we surrender our critical faculties—that we simply "romanticize resistance" (Ortner 1995) and ignore the contradictions, limitations, and internal divisions of activist politics. In Thessaloniki, for example, confrontation became so intense that it bordered on civil war, necessitating the secrecy and relative isolation of the most militant activists—who hurled an estimated ten thousand Molotov cocktails at the police. I consider whether the organizational possibility of the "movement of movements"—requiring collaboration among quite different constituencies—may have been compromised at the very moment when its existence seemed most self-evident, when the "us" and "them" of movement and state were at their starkest. What is more, the reference to video footage of confrontational protest as "riot porn" was part of an activist critique, in a feminist register, of the fetishization of violence among activists. Though this footage was used in important ways by activists to prepare themselves emotionally for the "low intensity state terror" (Juris 2008:162) to come, images of political violence nevertheless valorized hegemonic notions of masculinity associated with ideals of physical strength, courage, emotional passivity, and competiveness (Connell 2005; cf. Sian 2005; Razsa 2013).[17] Though most activists, especially on the anarchist scene, understood themselves to be feminists, these gendered tensions persisted within the movement, across a range of interactions and initiatives—including especially between Jadranka and Rimi—and they cropped up repeatedly during my fieldwork.

The fifth chapter, "The Occupy Movement: Direct Democracy and a Politics of Becoming," is based on nine months of new fieldwork, conducted since the documentary film was completed, with, among others, the Slovene activists who organized that first Noborder Camp where I met Pero. The Occupy Movement in Slovenia provides a critical comparative perspective on my earlier research. Whereas activists in Zagreb spoke in prefigurative terms, of "being the change you want to see in the world," those around Occupy Slovenia described engaging in activism so that you would be transformed, so that you would "become other than you now are." Occupy Slovenia activists' self-conscious decision to sidestep political institutions and confront financial ones directly, establishing an encampment in the square in front of the Ljubljana Stock Exchange, echoed other protest movements of 2011 in North Africa, Southern Europe, and North America. They also paralleled other movements in embracing direct democratic methods in response to a perceived crisis of electoral politics. As the name "Occupy Slovenia" as well as activists' preparatory trips to Tunisia and Spain indicate, protesters remained committed to transnational coordination and cooperation. But there were also innovations in activist practice that set Occupy Slovenia apart from contemporaneous campaigns like Occupy Wall Street or the earlier alter-globalization struggles of the 2000s. In particular, activists came to work closely with a range of migrant and minority activists. Rather than striving for ethical purity as Zagreb activists had, activists associated with Occupy Slovenia tried to organize activism so that it would be open to the participation of and transformation by activists with very different experiences than their own.

In conclusion, I reflect at more length on radical politics and the turn from a critical to an affirmative anthropology. I consider the implications of my collaborators' emerging political imaginaries and the practices that embody and sustain them. Crucial to all their efforts has been activists' commitment to direct action and direct democracy, as well as what I describe as the subjective turn—the struggle to develop individual and collective subjects who are antagonistic to dominant social relations and yearn for radical change. In this changing emphasis, we can discern a new terrain of struggle, which extends out from daily practice across the wider social landscape—but at its center is a struggle over the constitution of hopes and desires. Given the continuing crisis of the political imagination, in which, despite years of persistent economic crisis, it seems so difficult to imagine alternatives, I argue that scholars, if they truly wish to contribute politically, must move beyond the critique of neoliberalism and toward the affirmation of political alternatives. My focus here on the affirmative versus critical stakes of scholarship—and more generally the theoretical and political implications of radical activism—should not give the reader the wrong impression, however. This is a narrative ethnography, following closely the lives and political development of a small group of activists, especially Rimi, Pero, and Jadranka, over more than a dozen years as they pursued their hopes and desires within the volatile transnational dynamics of alterglobalization. If this book makes any political contribution whatsoever, it is because they were willing, at great personal cost, to model that other forms of cultural, political, and economic life are possible. They have pushed me, therefore, to return to anthropology at its best: the exploration of other ways of life, ways of life that seem unimaginable from within the current order.

*　*　*

Before you begin to read about activist life in Zagreb—and interventions in the urban landscape of national culture in particular—you might find it fruitful to get a more sensory "feel" for the city. You can experience morning at the central farmers market (watch "Vegetable Central"), get a taste of the less quaint but much vaster Zagreb flea market (watch "Antler Salesman"), tour the city center by funicular and tram (watch "Rails"), or explore the city's periphery of endless high-rise neighborhoods by car (watch "Wheels"), and see the increasingly ubiquitous shopping centers (watch "Big Box Stores Grow like Mushrooms"). In any case, welcome to Zagreb, at least the particular Zagreb that emerges through my collaborators' critical engagement with their city.

CHAPTER ONE

GRASSROOTS GLOBALIZATION
IN NATIONAL SOIL

A nation[al people] without a state is like a shit in the rain.

—FATHER ANTE BAKOVIĆ, FOUNDING HDZ PARTY CONGRESS 1990[1]

The most honest fucking statement I've heard about nationalism
. . . from a fascist. What does that make the Croatian state? The roof
they built over their shit? . . . And where does that leave me?

—PERO UPON READING BAKOVIĆ

Every individual is compelled to find in the transformation of
the imaginary of "his" or "her" people the means to leave it, in
order to communicate with individuals of other peoples with
which he or she shares . . . to some extent, the same future.

—ETIENNE BALIBAR

On May 2, and again on May 3, 1995, rebel ethnic Serbs fired surface-to-sur-
face missiles at Zagreb. Loaded with antipersonnel cluster bombs, each mis-
sile showered more than a hundred thousand deadly steel pellets down on the
city center of Croatia's capital. Several hundred were injured and seven were
killed (Hayden 2012:216–217).[2] A crowded tram was struck only a hundred
meters from Pero's apartment. While Croatia underwent far-reaching social
changes in the wake of state socialism's demise—the wrenching "triple transition" (Offe 1991)—it is the "ethnic violence" that accompanied the transition
to independent statehood for which the former Yugoslavia is known. Unlike

the relatively peaceful dissolution of other multinational socialist states, like the Soviet Union[3] or Czechoslovakia, Yugoslavia was violently dismembered, and there was widespread targeting of civilians. A complete accounting of the historical conditions that made the wars of Yugoslav succession so bloody is beyond the scope of this book. Given how much of the organizing efforts of the alterglobalization movement were directed against the institutions of the Washington Consensus, it is worth noting the significant role of the IMF in the destruction of Yugoslavia. IMF-imposed structural adjustment policies in the 1980s precipitated the first conflicts between the republics of the Socialist Federal Republic of Yugoslavia (SFRY), which emerged over assistance given by more developed republics like Slovenia and Croatia to less developed ones like Macedonia and Bosnia (Woodward 1995). One dynamic, however, charged the reciprocal violence that developed more than any other: competing efforts to found independent nation-states from multinational SFRY. Nationalists in each republic demanded what Thomas Hylland Eriksen has defined as the core belief of nationalism: that "political boundaries should be coterminous with cultural ones" (2010:131). Such demands, always intrinsically violent (Balibar 2002), were especially dangerous in the context of Yugoslavia's remarkably heterogeneous ethnic composition. SFRY inherited kaleidoscopic maps of religious and cultural difference in many areas—legacies of the Habsburg and Ottoman Empires.

Paradoxically, it was the reciprocity of the hatred and violence that led many on the left to claim, as Pero often did, that the Serbian and Croatian nationalists were one another's most essential political allies. This certainly appears to be the case for the respective wartime presidents of Serbia and Croatia, Slobodan Milošević and Franjo Tuđman. The victory of Franjo Tuđman and the HDZ in the first Croatian democratic elections in 1990 would have been unimaginable without the increasingly polarized atmosphere created by the threatening stance of the Slobodan Milošević regime in the neighboring republic of Serbia. Tuđman, with financial backing from extremist elements of the Croatian diaspora in Argentina, the United States, Australia, and especially Canada, promulgated a classically nationalist platform, arguing that multinational Yugoslavia—as a unified state for all South Slavs—was an unnatural imposition; Croatians must have their own state. The election of an avowed Croatian nationalist, who went so far as to claim that the fascist Ustaša regime, which had carried out genocidal policies against Serbs, Jews, Roma, and antifascist Croats during the short existence of the Independent State of Croatia (NDH—*Nezavisna Država Hrvatska*, 1941–1945) was not only a quisling state "but an expression of the political desires of the Croat nation for its own independent state" (Biondich 2004:70). Such statements allowed Milošević, in turn, to claim that Croatia was reviving Croatian fascism and that, therefore, minority Serbs were again in danger and only his strong hand could protect them. Eventually, the partnership in enmity between Milošević and Tuđman moved on to direct and secret agreement to divide the neighboring and ethnically mixed republic of Bosnia at the expense of its largest ethnic constituency: its Muslim population.

Immediately upon election, Tuđman set about realizing Croatians' "millennial desire" for an independent Croatian state. The new constitution he promoted defined Croatia as the state of the Croatian nation (*narod*) (Hayden 2000). While there were still significant portions of the population that saw interethnic coexistence as possible—and preferable—these constituencies were successfully demobilized, intimidated, and silenced by the outbreak of armed conflict (Gagnon 2006), especially once the Serb-dominated Yugoslav People's Army (JNA) intervened militarily to support the seizure of one-third of Croatia's territory by rebellious minority Serbs.[4] By the time Croatia recaptured this territory in 1995—finally realizing the nationalist dream on the ground—Croatia's political climate was overwhelmingly nationalist and xenophobic (Denich 1994; Hayden 1996) and alternatives had been effectively silenced (Gagnon 2006).[5] Even in 2013, one would find wide swaths of the Croatian countryside pockmarked with the shells of Serb homes that were dynamited to ensure Serbs would never return to contested territory. The violent conflict in Croatia serves as an important historical backdrop for this book; it was also the formative political experience for Zagreb's radical activists—including my three key collaborators—who all came of age during the war and its aftermath. To be sure, the war formed them differently than it did activists of an older generation, those who were involved with the Antiwar Movement of Croatia (cf. Bilić 2012), who generally had a more modest agenda, even a relatively depoliticized orientation, as becomes clear when I discuss intergenerational tensions on the left, especially during the campaign against the U.S.-led invasion of Iraq.

In the unlikely conditions of extreme ethnic polarization and hegemonic nationalism, activists in Croatia developed a small yet militant strain of antinationalist expression, initially from within the anarcho-punk subcultures in Pula, Rijeka, and especially Zagreb, sometimes intermingling with other spheres of activism, including antiwar activism and publishing.[6] Incidents like the 1995 rocket attacks aside, Zagreb was spared the generalized shelling that cities like Vinkovci, Vukovar, Slavonski Brod, and Karlovac endured. Developing antinationalism in these cities would have been much more difficult because, as the anthropologist Tone Bringa has demonstrated in Bosnia, it is existential fear more than hatred that accounts for ethnic mobilization (2005:72). As her documentary "We Are All Neighbors" (Granada TV 2003) makes heartbreakingly clear, there is a tipping point beyond which—no matter how strongly one may have supported coexistence previously—one must align with one's own co-nationals if one wants to survive. What is more, as a city of a million residents with the strongest subcultural and activist traditions in Croatia, Zagreb offered, relatively speaking, a hospitable social terrain for political alternatives.

Nonetheless, we should not underestimate how difficult it was in the face of the broader rightward turn in Croatian political culture for activists to develop and personally embody the oppositional practices and alternative desires of this committed antinationalist and antifascist youth culture. Their responses to the nation-state were not only reactive, however. Just as important as activists' critical attitudes toward local nationalisms were the variety of proactively transnational collaborations in which they participated—their "globalization from below" (*globalizacija odozdo)*. These collaborations in alternative publishing and electronic communications, self-education, music distribution and performance, protest organization, and video production afforded them a vivid sense of working to produce different values in themselves and others, of contributing to a global "culture of resistance," and of belonging to a political community—the alterglobalization movement—that stretched far beyond Croatian territory. Antinationalists' alliances, inclusive metaphors of collective action, and agonistic and participatory sense of do-it-yourself culture offer a stark contrast to the exclusionary, homogenous, and traditionalist cultural politics of nationalism. Aside from any political or theoretical contrast, their antinationalist subculture allowed activists to cultivate and sustain values fundamentally at odds with those of the broader society in which they lived.

Antifascist Action in Zagreb: January 12, 2002

Since beginning fieldwork eight months ago, I have regularly filmed activists' public actions, but I have not proposed recording activists' everyday lives—or their more furtive late-night "interventions." In part I have hesitated to in-

trude with my camera on less public aspects of anarchist life for fear of in-
flaming suspicions that I am a spy. On the one hand, this distrust—usually
raised half-jokingly or retroactively admitted by collaborators who said that
they had initially feared I was a spy but now trust me—highlights the skepticism with which Americans are increasingly viewed as the contours of the
Global War on Terror become clearer and the U.S.-led invasion of Iraq appears increasingly imminent. On the other hand, activists' suspicions are evidence of the ways the close surveillance they face from Croatian security services, evident in Pero's post-arrest interrogation, corrode trust and openness
among movement participants.

This particular winter evening is different, however, because Pacho, with
whom I co-produced an earlier documentary (Razsa and Velez 2002), is in
Zagreb for a brief exploratory visit. He wants to see for himself if the local anarchist scene warrants the years of work another feature film will demand—
plus Pero predicted a "night action" (noćna akcija), piquing Pacho's interest.
In the end no one objects to his request to film, so Pacho teases me that I
have "gone native," meaning that I have become unnecessarily paranoid "like
Rimi." He now shoots unobtrusively from the corner of Pero's crowded living room, leaning lightly on a pile of silkscreen frames to stabilize his shot.

Seven activists from *Antifašistička akcija* (Antifascist Action or AFA),
all men in their late teens to midtwenties, are sprawled on a foraged couch or
hunkered down on the floor. Pero's place, sometimes sardonically referred
to as AFA "headquarters" (*generalni štab*)—or derisively as "the boys club"
by some anarcha-feminists[7]—is where activists most often assemble antifascist zines, research, and graffiti stencils, and where they plan their sometimes
more forceful actions against neofascist youth. Pero takes in the banter as he
organizes a heap of papers, discarding old magazines and newspapers, fil-
ing activist publications, fliers, and press releases in AFA's archive of heavy
three-ring binders. His chunky dark-framed glasses, held together with electrical tape on one side, give him a look of disheveled yet thoughtful erudi-
tion. They belie his failure to finish secondary school and the glue sniffing
of his hardest days living on the street. Perhaps giving this background too
much weight, I am sometimes caught off guard by his subtle wit, keen sense
of self-irony, and uncanny knowledge of Zagreb's urban landscape. I never
learn more about the city than when I walk the streets with Pero as he tears
down announcements for religious meetings by the far-right priest Zlatko
Sudac, narrates the history of neglected buildings, sabotages billboards he

Figure 1.1. Rimi silkscreens anti-Bush T-shirts at Pero's apartment. The history of recent European protests is chronicled in the posters papering the walls behind him. *Photo by author.*

deems sexist, and recalls street fights with Zagreb's football hooligans and skinheads.

Pero's years on the street were not the result of a "broken" or abusive home life, as they are for many homeless youth. In fact, Pero is from a stable and relatively wealthy family. Politically and socially conservative, his parents own a successful wholesale ceramic tile firm. In his words, Pero broke off contact for several years beginning at age 15 "because of brutal political fights." He was periodically homeless until a social worker intervened, convincing his parents to allow him to live here in the apartment of his recently deceased grandmother. He now sees his parents for occasional Sunday meals—where his strict vegetarianism is a constant source of conflict.

Vintage brass light fixtures aside, there are few signs that this was once an elderly grandmother's apartment. The space has been "collectivized" and in its decoration—and cleanliness—it feels like many European squats. Radical posters paper the walls. Zines, fliers, CDs, patches, and T-shirts—the sale of which funds their activities—are stacked in every available space (see figure 1.1). While Pero cleans up, Marin and Ljubo debate whether or not to participate in this year's Gay Pride Parade. AFA marched last year during the first Pride, when extreme right elements in the Catholic Church organized a counterdemonstration and successfully disrupted the parade. The howling-mad crowd first threw ashtrays and bottles from nearby cafes. Then two men hurled teargas canisters into the center of the Pride march, "in complete coordination with the police," Rimi insists. With the Social Democrats now leading the ruling coalition in parliament, however, Pride will enjoy substantial police protection this year. Rimi, who is rolling another weak homegrown joint, looks up to declare that he "won't be caught dead with police protection. . . . They would rather beat us than the skins any day. They are just worried about their EU [membership] application."[8]

While much of my attention in the field was drawn to activists' innovative forms of direct action—actions that often generated dramatic clashes, like those with counterdemonstrators at Gay Pride—daily life with my collaborators was by no means always eventful. More often, days passed like this evening, revolving around socializing, chatting, hanging out, even explicitly wasting time together—sometimes referred to as čamanje, an "empty mood, the inability to escape boredom, a state without action" (*Hrvatski enciklopedijski rječnik* 2002). In other words, Pero's prediction of a night action was many dawdling hours ago, and it is seeming increasingly unlikely that this night will generate anything very cinematic. By midnight, Pero is preparing a third round of Turkish coffee—which he insists on calling *kafa,* using the Serbian rather than the properly Croatian *kava*. In fact, those around AFA regularly use a self-conscious mix of Serbian, Bosnian, and Croatian rather than the officially promoted "pure Croatian." Despite the coffee—and perhaps my very American impatience with inactivity[9]—I try to settle into the loose flow of *čamanje*. No sooner have I begun to relax, however, than I am caught off guard by an intense flurry of activity, as so often happens during fieldwork with these militants.

The music is off. Everyone is pulling on jackets and boots. It is three AM and we are on the street before I can hand Pacho a fresh battery for the camera.

Rimi, Pero, and Marin scan the walls with care as we near the most politically charged terrain in Zagreb's urban landscape: the Square of the Victims of Fascism. After the HDZ came to power in 1990, they renamed this intersection of six streets—all converging on a traffic circle around a dramatic columned pavilion,[10] the Square of Croatian Greats (see figure 1.2)—as part of a larger strategy of recasting the urban landscape with nationalist nomenclature. A coalition of human-rights NGOs, younger activists, and the elderly Alliance of Antifascist Fighters (SAB) protested this decision. The participation of the SAB in these annual demonstrations incensed the right because the aging veterans of the successful World War II antifascist resistance fought the quisling Ustaša regime and occupying German forces under Marshal Tito's leadership, helped found SFRY, and enjoyed the status of national heroes during socialism. Rimi described the violent clashes with far-right counterdemonstrations as the first time he had "faced off with fascist trash." When the former communist Social Democrats returned to power in 2000, this square was rededicated to the Victims of Fascism. If the right-left conflict is no longer fought openly here, it is carried on by other means: spray-paint.[11] We find one of Pero's graffiti, "Freedom Begins With the Death of the State," altered to read, "Freedom Begins With the Death of the *Communist* State." "Skinheads (*skinjari*)," Pero mutters, shaking his head. This rightist graffito editing aside, the left appears triumphant in our immediate vicinity: "No war between nations, No peace between classes!"; "We don't recognize national identity!"; "Destroy all nations, your 'own' first"; "Another world is possible"; "Viva Zapata"; "Destroy banks and corporations!" (watch "The Walls Are Our Newspapers" and "The Walls Are Our Sponges").[12] If you did not know that the few dozen activists with whom Pero associates are responsible for nearly

Figure 1.2. The Square of the Victims of Fascism came to be one of the most politicized urban spaces in Zagreb. During the 1990s, there were annual confrontations between antifascists and neofascists over its renaming as The Square of Croatian Great Men. *Photo by author.*

all the anarchist graffiti in town, you might imagine that Zagreb was on the verge of a leftist uprising. You would be sorely mistaken.

Pero drops his voice conspiratorially and we are soon headed west away from the square. I only make out, ". . . it's even rusted in place! It's been there a hundred years and no one's done anything about it!" When we turn off the broader thoroughfare, we are on a quiet street of five-story late-nineteenth- and early-twentieth-century apartment buildings. Rimi looks over his shoulder every few strides and Marin scours the walls for video cameras. Pero keeps his eyes to the ground. The minimal illumination of the few working streetlights is either diffused by Zagreb's chronic winter fog or absorbed by the exhaust-gray façades.

We walk the block twice before Marin is sent to the corner as a lookout. Pero moves decisively to the front of a building adorned with what appears to be a large Croatian flag. Rimi crouches down, hands together, fingers interlaced, so he can offer Pero a foothold and boost him up the wall. Grabbing the bars on the ground-floor window to his left, Pero manages to shimmy his way up, right foot on a drainpipe. The scrape of his puffy jacket on the façade is unbearably loud in the dead quiet. He gets one foot up onto the windowsill to his left and then swings out—spread-eagle—right foot on the next windowsill to his right. Only once he is perched a good two meters above the sidewalk do I see the heavy brass plaque.

While the Croatian Party of Rights (HSP) played a notable role in the nineteenth-century struggle for Croatian statehood (Banac 1988), this is the headquarters of a more recent incarnation of HSP, dating to 1990. A relatively minor far-right party today (with 8 of 151 seats in the Sabor), HSP claimed a 10,000-strong paramilitary force[13] at the beginning of the "Homeland War." Funded by Croatian émigrés in Germany, Canada, Australia, and Argentina,[14] its armed wing openly declared that it would reconquer lands held by the minority Serb uprising, as well as seize large swaths of the neighboring republics of Bosnia and Serbia to create a Greater Croatia on the basis of the borders of the Nazi-backed Independent State of Croatia.[15]

If we were standing in front of HSP headquarters in 1991–92—at the beginning of the war, when Pero and Rimi were in primary school—an action against their building would be unimaginable. Heavily armed troops—including artillery—defended HSP headquarters then. Even at three in the morning, paramilitary units would be coming and going from the "front," which for them extended to Serb-owned apartments in Zagreb's high-rises.[16] The rebirth of the HSP in 1990 was part of a broader societal shift rightward during a period in which Croatians simultaneously fought for independence from Yugoslavia and dismantled their socialist and multinational heritage.[17]

Though the HSP recently moderated its public image in preparation for the 2003 parliamentary election campaign, Pero is not reassured. The footage from this action—Pacho films so closely below Pero's perch that a fine dust from the façade settles visibly onto the camera lens—is the only material from the more than two hundred hours of footage we eventually record while making *Bastards of Utopia* that Pero insists we never show publicly.[18] Pacho, still unfamiliar with the Croatian political landscape, asks why. Pero replies flatly, "They pull out teeth."

Tonight, however, there is no sign of fear. Pero works patiently at the rusted bracket, which holds the HSP party flag that, with its field of red, white, and blue and prominent red-and-white checkerboard, looks much like the national one. Pero pauses only to shift his weight from one leg to the other and to confirm with Marin that no one is coming. After an excruciatingly long minute, he manages to slide the HSP flag from its base and hand it down to Rimi, who pivots and walks off down the sidewalk, flag held close and low. Pero lets himself drop and, without looking back, follows Rimi down the street.[19]

Only when Pero is ten meters away does he turn back toward the camera. With a sly grin, what I take to be an acknowledgement of the "tilting-at-windmills" quality of this *akcija*, Pero raises his right arm in a sweeping gesture of victory, and says, "Here we go!"[20]

The eventual fate of the stolen flag, which I return to below, provides a fuller sense of Pero and his comrades' fierce antinationalism, but this dead-of-night flag theft—which many observers would likely see as an act of mere vandalism—offers a glimpse of the far-reaching political changes Croatia has experienced since the early 1990s as well as a snapshot of the antinationalist sensibilities my collaborators have developed in response. To begin, the activists' night action highlights the dramatic political shift to the right Croatia has undergone and the degree to which the ideological underpinnings of socialist Yugoslavia have been dismantled: from an insistence on interethnic harmony, glossed as "Brotherhood and Unity"; through Serbo-Croatian as a large common linguistic area, cutting across key ethnic fissures; to an emphasis on the WWII Partisan struggle as antifascist resistance, social revolution, and the founding myth of the postwar order. What is more, urban space, holidays, patterns of socializing and residence, key areas in which ruling ideology intersects with the practice of everyday life, have been reorganized, often violently, such that public life came to stress national belonging at every turn (Rihtman-Auguštin 2000:52). Such changes confirm Verdery's claim that state building should always be understood as more than a technical process

> of introducing democratic procedures and methods of electioneering, of forming political parties and nongovernmental organizations, and so on. The "something more" includes meanings, feelings, the sacred, ideas of morality, the nonrational—all ingredients of "legitimacy" or "regime consolidation" (that dry phrase), yet far broader than what analyses employing those terms usually provide (Verdery 1999:25).

Zagreb activists are the most militant resistance to what Krohn-Hansen and Nustad describe as the "cultural revolution" of state formation, which profoundly reorganizes social life across national space (2005), and which local ethnologists have been at the forefront of documenting and analyzing in Croatia.[21] While activists were in no position to challenge nationalism's hegemony, they did manage to resist their own incorporation into the national body politic. First, nationalism sets the bounds of the community for which adherents should be concerned and, concomitantly, those outside the community who can be treated with indifference (Herzfeld 1993). Second, given the ways that it remakes time and space, as seen in the struggles over Zagreb's urban landscape and collective memory, nationalism has cosmological implications, positioning adherents within a national community that stretches far into the past and infinitely into the future. In this way, national belonging promises, like religion, an escape from the limits of individual mortality—which helps explain why the most perceptive scholars of nationalism argue it is analogous to religion (Kapferer 1988; Anderson 1991; Herzfeld 1993). Anderson even argues that it is this implicit promise of immortality, in which one's acts on behalf of the nation serve a larger and perhaps even timeless good, that is the source of people's willingness to die for the homeland (Anderson 1991). Given such implications—and these were not abstractions in Croatia, where mortal sacrifices for the national project were very fresh in everyone's minds—we can see just how high the subjective stakes of activist resistance to nationalist identification were. Understood in relation to this powerful national narrative, Rimi and Pero are contesting nothing less than the moral claim of Croatia on the fate of their souls in the universe.

An encounter with a documentary-programming executive from Croatian national television (HRT) drove home just how fundamentally at odds my collaborators' antipathy to nationalist sentiment was with the broader Croatian political culture. The executive had expressed interest in HRT coproducing *Bastards of Utopia,* so we showed him, among other scenes, the one of Pero stealing the flag from the HSP headquarters (with activists' faces digitally masked to hide their identities). He watched the video intently but he posed only one question: Are they of mixed background? I needed a moment to understand what he meant by "mixed background." He looked pained that I was compelling him to be more explicit: "Are they from [ethnically] mixed marriages? Or are they Serbs?" While there were activists of Serbian "background" involved in radical Zagreb activism, not least because of the welcoming antinationalist culture, all those who participated in stealing the HSP flag happened to be from families that identified as Croat. The TV executive's assumption, however, was that such an action could be motivated, at best by experiences of ethnic exclusion, and at worst by ethnic hostility. Even when I tried to explain their positions, he remained skeptical that this opposition to Croatian nationalism could come from an *antinationalist* rather than a nationalist outlook. While this inability to comprehend activists' oppositional politics reveals much about the wider nationalist consensus, it may also expose something crucial about Rimi and Pero's antinationalism. Their intervention could be interpreted as a failed attempt to communicate across a wide ideological divide, but the ways they discussed the flag indicate that Rimi and Pero did not necessarily intend their theft of the flag as a primarily communicative act. Their night action was, as much as anything, an effort to enact, together with others, antinationalist values—as becomes clearer in the eventual fate of the HSP flag.

Anarchist Punks and Bad Blue Boys

Ten days after the night action at HSP headquarters, I receive Rimi's text on my mobile phone: "AK47 @ Attack tonight." In other words, the band he fronts, in which Pero plays bass, is again performing at the Autonomous Factory of Culture (*Autonomna tvornica kulture*), commonly known as Attack. Tucked in the basement of *Jedinstvo* (Unity), a former vegetable oil factory, wedged between the sprawling HRT television studio complex and the Sava River floodwall, this club has been a center of social, political, and especially musical life for the local anarchist scene since 1998 (Janković and Strpić 2013).[22] The Trnje neighborhood hosts important national institutions—in addition to HRT, the National and University Library is nearby—but it is relatively far from the center, a good half-hour walk from Ban Jelačić Square. What is more, to reach Attack one must navigate a snarl of roads through a mix of "wild building" (*divlje gradnje,* i.e., homes and businesses erected without building permits), older farms with their chicken coops and apple trees, as well as socialist-era high-rise developments.[23] Perhaps such an urban amalgamate is to be expected in a city that was in a constant state of transition for the past century, growing twentyfold (Blau and Rupnik 2007) in successive regimes as varied as the Habsburg Empire; the first Yugoslavia, organized around the Serbian monarchy; the fascist Independent State of Croatia; the Socialist Federal Republic of Yugoslavia; and, finally, the Republic of Croatia. In any case, among activists, Trnje has a reputation of being a dangerous neighborhood, and many punks have stories of violent encounters with skinheads on their way to or from Attack (watch "Pink Star").

On this night we arrive safely at *Jedinstvo,* and make our way to the rear of the hulking industrial structure, down a ramp and through a pair of heavy steel doors into the basement. Miss Helium, a French Basque band, is opening for AK47 with an electronic punk show,[24] and I can make out the chorus, *"Attaque la banque, attaque la banque,"* (Miss Helium 2002) even before I push open the exterior door. Entering the first hall, which houses an infoshop,[25] meeting space, and bar,[26] I see that Rimi has spread his wares along the left wall, beside the bar and opposite a floor-to-ceiling mural of Carlo Giuliani, the protester shot dead in Genoa.[27] Approximately forty people are here taking a break from the high-decibel concert hall. Some recline on salvaged furniture, some crowd around the bar, and five or six cluster around Rimi's *distro*. Hanging above the folding table, on a wire tied taut between two pillars, are his T-shirts, including freshly silk-screened George W. Bush ones, featuring a stigmata on the U.S. president's forehead and the text "World Terrorist." There are neat stacks of anarchist patches, pins, zines, books, fliers, audiocassettes, and music CDs. The English-language publications include an activist video handbook and a brief history of the Black Bloc, a militant protest tactic frequently associated with anarchists (Highleyman 2002), and toward which Rimi and Pero have gravitated when attending large transnational protest mobilizations. There is a large collection of books and zines in the closely related and mutually intelligible languages of Serbian, Croatian, Bosnian, and Montenegrin, known collectively as Serbo-Croatian prior to Yugoslavia's dismemberment. Former Yugoslav bands are also well represented in the CD bins; Rimi regularly organizes tours throughout the region. Almost everything on the table is homemade in accordance with the anarcho-punk DIY ethic. The blurry black-and-white pamphlets and zines are clearly many photocopy generations from their original masters.

Among such conscientiously low-tech items, the CD-ROM "10,700 Political Motifs" stands out. The cover features a grainy image of a masked, black-clad protester facing police lines with a lit Molotov cocked back in his right arm. When I later go through the CD—if nothing else, Rimi appreciates that I am one of his best customers—I find that it contains thousands of posters, photos of punk bands, protests, graffiti, antimarketing or "subvertising," and many short videos.[28] Rimi tells me the CD is part of a fundraising effort by the magazine *Abolishing the Borders From Below* (ABFB), which publishes an eponymous "East European anarchist courier" featuring "scene reports" from anarchist groups throughout once-socialist Europe (see figure 1.3). Since he was able to meet the ABFB editorial collective in person at the November anti-NATO protests in Prague, Rimi expresses a renewed commitment to sustaining the journal. He notes that for political coordi-

Figure 1.3. The cover of *Abolishing the Borders from Below,* an "Anarchist courier from Eastern Europe," features a report on a Polish miners' strike, October 2003.

nation anarchist email lists are far more practical than ABFB, as was clear in the planning that went into the regional anti-NATO demonstrations and countersummit, which protested NATO's admission of much of postsocialist Eastern Europe to the security pact. But, he adds, "for getting a feel for what is happening around the region," ABFB's longer articles and analysis are much better. Funding ABFB is a constant struggle, however, and Rimi is often short the monthly ten-Euro contribution that is an obligation of all those in the editorial collective. But, he notes, this is just part of a "never-ending scramble" to cover activists' costs. This generalized lack of funds often fuels heated debates about the prices of tickets, T-shirts, zines, and audiocassettes (including allegations of "profiting off the movement"), as well as the appropriate allocation of funds raised. Tonight, if Rimi succeeds in covering Miss Helium's travel expenses and free drinks, proceeds from the show will help to defray a 650 kuna ($100) debt from the "Anti-NATO Street Party" three months ago.

Knowing that distro sales and concert proceeds fund a significant portion of activist initiatives, I had assumed they also served as Rimi's primary income. A few weeks ago, however, I had a chance encounter with him outside a local employment office of the Ministry of Labor and Social Welfare. With his black hoodie, patched camouflage pants, and dreadlocks, Rimi stood out among the small crowd of unemployed who were scouring the job listings taped up in the plate-glass windows. He expressed relief that he, along with four other laborers, had received temp assignments unloading trucks for the next few days. As Rimi is more guarded than Pero—and has never invited me to his home, or spoken at great length about his personal life—I was pleased when he also disclosed that his mother, who raised him after his father passed away, has lately been able to secure him shifts operating a forklift for Kraš, her longtime employer and Croatia's largest confectionary.

On Zagreb's western periphery, in the working-class suburb of Špansko where he grew up, Rimi's radical activism, and especially his militant antinationalism, are almost unknown. On the contrary, he describes his neighborhood as "infested" with Bad Blue Boys, the self-described "football hooligan" supporters of Zagreb's Dinamo soccer club. In many ways, such rightist youth (including the skinheads, who recruit heavily within the ranks of the BBB) are the youth subcultures against which AFA defines itself (Perasović 2001; cf. Brentin 2013).[29] After all, the BBB "football firm"—as such clubs are often known among hooligans—takes great pride that it was central to what many see as the opening violence of the Serb-Croat war (Sindbæk 2013). During a match with Red Star Belgrade in May of 1990, BBB fought Serbian supporters (known as *Delije*), who were led by none other than Željko "Arkan" Ražnatović, who would soon become one of the most infamous paramilitary leaders and war criminals of the wars of Yugoslav succession (Bellamy 2000). In recent months, those around AFA have become increasingly anxious that the far right is—in reaction against the center-left government—gathering force as they did in the early 1990s. We chat as people peruse Rimi's table and he tells me that he is especially worried about press reports that skinheads have published a fanzine that explicitly maps the locations of gay bars, Serbian Orthodox churches, Chinese restaurants, and Albanian-owned businesses around Zagreb (*Jutarnji list*, December 28, 2003). Rimi's fears might seem alarmist, but there has been a string of recent assaults by skinheads, including the beating of the eleven-year-old son of an Egyptian diplomat.

As we hear Miss Helium wrap up their show, Rimi hands responsibility for his table to Sabina, his girlfriend of several years, and heads for the stage. Sabina is at the center of Anarchofeminist Action (*Anarhofeministička akcija* or Anfema), which organizes a regular anarcha-feminist reading group in Zagreb and publishes a zine. Lately, with behind-the-scenes help from Rimi, Anfema has organized a series of workshops that are open to women exclusively and teach some of the technical skills of the scene that are often seen as "men's work" (*muški poslovi*), including lighting, sound-mixing, bike repair, and printing. So while some are critical of perceived male chauvinism around Rimi's "boy's club"—and this was not groundless in my experience—it is difficult to read these activists as sexist in any simplistic sense given Rimi's close relationship with Sabina, AFA's participation in the first Gay Pride, and Pero's vigilance in attacking sexist advertising. Given the strong reassertion of patriarchal values that accompanied the nationalist revival in Croatia, and the more general mutual reinforcement of masculinity and nationalism (cf. Aretxaga 1997; Nagel 1998), as well as their upbringing in what almost all described as patriarchal families, it is perhaps not surprising that the divisions and contradictions of gender reemerge, even among activists who nominally espouse feminism.

While Željko warms up on the drums, Rimi, Ante, and Brane don masks: balaclava, Palestinian keffiyeh, and a spare T-shirt respectively. When I ask the band about this practice, Željko explains the symbolism of the mask with reference to "everyone's right to be political without being registered by the police": "The masks remind those in the audience that the police are always present." Ante chimes in that the mask also signals solidarity with militant struggles around the world, including Palestinians and the Zapatistas. Rimi emphasizes a different aspect of "masking up":

> The masks signal that we are all equal within the band. And for pretty similar reasons, the masks confirm our commitment to do-it-yourself culture (*uradi sam kultura*). We're not rock stars and we're not professionals. I don't mean that we don't work hard at what we do, but what I'm trying to explain is, you know, the mask is a symbol of our refusal of any distance between those watching and those performing. Anyone could be doing what we're doing, and they should be.

Standing at the lip of the stage, Rimi turns back to the band and calls for "On the Backs of the People" as the opening number. He then pivots to urge the audience to be more active, to be more involved.

> Some people don't think we have to worry about a few stupid skinheads—well, actually no one denies there are a lot of them—but some people think they are just *marginalci*. Well, that's what people said in 1990 about all those loud patriots who started to call themselves Ustaše and Četniks [Serb ultranationalists]. And they all turned out later to be war criminals, murderers, war profiteers, and mass rapists. So this next song is for all of you who take your antifascism seriously, who take the time to animate Antifascist Action.

These final words are almost drowned out by the rising thunder of Željko's drum intro—and the crowd of 150 stirs in anticipation of the feverish mosh pits that always seem to accompany AK47 concerts. Then another masked man steps up onto the stage and unfurls the HSP flag. Standing impassive in the face of the crowd's excitement, gripping the flagpole at a forty-five-degree angle out over those in the front row, he is a masked public executioner, ax in hand. Then Marin steps out of the crowd. He is so stone-faced that he might as well be masked. He lifts an aerosol can of insecticide in his right hand and a lighter in his left. For a split second there is only aerosol mist—which you can hardly make out in the dark club. Then it ignites in billowing blue-and-orange flame around the HSP flag. The crowd howls approval.[30]

As the flames subside, Rimi doubles over in a stomach spasm of rage, clenching the mic in both hands, white-knuckled. He shreds his vocal chords against the coarse refrain: "Freedom begins with the death of the state, Freedom begins with the death of the state."[31]

* * *

With its physicality, militant flair, theatricality, and its air of politicized underground criminality, the punk scene at Attack—especially when an anarchist band with a strong local following plays—always produced a striking spectacle. But I experienced both the AK47 concert and the earlier AFA action at HSP headquarters against the backdrop of a very different public spectacle, one which put the antifascism and antinationalism of Rimi and Pero's circle into particularly stark relief. Five weeks earlier, I was invited to accompany an old friend—the Zagreb correspondent for *Delo,* the leading Slovene daily—to a concert by far-right singer Marko Perković. Riding the coattails of my friend's press pass, I was admitted to the show as his photographer (I had promised I would share my stills and video with him, so this was not a complete falsehood). Perković, more commonly known as Thompson, takes his stage name from the antique U.S. machine-gun (a.k.a., the Tommy Gun) with which he claims to have defended his Dalmatian hinterland village of Čavoglave from the Serbs. His first hit, an early wartime anthem named for his village, broke mainstream Croatian media taboos (Baker 2010). First, Čavoglave was explicit in its far-right sympathies—the Ustaša salute, "For the Homeland, Ready!" (*za dom spremni*) echoes through the track—at a time when such open neofascism was still seen as detrimental to Croatia's international standing. Second, the song has strong Balkan folk influences, at a time when Croatia's Europeanness was insisted upon, in contrast to the Serbs, who were represented as Eastern, Balkan, and backwards (Razsa and Lindstrom 2004).[32] Although he had fallen into relative obscurity after the war, in late 2002, Thompson enjoyed a notable resurgence in popularity by embracing, and in turn being embraced by, far-right critics of the center-left coalition's cooperation with the International Criminal Tribunal for the former Yugoslavia (ICTY). He explicitly aligned the national tour promoting his new album, *Oh, my people! (E, moje narode!),* with veterans' associations' ongoing protests against the extradition to The Hague of Croatian officers indicted for war crimes.[33] At the opening show in Split, the week before the Zagreb concert I attended, Thompson left two empty seats in the front row, one for General Mirko Norac, awaiting trial in jail, and one for General Ante Gotovina, a fugitive from ICTY prosecution (watch "Heroes and Criminals"). Within a matter of weeks, Thompson appeared to have become one of the most popular domestic performers, selling out Dom športova, Zagreb's largest indoor arena, overnight. The concert felt less like popular entertainment than a fascist political rally. Everywhere I turned, I was confronted with Ustaša insignia, black shirts, Nazi salutes, and chants. In sharp contrast to the anarchists' treatment of the flag, many concertgoers literally wrapped themselves in Croatian, HSP, and Ustaša flags (watch "A Real Croatian Public").

Before the official program began, different neighborhood contingents of Bad Blue Boys initiated competing chants, shouting themselves hoarse in the hope that their slogans would be taken up by the whole thundering crowd of almost ten thousand. In reference to liberal president Stipe Mesić, the crowd chanted "Mesić, you gypsy" (*Mesiću cigane*), which they sometimes alternated with "Mesić, you fag" (*Mesiću pederu*). The Trnje Bad Blue Boys, nearly all shirtless and with shaved heads, just kept starting the same chant over and over: "Kill the Serbs, Kill the Serbs."

* * *

The stark contrast between the anarchist punk scene and wider social attitudes toward national belonging, let alone with the vast audience for Thompson, inevitably provokes the question of how these activists came to see the world so differently—though this question may be impossible to answer with any certainty. Based on my earlier research on the politics of memory, especially the struggle over the WWII Partisan legacy, I had initially hypothesized that attitudes toward Croatian nationalism, especially toward its more overtly fascist articulations, would correspond to family affiliations. As one longtime Croatian friend described this relationship to me: "It depends on who your grandfather was. Did he collaborate with the NDH [fascist puppet state]? Or did he join the Partisan resistance? That decides your attitude toward history most of the time." Rimi, in fact, came from one such squarely antifascist family; his grandfather slipped into the hills to join a Partisan unit in 1942 and later endured seven months in an Ustaša concentration camp. Rimi said his mother's family tie to the WWII struggle was the source of her critical political outlook and antinationalism, and was a reason she was relatively understanding of the iconoclastic positions he staked out. What is more, Rimi said, "I was from the last generation of Yugoslav kids, the last ones to play Partisan and Germans, like you probably played Cowboys and Indians as an American, before all the kids started fighting [Serb] Četniks instead." When Rimi narrated his own political development, however, he deemphasized family traditions and his relationship with this socialist pop culture, which many others stressed as part of deeply ingrained antifascist sensibilities (see Razsa 2001). Instead, he spoke more emotionally about aspects of his own childhood. Rimi spoke, for example, of a Serbian friend from primary school. When the war began in 1991, this friend was hounded from school by threats from some students. "They just kept telling him that, 'this is independent Croatia now,'" Rimi recalled. "'It's not for Serbs like you.'" After repeated death threats and an attack on his father's business, the friend and his family left Croatia. "He just disappeared one day. No good-bye, nothing," Rimi recounted. When asked explicitly about his view of the nationalism, which he saw as the ideology that was used to justify his friend's ostracism, Rimi said,

> [Nationalism] isn't like a normal feeling. How should I explain it to you? It's imagined, you see. It's not like, say, the feeling of solidarity, respect, equality, or love, which a person has inside them. Nationalism is artificially created, promoted through schooling, the legal system, all kinds of ways. It's planted, exercised, so that you feel it.[34]

Many activists spoke of such formative experiences of ethnic hatred, of the everyday forms of violence that accompanied Croatia's secession from the multinational and federal state of Yugoslavia. They told stories of childhood encounters with "Croatian patriotism": someone repeatedly vandalizing the front door of Pero's Serbian neighbor, Jadranka's parents forbidding her to socialize with "those children," Ljubo's older brother returning from the front forever changed. Some activists explicitly attributed their antinationalism, even their view of the state as fundamentally violent and exclusionary, to these early experiences of Croatian state formation. The precise causes of individual ruptures with the dominant politics of the period, however, are difficult to identify with any certainty. Such accounts are retrospective, narrated years after the war, when activists are already deeply involved in antinationalist activism—when they have already reinterpreted social life with the critical tools of anarchism. After all, many Croats witnessed (or participated in) similar ethnically charged hostility, and most became, to varying degrees, committed to the project of national statehood.

It is important to note that for Rimi, and for many of the most militantly antinationalist activists I met in Zagreb, music figured prominently in how he narrated his politicization, the development of his critical sensibility. "I was never willing to just do what I was told, even as a kid," he told me.

> But this was never so political until I was introduced to anarchist punk by a friend. . . . That was before punks even had real places to go to shows. Nineteen ninety-three. In the darkest fucking days of the Tuđman era. He brought me to an air-raid shelter in a friend's apartment block, where we heard Apatridi [re-

putedly the first anarchist punk band in Croatia, dating from 1989]. We squatted *remiza* [a large complex of buildings just west of the city center, an early punk attempt at squatting] not too long after that. But we only held it for a few months before the police organized skinhead attacks to drive us out. They firebombed that squat four times before we gave up on it. It was in those days I started to really listen to the lyrics of bands, first punk classics like Crass, then much less known stuff. [. . .] I was sending blank tapes and postage all over the place, collecting punk from Ukraine, Russia, Boston, Canada, Mexico. [. . .] But when I really started to listen to the lyrics, it just all fell into place. This led me to anarchist zines, then to some of the anarchist classics. I started to make sense of all my anger about what was going on around me. . . . I understood that my friend's terrorization was not some isolated act of childish bullying but was the face of the state (*lice države*). This is the way we see the state in our lives.

Bearing in mind this subcultural facet of his political development, one can better understand why Rimi continues to see his activities at the center of the local punk scene—whether he's producing, distributing, promoting, or playing this music—as "equally important to my more direct political engagement." Similarly, the strong anarchist orientation of the punk scene helps clarify why Rimi did not understand his antinationalism as having roots in the WWII antifascist tradition, organized in large part by the Communist Party, and why he expressed little nostalgia for the Yugoslav socialist legacy— as was more common in the more mainstream, if still vilified, forms of antinationalism that the regime often branded as "Yugonostalgic" (Bošković 2013; cf. Velikonja 2009).

Ironically, despite their disavowal of the kind of Yugonostalgia common among the older generation of antinationalists, this anarchist youth subculture has been more successful than any other social group in the postwar life of the region in producing strong cross-border links—effectively recreating a transnational cultural space among former Yugoslavs.[35] Such transnational collaboration and exchange is one indication that Zagreb activists' antinationalism was based not only on the negation of Croatian national belonging. As Juris and Khasnabish (2013) have argued, the transnational is not simply a scale outside or beyond the national. The transnational, they observe,

is also a space of action and imagination, a new political horizon on which projects for social transformation are arrayed. As a scale that derives meaning, presence, and force from lived processes of articulation, the transnational—

and the possibilities it offers for radical social change—has to be understood as an outcome of lived relationships.

There were a number of ways that activists living in Croatia actively produced relationships that exceeded national borders: through the circulation of punk music and subculture, alternative publishing, DIY consumer goods, and an international anarchist cultural tradition. As we will see below, one resonant way that activists affirmed a positive sense of international community was through direct collaboration with activists across state borders to organize direct action and then take up these tactics at home. This story of how this transnational community was built could be told in different ways with regards to each of these collaborations. Video, however—because of my own intensive involvement, as well as the innovative and rich activist video practices of this period—was especially striking for the ways it, on the one hand, made possible the sharing of modular tactics developed by activists elsewhere and, on the other hand, provided a vivid sense of participating in a larger movement (Razsa 2014).

Video and the Production of a Global Movement

The commercialization of digital video technology in the late 1990s made the production of high-quality moving images affordable and widely accessible for the first time. The subsequent embrace of video by alterglobalization activists—like the contemporaneous boom in new-media activism within human-rights networks (McLagan 2003; Gregory 2007)—depended in large part on realist understandings of the medium. They depended, in other words, on the conviction that "seeing is believing" and that video is therefore uniquely suited to forms of witnessing, documenting, and reporting (McLagan 2003). By the time I arrived in Zagreb, video production, distribution, and consumption were woven thoroughly into the fabric of activist life. Following the skinhead attacks on Gay Pride, for example—when right-wing counterdemonstrators hunted and beat marchers who scattered into side streets to escape the noxious teargas cloud—AFA was able to draw on a range of activist footage to build a dossier of skinheads who led the attacks. These images were then used to plan AFA's "skinhead hunts," clandestine night actions during which neofascists were caught, beaten, and warned to stop their activities in Zagreb. These hunts were, in turn, recorded and shared with AFA activists in Germany, Russia, and Serbia. In a much less confrontational vein, activists from the Bicycle Section of Green Action (*Zelena akcija*) videotaped many

Figure 1.4. The author is conveyed in the Green Action video rickshaw as he records a Critical Mass protest. *Photo by anonymous.*

of their public actions. They even built a rickshaw with a large basket on the front for the specific purpose of conveying a cameraperson. The videographer in this basket was able to record actions, such as Critical Mass, from within the moving cluster of bicyclists (see figure 1.4). The Fade In collective, which emerged from video activism that was initially centered in Attack, produced an extensive catalog of video shorts documenting activist and civil-society initiatives. Fade In had even secured a regular contract to broadcast their productions on HRT following the election of the center-left government.

Reaching such a large and diverse public was, however, extremely rare for activists during this period. The advent of video-hosting services like You-Tube and Vimeo, as well as the popularization of social media like Facebook and Twitter—which made online grassroots video distribution feasible, and which played a highly visible role in the later wave of "global uprisings" in Tunisia, Egypt, Spain, Greece, Israel, Chile, and the U.S.—was still several years off. In short, the democratization of access to the means of video production was not initially accompanied by access to video distribution infrastructure (and in important ways, this remains only partially accessible today). In the spring of 2003, in an effort to address this challenge, free software and alterglobalization activists collaborated to found IndyMedia Croatia, a new node in a global network of participatory journalism collectives that grew from the Independent Media Center first established during the 1999 Seattle protests (Smith 2001; Juris 2005). Croatian activists hoped to use IndyMedia's free software to create an open platform for disseminating user-generated media, including video.[36] While activists already embodied the IndyMedia slogan "be the media" in a variety of text, audio, and video initiatives, most activists did not have the high-speed Internet access to make video uploading and downloading practical on the site. In the absence of such online distribution, activists regularly burned low-resolution copies of videos to CD and mailed them to contacts in the alterglobalization network, much as they had with punk audiocassettes a few years earlier. When Rimi learned that I would be returning briefly to Cambridge, Massachusetts, for example, he asked me to carry package of patches, T-shirts, and VCDs to a Boston-based anarchist punk (who reciprocated with a package for Rimi). Green Action was somewhat more systematic in their distribution efforts, regularly mailing copies of their videos to Undercurrents, a London-based video activist network that, in addition to video trainings and festivals, compiled regular video compilations called "European Newsreels." Undercurrents selected one Green Action video, which they described as "DIY urban planning," for Volume 22. The video documented how Green Action, in the face of the city's failure to address accessibility issues, would destroy sidewalk curbs with a sledgehammer and convert them to handmade bike and wheelchair ramps (watch "DIY Urban Planning"). When I traveled to alterglobalization gatherings elsewhere, international activists were sometimes familiar with the Zagreb scene from these video shorts.

One aspect of these productions stood out, especially in contrast to contemporaneous human-rights media practice: alterglobalization activists had radically decentralized the production of video for the first time. This marked a dramatic shift away from the industrial model of producing film, long dominated by state-owned or major private enterprises, but it also marked a break from radical film practice. To be sure, there is a long and vibrant tradition of experiments in radical filmmaking, in the USSR (Vertov 1929), postcolonial Africa (Gray 2012), and the U.S., from the New Left (Nichols 1980) to the LA Riots (Gaines 1999). These earlier productions, however, were created by a political or artistic vanguard, unlike the video made by my informants. The experience of watching videos such as *This is What Democracy Looks Like*—a film made by the Seattle IndyMedia collective and that draws on footage from more than a hundred media activists (Big Noise 2000)—drives home how different contemporary activist productions are. The viewer finds herself jostling among protesters because the cameraperson was filming from within the crowd. When one watches television coverage of protests, in contrast, one is inserted behind police lines, with profound implications for how one's political sympathies are positioned.

The technological and logistical barriers to sharing activist videos more widely came with one unexpected benefit in the days before social media: viewing typically remained a collective activity, tied to explicitly political gatherings. In Zagreb, as well as Ljubljana, activists had programs of self-education that centered on watching documentaries shot from within activist struggles, videos from Chiapas, Italy, Korea, India, and Brazil. Indeed, "*Subverzije* (Subversions): Evenings of Media Guerilla Warfare and Poetic Terrorism*,*" was one of the most regular and well-attended events in anarchist life in Zagreb. The videos screened in this series served to inform activists about movements elsewhere. Indeed, activists were so well informed about radical movements that they often embarrassed me, a social movement scholar, by knowing U.S.-based movements better than I did. At an early December 2002 Subverzije, for example, nearly fifty people gathered to watch *Argentina in Revolt* (Massproduced Video 2002), which chronicled popular responses to the Argentine financial collapse in December 2001.[37] In the final minutes of *Revolt,* a *piquetero,* a member of one of Argentina's unions of unemployed laborers, burns tires at a barricade on a highway near a refinery. The *piquetero* stares directly into the camera lens, so he stares out of the television screen at the gathered Croatian activists. "I've heard about the protests in Seattle and Genoa against corporate globalization," he says, face smeared with soot, "and I'm part of that struggle." Activists in a smoky room in *Studentski Centar*— a socialist-era student center—stare back.[38] Such experiences offered activists in Zagreb a vivid sense of belonging to a larger movement, of seeing their identification with the alterglobalization mirrored in the *piquetero*'s recognition from more than seven thousand miles away.

As much as it allowed Zagreb activists to become aware of, even knowledgeable about, a broader alterglobalization movement, video also linked activists to concrete forms of direct action. The weekly email announcement for Subverzije implied such a call to action: "The idea of Subverzije is the provocation of the imagination, the realizing of the dreams of utopia such that they become an everyday part of our lives. Discussion, collective reflection, video screenings, presentations, and socializing are what we organize. Everything else is up to you."[39] A January 2004 Subverzija was organized around the visit of Keith McHenry, one of the founders of Food Not Bombs (FNB). He showed a rough cut of a work-in-progress documentary on the history of FNB. Watching the history of the largely anarchist initiative, centered around feeding the public with collectively scavenged and cooked food that would otherwise go to waste, an initiative which dates to the U.S. antinuclear movement of the 1980s, gave activists a distinct sense of how tactics that were a regular feature of protest in Croatia were drawn from a global commons of tactics and creative organizational forms. Watching clips of FNB collectives in Seoul, Berlin, and Mexico City reaffirmed Zagreb's active participation in a global movement. The subsequent discussion also demonstrated that while the tactic has been adopted around the world, it had specific meanings in each locale, in Zagreb's case in relation to the postsocialist transformation of the city's urban landscape, including a growing wave of privatization, deindustrialization, and social stratification.

Sometimes video provided more than a sense of global movement—that is, as a sentiment or idea. Sometimes it also provided a catalyst for further action. It was in August 2002, in the opening weeks of my primary fieldwork, that I encountered the most dramatic and immediate instance of activist video sparking further action. I traveled to Slovenia at the invitation of Barbara and Andrej, who would become two of my most important collaborators. They had organized a gathering of one hundred leftist radicals—Italians, Austrians, Swiss, French, Slovenes, and Croatians—in a former Yugoslav army base only a hundred meters from the Hungarian-Slovene border. Associated with the informal Noborder Network, which demanded complete freedom of movement for human beings, the weeklong camp was one in a broader series of protests at the borders, detention centers, information hubs, and airports that comprise what has been described as the global North's "migration regime" (Jileva 2003).[40] Those associated with the network sought to draw attention to what they perceived as a contradiction at the heart of neoliberal globalization between the mobility developed for goods, services, and capital on the one hand and ever-greater surveillance of and physical control over human movement on the other. In this case, Slovene activists selected Goričko, one of the poorest and most geographically isolated regions of Slovenia. Refugees, "illegal migrants," and asylum seekers were crossing into Goričko from Croatia with ever-increasing frequency even as Slovenia enforced the EU's Schengen migration controls in preparation for accession in 2004. Though I did not yet know him well, I met Pero at the previous year's Noborder Camp in Slovenia, only a few days before we traveled together to Genoa, Italy, and was not surprised to find him at a Noborder Camp again.

As activists in Goričko convened for the final evening of video screenings—which Andrej and Barbara had dubbed "Images of Global Struggle"—they watched *Holiday Camp* (2002). The documentary, shot only two months earlier, showed fifteen hundred demonstrators converging in the remote South Australian desert for a Noborder Camp outside the Woomera Detention Center. Hundreds of inmates began to demonstrate when they realized that there were sympathizers outside. Inspired by the response inside, Noborder campers overran a perimeter fence before pressing through police lines toward the detention center.

The next twelve minutes of *Holiday Camp* feature shots of the physical struggle to liberate detainees. They bring to mind the scenes of activists trying to penetrate temporary security walls thrown up around global summits, scenes we watched in videos earlier in the week, scenes that many of the Noborder campers witnessed firsthand when they participated in the previous year's G8 demonstrations in Genoa. The camera pans from the young, mostly white faces outside to the mostly brown faces inside. Staring at one another through a final barrier of four-meter-long aluminum slats, they chant, "Freedom! Freedom!" Tears streak two Afghani men's faces in a medium close-up; hands clench razor wire and rivulets of blood run down forearms onto bare knees and soak into white tube socks. "We are human too. We are human too," they cry.

From within the detention center, inmates pry the slats apart with steel piping. Immediately police move in, trying to wrest control of the breached area from protesters with a pincer movement. Many demonstrators clutch video cameras as the crowd chants, "The whole world is watching. The whole world is watching." Detainees dive into the waiting arms of the crowd like ardent fans from the stage of a punk concert. Nearly fifty escape into the embraces of the protesters (watch "Through the Wire").

After watching *Holiday Camp,* a young woman in her early twenties asked those assembled in Goričko, "What will we do about the detention camps in *our* midst?" Consensus was quickly reached around the first proposal for action. The campers packed their tents and marched on the Vidunci Center for the Removal of Foreigners. Echoing Woomera, activists chanted, "No border! No nation! Stop deportation!" My video camera was one of a half dozen recording protesters as they ripped up a chain link fence and entered the compound to speak with those imprisoned inside. A video of this action was in turn edited and distributed (watch "Noborder Camping").

To be sure, these video images also had affective, sensory, and bodily dimensions that were crucial to their effects, especially on individual and collective subjectivities. These dimensions of video, which exceed sober and realist assumptions (Nichols 1991) will become clearer when I discuss the politics of direct confrontation with state security forces in chapter 3. It is important to note here that the production and consumption of activist videos made varied contributions to the formation of a militant and transnational movement—through the sharing of tactics, the study of movements elsewhere, the formation of transnational counterpublics, and the experience of participating in a simultaneous if geographically dispersed movement.

Clash of Culture Concepts

In response to the violence that accompanied Croatian state formation—as well as everyday forms of nationalist pressure to conform—activists developed a repertoire of antinationalist interventions. They marked public space with alternate meanings, spoke an "ethnically mixed" dialect, and staged antinationalist rituals, contesting what Balibar describes as "the nationalization of the population," those processes through which individuals are incorporated into the national community (1991:96). Beyond reacting against nationalism, they also produced alternative transnational communities, as was common among activists elsewhere during this period (Cunningham 1999; Juris and Khasnabish 2013). They developed and sustained networks of collaborative production that extended far beyond Croatia's borders and included anarchist punk concerts and tours, DIY publishing, email listservs, websites, trainings, self-education, reciprocal visits, planning meetings, speaking tours, protest mobilizations, and video production and consumption. These collaborations, as well as the enactment of modular tactics like Food Not Bombs, Critical Mass, Noborder Camping, even Antifascist Action—borrowed from elsewhere and often mediated by video images—were particularly important in confirming activists' sense of participating in a common global movement.

This participation was especially salient for radicals given their specific historical predicament in Croatia. Transnational communication and collaboration offered these relatively isolated activists—numbering only a few hundred in Zagreb—a larger, more dynamic, and more potent movement

than they could experience locally. What is more, Renata, a Croatian anarchist in her early twenties who helped coordinate the Goričko Noborder
Camp, stated that by working directly with Austrians, Italians, and Slovenes
to prepare the camp, participants were modeling the kinds of direct voluntary and noncoercive transnational relations that they hoped to achieve on a
larger scale. Finally, for Renata, part of the attraction of these collaborative efforts was the escape they offered from what she described as the claustrophobia of "nationalist conformity" in Croatia. The alterglobalization movement,
in other words, opened for Croatian activists what Deleuze and Guattari have
described as a "line of flight" (1987), a form of politically engaged desertion
from national community that Hardt and Negri have called "exodus" (2000:
213–217).

As an anthropologist, I was struck time and again by another dimension of radical antinationalism in Croatia. At issue was not only a struggle
over the content of Croatian culture—e.g., leftist vs. rightist symbolism in
Zagreb's urban landscape—but a struggle *against* culture as a form, at least
as it was understood by nationalists. I say "as an anthropologist" because, on
the one hand, nationalist articulations of "Croatian culture" seemed to echo
the anthropologically discredited (Gupta and Ferguson 1997; Steedly 1999),
but now broadly popularized (Cowan 2003) concept of culture developed by
early anthropology. Nationalist representations, in other words, shared much
with what Franz Boas and his most influential students, such as Benedict, Sa-
pir, and Kroeber, emphasized: cultures have distinct and incommensurate
forms of life (Kuper 1999:68).[41] The kind of antinationalism that anarchists
practiced, on the other hand, strongly resonated with contemporary anthropological critiques of the Boasian culture concept. Anthropologists now more
often stress that culture must be understood as dynamic, agentic, and histo-
ricized, as a field of struggle (Cowan 2003:67) rather than as a community of
cultural conformity. Anarchist practice embodied this insight and as such
undermined the principle ways that nationalists articulate Croatian national
culture: first, as a unified, exclusive, and organic community and, second, as
the collective inheritance of this community, that is, its material and imma-
terial patrimony embodied in particular shared language, values, heritage,
and traditions.

With regards to the first idea, nationalists represented Croatia as a unified, territorially bounded, and exclusive community—as if it were a natural
organism existing on a different (higher) plane than individual life and experience.[42] With its common origins and corporeal unity, the nation was a

political project fundamentally based on what Deleuze and Guattari (1987) critically describe as the arborescent metaphors of roots and origins, solid identities (trunks), and a known utopian telos (flowers and fruit) (cf. Malkki 1992). Just such a reification and objectification of national being—that is, understanding the nation as a unified being—was enshrined in the 1990 constitution, in which Croatia was defined as the state of the Croatian nation (*narod*) with a strong ethnic connotation that excludes those who are not ethnically Croat (Hayden 2000:70). These ideas of national culture—and the nation as the ultimate sovereign—rendered minority populations "foreign objects" within the body politic, easily portrayed, in Mary Douglas's terms, as filth, as human "matter out of place," (Douglas 1966; Hayden 1996). With such an objectified and naturalized framing of national culture as an organism, it is not surprising that "ethnic cleansing" is one of the most important contributions Yugoslavia's violent dissolution made to the global lexicon.

The alterglobalization movement, in contrast, was understood by participants to be fundamentally plural, deterritorialized, and open. Its metaphors of collective subjectivity were internally diverse—the network, the movement of movements, the multitude. It encompassed Zagreb anarchist punks, Western direct activists, unemployed Argentines, South African shantytown dwellers, and Mexican indigenous peasants. Those in the alterglobalization movement often spoke of "grassroots movements" or even "grassroots globalization" (Routledge 2003; cf. Appadurai 2000). The metaphor of "grassroots" is salient because it is bottom up, its standard implication, and the one activists most often stressed, in contrast with elite-driven "globalization from above." The root structure of grass also exemplifies biological rhizomes, the very form which Deleuze and Guattari affirm for its fundamental multiplicity, in contradistinction to the unity of the arborescent (1987:6–27). Grass has a rhizomatic structure; it expands underground horizontally, sending down roots and pushing up shoots that arise and proliferate not from a single core or trunk, but from a network which expands endlessly from any of its points (Mansfield 2000:143). While much of social life, including for nationalists, is probably more rhizomatic than arboreal, contemporary radical movements, especially anarchist ones, cultivate the rhizomatic in a self-conscious manner, preferring decentralized and horizontal forms to centralized and vertical ones (Juris 2008). But the antinationalist struggle against the nationalist concept of culture is not limited to the question of inclusive versus exclusive metaphors of community.

Antinationalists also contested the nationalist understanding of culture, as the shared, unchanging, and uncontested collective heritage of a distinct people, i.e., their customs, values, arts, traditions, language, and institutions. Nationalists represented Croatian culture as internally integrated and long-standing. For antinationalists, in contrast, culture was a field of struggle, as it was now understood by many anthropologists (Cowan et al. 2001). To be sure, there was some emphasis on, for example, the anarchist cultural inheritance, seen in the classic literature of Rimi's distro or the songs of revolutionary Spain sung by the ABFB editorial collective when they met in Prague. When activists spoke of culture, however, they were much more likely to emphasize DIY culture, broadly construed. In the musical and zine culture of the anarcho-punk scene, the participatory media production of contemporary video practice, and the prefigurative politics of direct action, this was a sense of culture not as an uncritically accepted heritage, but a space of active engagement. This DIY sense of culture resonated with that developed by anthropologists of indigenous media, especially those who have collaborated with community efforts to obtain and adapt video technologies to their own needs. Terrence Turner, for example, claims that video was a key technology through which the Kayapo of the Brazilian Amazon asserted control over the conditions of their reproduction as a people (1992). This is culture not as a conformity to one's own culture, as a shared code, but as a capacity for culture, a fundamental human capability to generate difference in collaboration with others (Turner 1997; Boyer 2006). DIY culture, so conceived, is a field of human activity in which one works to make and remake oneself and others through collective action.

I could end on such an affirmative, even self-congratulatory, note, in which Zagreb activists and contemporary anthropologists fight together, in (theoretical) alliance, against nationalist hatred and exclusion. Activists' remarks, and actions, sometimes indicated that they found themselves in a more complex predicament. The global was not always experienced as a dimension of libratory escape (Juris and Khasnabish 2013) and tradition was not always equated with the political right. What is more, the extreme polarization described in this chapter—in which activists felt they were living in fundamentally hostile territory—also served to cut off Zagreb's radicals from their neighbors by reinforcing some of their isolationist and identitarian tendencies and therefore precluding the possibility of a stronger and more inclusive movement.

While activists usually spoke about how much they gained from links to movements elsewhere, even sometimes referring to a "global commons" of movement ideas, tactics, and images, there were also times when activists expressed frustration that so much—nearly all, in fact—of what activists did in Zagreb was borrowed. One Slovene activist, describing the similar experience of activists in Ljubljana, lamented what he termed "franchising from below." In a longer conversation with Marko—an experienced Zagreb activist in his midthirties—about why such global activist "franchising" predominated, why there was not more effort to reclaim local traditions of resistance, he answered in a way that was echoed in many conversations.

> Almost every [older] radical tradition here has been discredited by its co-optation, and abuse, by the previous regime. The communists claimed that everything was "proto-communist," even the peasant uprisings hundreds of years before Marx's birth! So when you try to draw on these traditions now, it sounds like you're a communist, like you're nostalgic for the previous regime. You know, it sounds like you are naïve enough to believe what they taught you in their schools.

There was also sometimes resentment alongside respect for Western activists, who had experience with vibrant movements but worked in much less isolated, impoverished, and dangerous conditions (watch "Not Cool").

Finally, if activists understood their own cultural production as thoroughly open, internally diverse, and contested, they certainly did not usually see mainstream Croatian society in this way: Croatian nationalism was monolithic, unified, and almost universally contemptible in the eyes of radicals—understandably perhaps, given recent history. Ironically then, given what I have argued above, anarchists were often at their most subcultural, identitarian, and rigid when describing the dominant culture, or when they viewed the Croatian state as their tangible and mortal enemy. Such positions ensured that they would be widely alienated from many of their neighbors. For example, anarchists, despite numerous attempts, were never able to forge alliances with workers, even during wildcat factory occupations, because they could not stomach the nationalist rhetoric that workers so often adopted in an effort to lay claim to public legitimacy. Given the extremity of the nationalist terrain in which activists worked—and the ambitions they had for cultivating radically different values in this inhospitable soil—such Manichean tendencies were probably almost impossible to avoid but they had very detrimental consequences.

In 1990, a few weeks before the nationalists swept to power, ending forty-five years of Communist Party rule, it might have still been possible for them to see themselves in danger of being washed away, "like a shit in the rain" (*kao govno na kiši*), as the colorful Croatian saying has it. By the early 2000s, however, targeted by the police as well as by the extralegal violence of the far right—and often abandoned by the most important NGOs, as became clearer in the lead-up to the U.S.-led invasion of Iraq—it was the anarchists who felt, as Pero expressed it, "like those who are really left out in the gutter in a downpour."

CHAPTER TWO

UNCIVIL SOCIETY:
NGOs, THE INVASION OF IRAQ, AND THE
LIMITS OF POLITE PROTEST

Divisive Beginnings

Ante and Nina sit behind the small rectangular table reserved for lecturers at the front of the public hall of the United Nations Human Rights Centre. They outline plans for a Zagreb march to coincide with the February 15 (F15) "global day of action" against the impending U.S.-led invasion of Iraq. When we go around the room and introduce ourselves, I learn that the audience includes representatives from a Karlovac human-rights organization active in advocating for the return of Serbian displaced persons in the Krajina; several women from Be Active, Be Emancipated (B.a.B.e), a women's rights group; a law student from Center for Peace Studies who often advises Zagreb's anarchists on legal issues; two activists who work as programmers for ZaMir, a pan-Yugoslav electronic communications service dating to the 1990s peace movement that has recently been converted into a for-profit Internet service and content provider;[1] as well as several generations of anarchist activists. Marija, Branimir, and Ljubo, in their thirties, helped organize the Another World is Possible campaign (*Drugačiji svijet je moguć*), and represent the older generation in the front row. I am surprised to see younger generations also present. Rimi and Pero are slumped sullenly in folding chairs at the rear of the room. When Ante and Nina's invitation—sent to a range of activist, civil society, and political listservs—arrived in Rimi's inbox, he had looked up from the dusty desktop where he does most of his zine publishing and design. "Those two?" he asked, turning to Pero. With a long, exasperated whistle, he added, "I am so fucking tired of dealing with NGO types and their polite protests."[2] Jadranka is also here tonight, but this comes as less of a surprise. She responded enthusiastically to the invitation to plan a Zagreb F15 protest. In fact, I first met her four months ago on an international NGO-sponsored bus carrying former Yugoslavs to the European Social Forum (ESF) meetings in Florence—the very meetings that generated the F15 plans. Though she wears a Palestinian keffiyeh as a scarf tonight, Jadranka is usually less readily identified with the anarchist-punk subculture than Rimi or Pero. What is more, she is critical of what she describes as "isolationist" and "subcultural" tendencies in the alterglobalization movement, including in Rimi and Pero's circle. Instead, she cultivates a broad network of contacts among artists, intellectuals, and NGOs. Only twenty, she has already traveled to protests and activist gatherings in Brazil, North Africa, and Western Europe. Rimi and Pero have shunned the World Social Forum (WSF) in favor of more militant, antiauthoritarian, and directly democratic People's Global Action events. Jadranka, in contrast, has attended various continental, national, and local variants of the Social Forum process, which represents one of the broader and more inclusive strands of the alterglobalization movement. Despite tensions, this process has produced fora in which radical activists often commingle with more mainstream NGOs and left political parties (see Juris 2008).[3] In recent months, in part due to her transnational experience, Jadranka has also become one of the more widely recognizable faces of radical politics in Croatia. The media are drawn to what one male TV producer described to me as her "open and attractive character," and she has been featured in several newspaper stories and even a recent documentary short on national television.

In Florence, the war had seemed far off and avoidable; now it is increasingly clear that the U.S. is intent on invading Iraq—with or without UN Security Council approval. This impending invasion—and the U.S. government as a common target of abuse—have not unified Zagreb's activist scene, however. Arguments break out even before tonight's meeting is called to order. Rimi confronts Ante and Nina about what he sees as the implicit hierarchy of the seating arrangement: "You people stand there at the front and lecture us while we are supposed to sit obediently [in the audience] accepting another one of your plans to politely register your disapproval?" Then, contrasting their approach with the organization of the 2002 anti-NATO campaign, which opposed Croatia's membership in the Euro-American military alliance, he adds, "When *we* organize a meeting, we do so with respect and equality for those who attend." By the end of the first cigarette break, Rimi and many of the younger anarchists leave, intent on organizing a more militant response to the imminent war in the Middle East.

When I catch up with him later at his apartment later, Pero offers a similar response. "Did you see what they did to us?" he asks incredulously. "Those fucking NGOniks tried to *workshop* us! They think they have some moral authority [to lead] because they are paid professionals?" Turning more explicitly to concerns about NGO funding from Western governments—and from the U.S. Agency for International Development (USAID) in particular—Pero continues, "Everyone knows they're sleeping with the enemy and they expect us to respect them? Listen to them?!"

Rimi and Pero will disparage Jadranka's "sellout" decision to stay and become a key organizer within the antiwar campaign that emerges from this meeting. Jadranka's participation does not mean, however, that she simply accepts what she describes as the "NGO methods" she encounters at the meeting. She complains openly, for example, when Ante and Nina present fully formulated plans without consulting others first. Additionally, she questions their emphasis on inviting prominent civil society figures to speak at the planned rally. "We've heard from you people and what you have to say for fifteen years," she says during one particularly heated exchange. "We need new voices. We need more participatory approaches to politics." Such arguments will only intensify in the months to come, eventually rippling out across the wider political left in Croatia.

This first factious meeting will give birth to *Dosta je ratova!* or Enough Wars!, which will be designated as an informal "ad-hoc initiative." Enough Wars! will organize vigils, petitions, direct actions, and demonstrations, becoming the country's most dynamic, best publicized, and most popular leftist movement since Croatia declared its independence from Yugoslavia in 1991. Despite its internal divisions, the antiwar campaign will bring some fifteen thousand people onto Zagreb's streets for F15. *Zagrepčani* will join millions of protesters across the globe for what will become the largest protest in human history (*New York Times* February 17, 2003). F15 in Croatia is the product of weeks of common organizing and collaboration between those from the civil and anarchist scenes. Some anarchists, including Rimi and Pero, will nonetheless refuse to be associated with Enough Wars! They will organize a separate, almost exclusively anarchist, strand of the movement.

Together these activist strands channel deep public frustration with official responses to the war. While polling indicates that over 90 percent of the population opposes the invasion (*Vjesnik,* March 8, 2003), Croatia joins the ranks of President George Bush's "Coalition of the Willing." Alongside most of postsocialist Europe, Croatian Foreign Minister Tonino Picula pledges the country's support for the controversial Vilnius Declaration, which asserts that intervention against Saddam Hussein is urgent and need not wait for approval by the UN Security Council. By granting coalition forces access to national airspace, ports, intelligence, and army and medical facilities, Croatia's center-left coalition earns Defense Secretary Donald Rumsfeld's glowing approval[4]—and inclusion in the Coalition of the Willing. For many Croatian activists, official disregard for the will of its citizens—coming only a few years after the country emerged from a decade of authoritarian rule, preceded by five decades of Communist Party hegemony—points to a crisis in Croatia's democratization. For more radical activists, however, this crisis serves as definitive confirmation of the fundamental limits of representative democracy.

Activist disputes at the first antiwar meeting—which foreshadow the conflicts that will plague Enough Wars!—also point to another, perhaps deeper, crisis of democratization. Many theorists of democratic transition argue that "civil society" is the prerequisite for any democratic society, the living tissue of democratic culture (Tocqueville 1994 [1835]; Almond and Verba 1989; Putnam et al. 1993).[5] The skepticism about—even outright hostility toward—civil society from more radical activists, which will only intensify in the coming months, points to a crisis of legitimacy for NGOs, those organizations most often associated with civil society in the public mind. These tensions erupt in heated debates about NGOs as legal forms of organization, dependence on foreign funders, the proper relationship of the antiwar struggle to state officials, styles of public action—including official spokespersons and speeches by prominent public figures—as well as professional rather than voluntary organization.

It was in the wake of these rancorous debates, in the waning months of the campaign, that Pero was arrested for his part in the unruly Bicycle Caravan, described in the Introduction. By tracing the evolution of the Enough Wars! campaign, as well as the deeper social and political changes it exposes, we can better understand the misunderstanding of anarchist politics—as well as the implicit understanding about "those Fucking NGOniks"—that emerges from Pero's police interrogation. First, given that anarchists, who had played active roles in civic initiatives since the late 1980s—and who continued to declare their commitment to ethnic peace, social justice, and antifascism—came to have such a hostile view of NGOs highlights fundamentally changed historical circumstances. In short, global, regional, and national transformations altered the social position and political meaning of civil society in Croatia. Second, the specific anarchist objections to the political practices of NGOs make clear why they could no longer serve as vehicles for anarchist political hopes. As such, these objections help to distinguish the contours of the anarchist political imaginary associated with the most militant strands of the alterglobalization movement from the liberal one historically associated with civil society. Finally, at a more immediate and personal level, the bitterness, even desperation, that Rimi, Pero, and even Jadranka experience during the Enough Wars! campaign animates their participation in militant action at the transnational mobilization in Thessaloniki, Greece, a few months later.

Civil Society in Historical Context

The Death of Socialism and the Rebirth of Civil Society

Today's dominant—and overwhelmingly positive—understanding of civil society owes much to the historic role civil society played in the Eastern Europe's transformation and the ending of the Cold War (Hann 1996). As fledgling labor, ecological, church, and human-rights initiatives emerged in the early 1980s—especially in Poland, Czechoslovakia, and Hungary—they were met by systematic repression by regimes that jealously guarded the Communist Party's monopoly over associational life. Dissident intellectuals aligned with these initiatives came to see them as "civil society," which became a rallying cry in the struggle against state power and Soviet imperialism. Many went so far as to see *any* associational life outside state control as an important form of resistance because the state had, in their view, colonized all of society (Arato 1981). In other words, these intellectuals, echoing Gramsci's analysis (1971) of Fascist Italy forty years earlier,[6] insisted that civil society constituted a potentially emancipatory project of self-organization, independent of the state (see also Kopecky and Mudde 2003:4).

The dramatic success of the 1989 revolutions, whether nonviolent (Czechoslovakia) or otherwise (Romania), radically changed global views of Eastern Europe and civil society alike. First, the pivotal role civil society played in ending authoritarian state socialism lent a rosy hue to the concept and associated organizations. What is more, the dissident, often outlawed, status of civil society initiatives during late socialism reinforced the tendency of analysts to accentuate a fundamental separation of civil society from the state. Indeed, one of the few common denominators among the many definitions of this famously pliable concept[7] has been its nominal independence from the state (Hearn 2001). One of the greatest ironies of postsocialism, however, is the Western deployment of the civil society framework against the very peoples who had done so much to resuscitate it. As Janine Wedel (1994:323) has argued, "Because the lack of civil society was part of the very essence of the all-pervasive communist state, creating such a society and supporting organizations independent of the state—or NGOs—have been seen by donors as the connective tissue of democratic political culture—an intrinsically positive objective." In other words, after their successful struggles to end single party rule, the states of postsocialist Europe were judged to be fundamentally lacking in civil society (see also Rivkin-Fish 2004; Hemment 2004), despite the fact that many postsocialist states elected the very civil society dissidents whom socialist regimes had persecuted. Civil society, it seems, may always be better known for its absence or incompleteness (Comaroff and Comaroff 1999). Programs from USAID, Freedom House, the National Endowment for Democracy, and George Soros's Open Society Institutes were on a long list of Western foundations and embassies that claimed to be addressing this Eastern European deficiency by actively supporting the building of civil society institutions (Hann 1996; Junghans 2001). As Junghans has documented in Hungary, "the diagnosis of the ills of post-socialist society, and the claim that individuals and organizational patterns required drastic change in order to overcome a debilitating legacy" has justified these institutions prescribing strong doses of "civil society" (Junghans 2001:390).

Civil Society in (Former) Yugoslavia

In the years between the death of longtime president Josip Broz Tito in 1980 and the collapse of state socialism across Eastern Europe in 1989, civil initiatives developed in the former Yugoslavia as they did in the broader region (Gantar and Mastnak 1988; Mastnak 1994; Mesić 1991). These initiatives were more prominent in the more economically developed northwest where I conducted my research. A wide, informal opposition emerged, especially among the intelligentsia, that included "petitionism," the so-called "flying university," which met in private apartments to discuss taboo subjects, independent publishing (*samizdat*), and "protest evenings," centered especially on the protection of civil rights (Dragović-Soso 2002). This opposition included a loose coalition of dissenters—right-wing nationalists, liberals and radical leftists, anarchist and heretical Marxist alike—with a common goal of challenging the communist party's monopoly on associational life.

Following popular elections in 1990, it was the nationalists, led by former right-wing dissidents, who came to power in Croatia. Franjo Tuđman, who had himself been jailed for political dissidence, would rule Croatia throughout the 1990s. Despite his place in the earlier dissident coalition, Tuđman and his Croatian Democratic Union (HDZ) quickly moved to demonize Croatian civil initiatives, representing them not so much as nongovernmental but as antigovernment and anti-Croatian (Human Rights Watch 1995:99).[8] The nationalist press portrayed NGOs as foreign mercenaries (*strani plaćenici*) highlighting ties between Croatian organizations that criticized Tuđman's authoritarian policies and the funding these organizations received from USAID, foreign embassies, and George Soros's Open Society Institute. In Serbia, media loyal to President Slobodan Milošević went so far as to call local NGOs working against the wars his regime fomented in Croatia, Bosnia, and Kosovo anti-war profiteers.

In this intense climate of nationalism and militarization, the idea of civil society continued to be invoked by a loose coalition of liberals and more radical critics, including anarchists. Marko, one of the relatively few activists whose participation spans from the early 1990s Antiwar Campaign of Croatia (*ARK*) through alterglobalization and Enough Wars! activism in the 2000s, met me over coffee in his cramped one-room apartment to discuss these changes. He described how civil society became a rallying cry for many within the most radical circles of Croatian resistance—such as the Zagreb Anarchist Movement (*Zagrebački anarhistički pokret or ZAP*)—in a political context of nationalist war and authoritarian rule. In stressing a political identity rooted in civil society, activists emphasized that ARK was *civilian* in a highly militarized society at war.[9] The continued association of the term with civic initiative rather than state authority also remained important because a single authoritarian party was still dominant. Furthermore, civil society (*civilno društvo*), with the Latin-derived Croatian adjective civil (*civilno*), and civic initiative (*građanska inicijativa*) from the Slavic word for citizen (*građanin*), which derives from the Slavic word for city (*grad*), also emphasized political citizenship rather than ethnic belonging.

During the 1990s, politicians generally shunned both these civil variants and claimed instead to represent *Croatians,* implying ethnic Croats. Stipe Mesić's successful 1999 campaign slogan, "President of all Croatian Citizens" (*Predsjednik svih hrvatskih građana*), which finally helped dislodge the HDZ from its decade in power, broke with this practice by emphasizing the self-consciously ethnically neutral term *citizens.* But the campaigns by Mesić and the center-left coalition were more than rhetorically aligned with civil society. A countrywide coalition of 148 NGOs known as Glas '99, comprised of human-rights, women's, environmental, and student groups, is often credited with making a decisive contribution to the center-left victory (Irvine 2007:17). These NGOs benefited from substantial injections of cash contributed by foreign embassies and foundations. Indeed, we can see in the Croatian elections of 2000—in which NGOs backed by USAID, among others, played a significant role in mobilizing voters for "regime change"—a precursor to those mobilizations in Serbia, Ukraine, Georgia, Kyrgyzstan, and Lebanon that came to be known as the "colored revolutions," which also enjoyed significant Western funding and logistical support (Traynor 2004).[10] In any case, following the elections, the leaders of key Croatian NGOs found themselves, for the first time, close to those in power. Many received appointments in the new administration. After years of right-wing rule, many liberal and progressive Croatians were heartened by this electoral transition of power and its promise to bring substantial change (cf. Stubbs 2012:21).

In the meantime, as liberal civil society figures edged closer to state power, anarchists were experiencing new forms of collective action and power. By the late 1990s and early 2000s, activists read extensively, especially online, about struggles elsewhere and, in many cases, traveled throughout Europe, where they had personal encounters with the burgeoning alterglobalization movement. One Enough Wars! participant and social-movement scholar described the growing distance between NGOs and activists in these terms, arguing that a special problem was presented by the "poor communication between different generations of activists" (Šimleša 2006:147). He went on to delimit the two generations according to their political experience:

> A large portion of the older generation of activists grew up in the course of the war years and engaged with questions connected to the consequences of war as well as civil rights for many years. On the other hand a portion of the younger generation had absorbed images from Seattle and other protest gatherings (Šimleša 2006:147).

Like liberals in the U.S. after Obama's election, the older generation of activists was terrified at the prospect that the nationalist right—against which it had struggled for a decade—would return to power.[11] The younger generation, meanwhile, was not interested in the struggle between what it saw as two right-wing electoral blocks, the Social Democrats (who favored neoliberal market reform) and the HDZ (who promoted populist far-right policies).[12] Furthermore, as Šimleša states and as the frequent use of video in anarchist self-education makes clear, images from protest mobilizations were formative for Croatian radicals—something that was especially evident when they engaged in large-scale direct confrontation with state security forces. While images played a crucial role, it was the whole range of networks of collaborative production that gave activists a sense of belonging to an emerging radical multitude.[13] Many also gained firsthand experiences of protest mobilizations in Western Europe. The new political sensibility of these activists was at odds with the politics of demanding moderate reforms—at odds with the idea of addressing the state at all—seeking instead, in the spirit of direct action, to valorize forms of horizontal, networked, and grassroots power. It is only with this broader historical context in mind that one can understand why the relationships between "NGOniks" and anarchists came to be so fraught around Enough Wars!

F15 and the Second Superpower

The Enough Wars! March

By the cigarette break of that first meeting, five or six of the younger anarchists, Rimi and Pero among them, had left visibly frustrated—and those who departed would eventually organize a parallel anarchist march for F15. Among the twenty-five who remained at the planning meeting, however, more than half considered themselves anarchists. Jadranka, Danica, and Sunčana belonged to the younger generation. Several older and relatively experienced anarchists also stayed, key organizers in earlier Croatian mobilizations against corporate globalization. Indeed, the listservs, coalitions, and personal relationships and experience from several years of alterglobalization organizing in Zagreb would serve as the basic infrastructure for nearly all antiwar organizing, as Tarrow (2005) has argued happened in antiwar demonstrations globally. The anarchists who remained at that first conflictual Enough Wars! meeting challenged the approach to F15 that Ante and Nina had initially proposed. Their criticisms prompted many questions by those unfamiliar with anarchist political principles. Why distance ourselves from political parties? Because aligning ourselves with political parties would mean handing away our collective power to representatives before we've exercised it. Why not accept any allies, even far-right ones? Because we should only work with those who oppose war, not just this war. Shouldn't those with more experience set the agenda of the meeting? This will only ensure that they stay more experienced, that they become the authorities within the movement, monopolizing expertise, media attention, and contacts.

By the next week, in response to the vociferous criticism of participating anarchists, the group had assumed a quite different character than initially proposed. The need for horizontal organization, antiauthoritarian decision-making, and direct action were accepted. Plans included proposed blockades of Croatian military airports should U.S. or UK military aircraft land for repairs on their way to and from bombing runs over Iraq. Spokespeople would be "ordinary people" (no professional politicians) and rotating spokespersons would ensure that everyone learned to speak publicly and preclude the centralization of power in too few hands. Furthermore, Enough Wars! did not seek formal recognition from the state Office for Associations as is traditional for NGOs (*nevladine organizacije*). As anarchists had demanded, we sat in a circle.

Enough Wars! became a meeting ground, like the social forums, for those more oriented to what was often called the "civil scene" and those who were involved in more radical activism. This meant that not everything turned out as the radicals wished. The full name of the campaign would be the "Ad-hoc Civil Initiative, Enough Wars!" (*Ad hoc građanska inicijativa, Dosta je ratova!*), even though anarchists had argued against grounding the campaign in the language of "civil society," which they perceived as conservative, dependent on foreign funding, and linked the language of "citizenship." For those with ties to the Noborder Movement, citizenship was associated with "the border regime" and its system of deportation, which threatened the free movement of people. But Enough Wars! did not only adopt the nomenclature of civil society. The campaign drew on the expertise, infrastructure, personnel, resources, and legitimacy of the *civilna scena*. Enough Wars! declared itself an alliance of thirty associations (*udruga*), though it did not name these organizations, many of which hoped to remain silent partners. Debates about what constitutes the most ethical and effective means of political organizing and engagement, and specifically the relationship to "civil society," continued to divide the campaign throughout the next five months of activity.

In the weeks leading up to F15, those around Enough Wars! did the basic organizational legwork required for a large public gathering in Croatia. They held press conferences, produced press releases, made themselves available to reporters for interviews, obtained legally required protest permits, borrowed a sound system and small makeshift stage, "flyered" and "postered" extensively, and sent invitations to all relevant organizations and email lists.

Enough Wars! coordinated with activists in New York, Stockholm, and Ljubljana, establishing plans for mobile phone links that would enable guest speeches from other demonstrations to emphasize the global scale of F15. While they did not invite many of the "usual suspects" from the *civilna scena* to speak, there was, in the end, a mix of public speakers who could be seen as part of a marginal yet nonetheless publicly recognizable tradition of Croatian dissent.

The day of the demonstrations saw Dorino Manzin, a gay rights activist, Vesna Teršelič, longtime peace activist and nominee for the Nobel Peace Prize, and Ivan Supek, antifascist Partisan, theoretical physicist, and longtime nuclear weapons opponent and peace activist speak on behalf of Enough Wars! The crowd of some fifteen thousand was by turns somber, angry, and festive. They cheered, whistled and booed uproariously when speakers condemned the imminent invasion. As the Evil Drummers (*Zli bubnjari*)—decked out in bright yellow jumpsuits—pounded out fierce marching rhythms, others carried candles, and many chanted "not in our name," the Enough Wars! procession left the central square to follow a police-approved march route that snaked through lower Zagreb and past the U.S. Embassy.

The Anarchist March

Meanwhile, a kilometer and a half down Zagreb's main shopping street, Ilica, a march organized in punk hangouts, on anarchist listservs, such as the ex-yu-a-list, and at concerts gathered at the Square of the French Revolution. With its centuries-old tradition as a military parade ground, the square had certainly witnessed more disciplined formations. Activists approached the square in small groups to the rhythm of the 2, 6, and 11 trams. They carried rolls of hand-painted canvas and signs taped to rough dowels. At first there were only a dozen black-clad anarchists, almost all familiar from the past week's planning meetings. But soon there were a hundred milling about, many from further afield, including six or seven men from the small central Croatian town of Križevci, a few women in their midtwenties from the central Serbian town of Čačak, as well as three teenagers from Banja Luka, Bosnia. Each time the tram rolled by, a larger and more exuberant group emerged. By eleven fifteen, when we assumed marching formation, there were two hundred and fifty, most boasting the stylings of punk and radical culture: Palestinian scarves, black masks, piercings, army pants, anarchist patches, banners, and flags. By the time the march assembled, more than half of those gathered were not familiar to me despite eight months of fieldwork in the principle hubs of anarchist life in Zagreb.[14]

A Black Bloc of this size would be significant even at a major protest in Western Europe, and it certainly caught me off guard in Zagreb. What also surprised me, as much as the absolute size of the gathering, were some of the individuals who chose to participate. Here among the crowd were Branko, Ljubo, and even Jadranka, all of whom were critical of Rimi and Pero's rapid departure from the first Enough Wars! meeting, and all of whom were deeply involved in Enough Wars! organizing. Branko and Jadranka even served as Enough Wars! rotating spokespeople. I asked Jadranka why she'd chosen to march here and not with Enough Wars! "Well," she began, "I felt a responsibility to work with Enough Wars! so as to contaminate the *civilna scena* with antiauthoritarian principles. And we can probably reach more people with their moderate message. And there are few chances to reach out to a wider audience in Croatia." "But really," she continued, "this is where my heart is. I'm not interested in making a career in an NGO, and you saw what it's like around Enough Wars! It'll be such a predictable and polite protest (*pristojni demo*)!"

When the Black Bloc moved into the street behind the banner "No war between nations! No peace between classes" (*Nema rata između naroda, nema mira između klasa*), a few dozen police looked on with concern. Several ranking officers, flanked by cops in riot gear, ordered the Black Bloc onto the sidewalk. The energy surged when it appeared conflict was imminent; police grabbed at the banner and shoved those at the front row of the march. They yelled that this demonstration was unauthorized and could not proceed. In fact the anarchists' flier—which was being handed out to passersby—brazenly emphasizes that this march is not authorized, that they have not sought a permit for their protest. In the end, the Black Bloc easily pushed past the officers, sweeping down Ilica. The march took on a surreal quality as elderly women in fur coats, well-heeled young professionals, and designer-clad men—the regulars of this boutique shopping district—moved among banners touting class war (see figure 2.1). Hapless passengers abandoned their seats on trams, which were backed up, one after another, the entire length of Ilica, and joined the march. A dreadlocked woman distributed fliers from a commandeered shopping cart. The police made no further effort to interfere as the march swelled to five hundred. A dozen photographers scurried around the march snapping photos. One reporter, shuffling backward in front

Figure 2.1. The February 15 Black Bloc sweeps down Ilica, one of Zagreb's main shopping districts. *Photo by Markos.*

of the march, asked a masked Rimi why he did not seek the required permit to demonstrate. Rimi replied, "The government didn't ask our permission to support the war. I'm not going to ask their permission to oppose it."[15]

Despite the split into separate blocs, as well as the vitriolic attacks on the march by civil society and right-wing figures alike that came the next day, F15 was judged a wild success by nearly all participants, regardless of where they chose to march. Indeed, in some sense, internal political differences, manifested in the separate marches, were seen as contributing to the dynamism of the day's actions. Activists from both the Black Bloc and Enough Wars! described the moment when the two marches converged—as planned in a brief coordination meeting between representatives of both marches—as an emotional high point.[16] Beyond such experiential dimensions of the protest—and nearly all activists described a palpable sense of collective power and solidarity—organizers described F15's success in a variety of registers. Black Bloc participants expressed satisfaction that they had proven that well-organized activists could express themselves politically irrespective of state approval. What is more, on one of the coldest days of the year, an estimated 10–15,000 marched, making this—with the possible exception of 1999 protests against the closing of Radio 101—the largest progressive demonstrations in decades.[17]

F15 even edged out national hero Ivica Kostelić's World Championship gold medal in the slalom in San Moritz for the lead story in the press. Furthermore, the protests in Zagreb were coordinated with six other Croatian cities—Osijek, Pula, Split, Zadar, Vukovar, and Šibenik[18]—and the wider global protests that gathered an estimated 10 to 30 million people on all continents.[19] Such was the scale of the protests that the *New York Times* (February 17, 2003) opined, "The huge antiwar demonstrations around the world this weekend are reminders that there may still be two superpowers on the planet: the United States and world public opinion."

Broad Croatian participation in and support for this global protest held a special importance for activists, especially those who had been involved in antiwar activism since the Yugoslav wars of the early 1990s. The popularity of the campaign and opposition to the looming invasion, they insisted, must be understood in relationship to the Croatian experience of war. The campaign's name, Enough Wars!, as well as its most common slogan, "We've been through a war and we wouldn't wish one on anyone else," were calibrated to engage precisely this sentiment. Indeed, when I stood with Enough Wars! activists collecting signatures against the war, many of those who signed—and they numbered some fourteen thousand in three days—expressed seeing the U.S. threats against Iraq in terms of their own experience at the hands of the relatively more powerful Serb-controlled Yugoslav People's Army in 1991. This was the first time that Croats drew positive lessons from the war, according to Marko, moving beyond the "cultivation of old resentments toward a fundamentally anti-militarist stance." Jadranka, whose father lost a leg fighting Serb irregulars in the Dalmatian hinterland, described F15 as a break from an extended period of "claustrophobic provincialism," a turning outward from their own victimhood and an "expression of solidarity" with other (imminent) "victims of military aggression." Enough Wars! organizer and longtime anarchist activist Dražen Šimleša characterized Enough Wars! as

the best action ever organized by the *civilna scena* in Croatia. The spontaneity of organization, the maximal investment of energy and respect of difference, as well as the dedication of months of voluntary effort, resulted in an action that the whole *civilna scena* can be proud of. Here, in the best way, the linkages between global questions and local context were shown. It was important for activists to express solidarity with the global peace movement and express its position against the war in Iraq, but also, just as importantly, to force the Račan government to distance itself from the war and deny the support for the American war machine (Šimleša 2006:141).

The elation surrounding the demonstrations swept away, for the moment, the mistrust that had typified relations among different *civilna scena* actors, as well as between them and anarchists. Such unity would not last, but on the evening of F15 everyone celebrated together at a large party in Jadranka's squatted villa.

A series of disputes broke out in the weeks and months after F15. These disputes, prompted by the invasion of Iraq, served to expose a deepening crisis of civil society and the democratization with which it is so closely associated.

Conflicts, Controversies, and the Decline of Enough Wars!

A few days after F15, a dozen Enough Wars! organizers gathered to reflect on the successes and shortcomings of the demonstrations. The tone was still overwhelmingly positive but divisions were re-emerging. Besides logistical difficulties—such as running out of photocopied petitions when the protests grew beyond the most optimistic projections—many agreed that the burning of the U.S. flag, torched when the march passed the U.S. Embassy, was a mistake. Three Iraqis—someone said they were from the Iraqi Embassy—had pushed to the front of the crowd waving Ba'ath party flags and a stylized American flag with swastikas. With eager help from four Black Bloc protesters, they had doused the American flag in lighter fluid and then ignited it. The surrounding crowd howled approval as Enough Wars! marshals looked on, disapproving yet helpless.

The only immediate negative press about F15—a scathing critique of Enough Wars! by Drago Pilsel, a prominent civil society figure and a founder of the Croatian Helsinki Committee for Human Rights—centered on the flag incident. The terms of his attack reveal much about the NGO elites' assumptions about civil society and its role in Croatia. Under the title "Sloppiness and Vandalism" (*Šlamperaj i vandalizam*) Pilsel (2003) emphasized a lack of professionalism. He wrote that "the poorly organized protest held yesterday in Zagreb, coordinated by a couple of inconsequential nongovernmental organizations and a handful of anarchists and other autocrats, lost all legitimacy when these so-called peace activists burned the American flag" (Pilsel 2003). Pilsel went on to claim that the organizers had "embarrassed Croatia" and, significantly for the argument here, "all *civilized* people" (emphasis added) with their vandalism.[20] In fact, the civilized/barbarian opposition was central to his condemnation:

Jurić, Šimleša, Teršelič, and those *barbarians* who *shamed* us so have on their conscience that vandalism that did not have to occur, which insults the American nation, the American state, and us as *civilized people.*

I was there, Ambassador Rossin, because I don't agree with the politics you represent, but neither with the *savagery (divljaštvom)* in our ranks, and because of that I ask for your forgiveness (emphasis added, Pilsel 2003).

Pilsel's attack was framed in terms of Croatian national honor, propriety, civilization, and organizational professionalism. For many activists, it demonstrated that the unruly F15 protests were not the kind of spectacle with which some civil society elites believed they ought to be associated. When we discussed these elites after the meeting, Jadranka referred to them as the "civil society patriarchs," who "jealously controlled" access to funding, the media, and the center-left political elite.[21]

Within Enough Wars! the flag incident, and the Pilsel attack on it, exacerbated divisions, because ironically all three activists named in Pilsel's article agreed that the flag should not have been burned. They reminded those gathered to reflect on F15 that Enough Wars! had worked carefully to resist falling into any crude anti-Americanism.[22] Indeed, even I had been invited take a turn as a rotating spokesperson—and act as a "diplomat from below"—precisely because I was American and it was useful to show that the movement was not anti-America but rather part of a larger global movement against the war that included many Americans. An older organizer then suggested that the police should have stopped the burning of the flag, as it was carried out directly in front of a line of riot police. Younger anarchists, including Jadranka, were outraged at the suggestion that Enough Wars! would have welcomed police intervention. Over Jadranka's objections, it was decided that Enough Wars! would apologize publicly for the flag burning.[23] Divisions over the appropriate relationship of Enough Wars! to the Croatian authorities—and the representatives of other states—would continue to plague the campaign in the months to come.

Negotiating the Movement's Relationship to the State

When we spoke later, Jadranka expressed a "deep sense of betrayal" by those she had worked with in Enough Wars! especially when a spokesperson at the next press conference condemned the flag burning and faulted the police for not having intervened. Anarchists who had refused to work with the campaign felt their worst suspicions of "NGO types" were confirmed. When shortly thereafter Foreign Minister Picula invited Enough Wars! organizers to meet with him to discuss Croatian policy, these tensions were only further exacerbated. Older activists, especially those affiliated with Committee for Defascization (*Odbor za defašizaciju*) and Peace Studies (*Centar za mirovne studije*) argued for the need to meet with Croatian policymakers and make clear their objections to any support for military action against Iraq without UN Security Council approval. While some did not, in principle, believe in appealing to the state to change its policies—because this affirmed the state's right to make such policies in the first place—the older generation of activists, including some anarchists, felt it was more important to accommodate a wide range of tactics and political approaches within the campaign than to guard the political purity of the initiative. Younger anarchists opposed the meeting in general, feeling it legitimized Picula's policies and risked cooptation by the government. Rimi said such a meeting allowed the government to "appear open and democratic," even as it proceeded with the same undemocratic po-lices, effectively "white-washing their crimes." Rather than see the looming invasion of Iraq as an undemocratic aberration—and the purpose of Enough Wars! to demand a realignment of Croatian policy with public opinion—rad-icals saw an opportunity to highlight fundamental objections to liberal de-mocracy in Croatia. The text of their flier, titled "War Itself is a Crime Against Humanity," voiced these objections:

> We do not object to fighting in an unconventional manner or the reasons for which one kills. War itself is a crime. We who have survived a war are in the best position to confirm this truth. [. . .]
>
> They have committed Croatia to an offensive war—including the use of its entire infrastructure—in the service of an aggressive *(osvajački)* war. In this way the government has again assumed the right to make decisions with which the majority of residents of this country do not agree, openly displaying the ab-sence of democracy and the absurdity of the idea of "representation," the foun-dations of parliamentary democracy. The "representatives" only serve their own interests and those of other political and economic elites. [. . .]
>
> If we are not asked whether or not we want to participate in a war, then we do not need to seek permission for our disagreement with that war! Every dis-obedient action that can slow or stop the war efforts is legitimate.

In other words, the flier articulates a politics grounded in the anarchist no-tion of direct action. The issue was not, or at least not only, that the goals of

Enough Wars! were too moderate or reformist—they did not go to the root of political problems as radicals understood them. Rather, the mode of addressing the state, appealing to its representatives to change their policies, was problematic in and of itself for anarchists. For Rimi and the other coauthors of the flyer—written at their final meeting before F15—the Enough Wars! attacks on the Black Bloc were highly suspect. Given their critical view of civil society, some anarchists were suspicious that Enough Wars! organizers were raising their personal profiles and therefore their NGO career prospects with Enough Wars! After photos of Enough Wars! organizers meeting with the Minister of Foreign Affairs ran in the most widely circulated daily, I heard these suspicions voiced more frequently. Black Bloc activists saw Enough Wars! organizers' public repudiations of more confrontational tactics as an attempt to establish themselves as the reasonable representatives of public anger, representatives with whom the state could negotiate. "Their criminalization of us, their call for our exclusion," as Rimi expressed at Attack, over the blare of a punk show in the next room, "is what made them seem responsible, trustworthy. You know, [they became] the ones who could be relied on to police the 'dangerous elements.'" Rimi's argument echoes similar debates between civil society and militants, both elsewhere in the alterglobalization movement and more recently in the Occupy Movement.[24]

In short, more radical activists like Pero and Rimi, and increasingly even Jadranka, asked awkward questions about the motivations of those involved with NGOs. They challenged NGO claims to civil society's legitimacy: that it represented the public good and that it mediated between the public and the state. What is more, activists who gravitated toward Black Bloc tactics felt that those around Enough Wars! were not prepared to criticize representative democracy itself. They saw them as unwilling to highlight the crisis of democracy that Croatia's involvement in the impending Iraq invasion brought into view. Rather than restore the liberal democratic order, Black Bloc participants sought to discredit it and voice a need to establish the legitimacy of grassroots direct action and decision making.

The legitimacy of civil society would only become more vexed in the coming weeks as subsequent conflicts around Enough Wars! cast further doubt on the assumed independence of civil society from the state. Enough Wars!, already facing criticisms on one side from more moderate civil society elites and from more radical activists on the other, was soon also under attack from the nationalist right.

Western Funding and Croatian Civil Society

Max Primorac,[25] in a letter in the *Washington Times*—the right-wing paper owned by Reverend Moon at this time—voiced longstanding Croatian nationalist frustrations with U.S. funding priorities that favored Croatian NGOs focused on human rights and opposition to ethnic antagonism. Seeking to discredit those NGOs associated with Enough Wars! and reorient USAID away from "anti-U.S. demonstrators" and toward "patriots," Primorac wrote,

> As elsewhere in Europe, we find here the same motley mash of anti-war protesters—anarchists, anti-globalists, greens, Marxist peaceniks—shouting "smash capitalism" and "Bush is Hitler." [. . .] The rub is that this hate-America crowd is sponsored by the U.S. taxpayer.
>
> Protest organizers—Anti-War Campaign, Green Action, women's group B.a.B.e. and others—are a who's who of U.S. foreign aid grantees who, for a decade, have received millions of dollars, ostensibly to strengthen democracy. In fact, aid has been grossly misallocated to a marginal and extremist nexus of former communists, anarchists and extreme feminists that represent the core of anti-American political activity in the Balkans.
>
> Anti-War Campaign *(ARK)* fronts for numerous anarchist-Marxist groups, offering them office space, equipment, funds and training. They include Zagreb Anarchist Movement, anarcho-feminists ANFEME (sic), Croatian Anti-Globalists and others. Its PeaceNet *(ZaMirNet)* is a regional Internet link that is part of a global alliance to wage "netwars" against Western institutions. Radicals use it to coordinate activities, inform members on anti-capitalist and anti-NATO rallies, access donors and provide a steady diet of radical literature. Though ZaMirNet's manager is a self-described "anarcho-feminist," she also works for USAID clients Urban Institute, MercyCorps, CARE and others. CARE alone granted ZaMirNet $335,000, part of a larger sum received from the U.S. government. [. . .]
>
> In large part, we are paying the price for past policy that defined not communism as the threat to regional peace, but rather a vaguely defined nationalism. In turn, support was channeled to so-called anti-nationalists with little regard to what they actually believed. Pro-Western groups were disqualified from aid from the start because they were considered "too patriotic" (*Washington Times*, May 2, 2003).

To be sure, Primorac is sketching a crude and biased portrait of the recent history of U.S. funding in the Balkans. His attack nonetheless helps to bring into relief some unique aspects of that history, confirmed by much of my research in the former Yugoslavia in association with a range of progressive and self-identified civil society organizations. From the Belgrade Circle, an intellectual association dedicated to antinationalist and antiwar education, organization, and publishing (Razsa 1996), through the Antiwar Campaign of Croatia, to Arkzin, a radical publishing project that specialized in youth subculture, new-media technology, grassroots activism, and critical theory, nearly all leftist organizations enjoyed some official Western funding—including from USAID. This funding record was a peculiarity of U.S. civil society development support in the former Yugoslavia. Western governments prioritized support for antinationalists during the war years in hopes of stabilizing the region and staunching the flow of millions of refugees. So many of the organizations receiving funding in the former Yugoslavia did have a strong leftist slant, as Primorac alleges, though they were, in my experience, more likely to be initiated and led by individuals who had been leftist dissidents in Yugoslavia rather than members of the Communist Party elite, as he implies—though there were notable exceptions. In any case, many older activists and civil-society activists who worked within the "civil scene" (*civilna scena*) had enjoyed significant Western funding at one time or another.

Given this history of funding, Primorac's letter was worrying for many on the civil scene. Many anarchists—rather than seeing this nationalist hostility as evidence that the "civil scene" was an ally under attack by the right— saw this as evidence of their complicity with, and therefore vulnerability to pressure from, USAID. Suspicions were further aroused when two anarchists working for one of the organizations targeted in Primorac's attack spread the word that USAID grants required a loyalty pledge that organizations would not work against "the national interests of the United States." The case of Green Action (*Zelena akcija*), which, it was widely believed, had been denied further USAID funding when it organized an anti-GMO campaign, had already generated considerable cynicism about the political independence of those accepting U.S. funding. All of these issues remained matters of private rumor and speculation until they erupted into the national press with calls to boycott U.S. funding.

Before I turn to these calls, it is worth remembering the dramatic shifts in the perception of the U.S. during this period. The decline in U.S. popularity was striking given the previously high opinion of the U.S. in Croatia, especially strong in the wake of extensive U.S. support for Croatia's military efforts to recapture territory seized by the rebellious Serbian minority in the mid-1990s. While there are some longstanding forms of Croatian anti-Americanisms,[26] the perception of the "Global War on Terror," of which it was argued "Operation Iraqi Freedom" was a part, as well as shifts in U.S. policies toward Croatia during the period of my fieldwork, were central to how many Croats articulated their changing attitudes. The press coverage from these months tells part of the story. A brief survey of headlines—which were forwarded extensively through activist networks in the months before and after the invasion of Iraq—helps to illustrate why the global standing of the U.S. declined so rapidly during this period: "USA Will Release Teenagers from Guantanamo?" (*Jutarnji list*, August 25, 2003); "In Guantanamo: Admit Guilt or Die" (*Jutarnji list*, July 7, 2003); "U.S. Will Not Rule Out Use of Tactical Nuclear Weapons in Iraq" (*Jutarnji list*, January 27, 2003); "Donald Rumsfeld: France is the Problem, Germany is the Problem" (*Feral Tribune*, February 23, 2003); "International Law of the Strongest" (*Feral Tribune*, January 29, 2003:28–31); "Freedom Fries: Potatoes also Victim of France-U.S. Dispute" (*Vjesnik*, March 13, 2003); "U.S. Bugs the UN Security Council" (*Feral Tribune*, March 15, 2003:15); "Jessica Lynch's Rescue Invented" (*Jutarnji list*, May 19, 2003).

It was the Zagreb-based Multimedia Institute, however, that gave questions about U.S. funding of Croatian NGOs a new urgency. The Multimedia Institute, whose most public face was MaMa, the Internet café, social club, lecture hall, and meeting space, was a crucial resource to many of Zagreb's political and social subcultures. MaMa was a regular stomping ground for Zagreb's anarchists, who held their weekly self-education series Subverzije there. Only days after the U.S.-led invasion of Iraq began in earnest, the Multimedia Institute announced that it was returning a $100,000 USAID grant. In its public statement, the Multimedia Institute[27] was outspoken in its criticism of U.S. policy,[28] writing that they could not accept U.S. funding because the war represented

> a) a precedent based on the rationale of pre-emptive war, b) being waged in disregard of legitimate processes of the international community, and c) guided by corporate interests to control natural resources (Multimedia Institute 2003).[29]

While the moral clarity of this decision would be clouded when the institute received a $100,000 grant from the German state a few weeks later, leading some to allege that the institute had simply realigned politically, swapping

U.S. for Western European patrons,[30] the decision nonetheless sent shock waves through the "civil scene." Recipients of U.S. funding were immediately on the defensive.

Reporters pressed representatives of NGOs for their response to the Multimedia Institute's declaration. Their answers involved some awkward rhetorical contortions.[31] Jadranka was particularly incensed by the "rationalizations" of Žarko Puhovski, whom she characterized as "one of the patriarchs" of civil society. Puhovski had served as president of the Croatian Helsinki Committee for Human Rights as well as a key figure in the George Soros–endowed Croatian Open Society Institute, which had been a funding source for nearly every civil society initiative in the 1990s (Stubbs 2012). Puhovski condemned the Multimedia Institute's decision, writing that "the time has not yet come for returning donations" (Kršić 2003:20). He enumerated several reasons for his position:

> First, that money belongs to American taxpayers, many of whom oppose the war. Second, such [returning of donations] assumes the perverse moralizing position that associations ought to be moral activists in the name of the whole of society. Third, so far there are fewer killed [in Iraq] than in Yugoslavia during NATO bombing, in Somalia, or in the first Gulf War. Now isn't worse than the period of daddy Bush or Clinton, and I didn't hear anyone asking (. . .) why we should accept money then (Kršić 2003:20).

Puhovski went on to write that the Multimedia Institute's refusal of funding seemed to assume that "financers directly influence the whole operations of those they finance, that the numerous activists of nongovernmental organizations are simply 'foreign mercenaries' [*strani plaćenici*]" (*Novi List* March 29, 2003). Puhovski's use of the term *foreign mercenaries,* invoked repeatedly in his critique of the Multimedia Institute's refusal of the U.S. grant, was especially telling. The pejorative foreign mercenaries had been central to attacks on civil society figures by rightist intellectuals and officials close to the Tuđman regime. Foreign mercenaries, it was understood, were essentially the agents of foreign governments because of their funding and their "anti-Croatian" politics.[32] Indeed, for many nationalist Croats the term *nongovernmental organizations (nevladine organizacije)* was itself suspect, necessarily associated with unpatriotic activities precisely because it was nongovernmental (Bežovan 2001) and often understood as antigovernmental. By linking the Multimedia Institute to earlier attacks on foreign mercenaries, Puhovski was associating their decision with the populist and xenophobic politics of the right—even going so far as to imply that those around the Multimedia Institute were Luddites and isolationists.[33]

Indeed, many on the right were also asking uncomfortable questions of civil-society figures like Puhovski in the weeks before war in Iraq began. Why were human-rights activists not as vocal in attacking this U.S.-led invasion when they had been so outspoken about Croatian war crimes—which to their minds were not war crimes at all, as they had taken place during a defensive war against a much more powerful enemy? Had they just been tools of a U.S. foreign policy agenda when they had helped unseat of the HDZ in the 2000 elections (*Novi List* March 29, 2003)? While these rightist critiques were highly selective in their choice of facts, they did indicate the unstable position in which those organizations most associated with civil society in Croatia found themselves in these new political circumstances.

Rightist and civil-society elite attacks on the organizations and individuals associated with Enough Wars! did not convince anarchists that these organizations and individuals were political allies. Instead of viewing these attacks as unscrupulous ones by common political enemies, radicals saw what Pero described as "a tightening of their [NGO] leashes." Given these organizations' funding histories, this was to be expected. In other words, many anarchists expected that U.S. support would come with strings attached and that NGOs would be called to account sooner or later. This was precisely why they were concerned with NGO political and funding dependency in the first place.[34] One anarchist from Belgrade wrote to the ex-yu-a-list that he found it strange that some people "need to see a text like [Primorac's] published to start thinking about the fact that the U.S. and EU are not interested in promoting freedom of speech, democracy, or real human rights." "Do people really think," Pero asked me, "that they are free to criticize the U.S. when the U.S. bankrolls them? Of course a time of reckoning will come." "Some of them seem to know this anyway," he added, "Or else they wouldn't feel the need to hide their participation in Enough Wars!"

The Limits of Polite Protest

In contrast to the opposition to the U.S. war in Vietnam, which grew over a decade, the global movement against the U.S.-led invasion of Iraq crested before actual armed hostilities had even commenced. The dynamism and scale of protests in Croatia—like in much of the world—never again reached the levels of F15. In the months after President Bush declared "mission accomplished" on the deck of the aircraft carrier USS *Abraham Lincoln,* Enough Wars!'s most consistent actions were its weekly vigils outside the U.S. Embassy. Activists stood in silence, holding signs with the growing number of estimated civilian victims of the war. Some anarchists, including Rimi, Pero, and Jadranka, were critical of this style of protest, which they described as "moralistic," "muzzled," and "submissive." They tried repeatedly, with increasing anger, to organize direct action against the war and official Croatian support for it.

When student leaders at Zagreb University's Faculty of Humanities and Social Sciences organized an outdoor antiwar concert featuring prominent rock and hip-hop acts, Pero and Rimi attempted to mount the stage and invite those in attendance to march on the U.S. Embassy and Ministry of Foreign Affairs. When private security prevented them from taking the microphone, they were left yelling into a handheld megaphone, largely drowned out by the concert's wall of speakers. Riot police quickly stopped them when, despite everything, they attempted a breakaway march. Seven activists were thrown to the ground and arrested as a small crowd of bemused students, beers in hand, looked on.

By late spring of 2003—with Saddam Hussein still at large and the first signs of the Sunni insurgency emerging—Pero and Rimi began to report close police surveillance. They described occasional stakeouts at their apartments, "tails" on the street, and tactical police units at all their public gatherings. I was initially uncertain what to make of these claims as Pero and Rimi sometimes seemed a bit paranoid and conspiratorial. They often made remarks, for example—even though they had known me for years at this point—that implied that they feared I might be a spy. I tried to not take such suspicions personally; they were indicative, after all, of the broader European (and global) climate of anti-Americanism that characterized this period. I soon realized that these suspicions also indexed very real fears about police surveillance when I, too, witnessed a conspicuous undercover police presence at MaMa during Subverzija, their weekly video screenings. For Pero and Rimi, anger was apparently stronger than fear of police surveillance; at least, fear did not seem to inhibit them. On one occasion, shortly after the arrests at the Faculty of Humanities and Social Sciences, I was walking with them in central Zagreb when they recognized an SUV associated with the U.S. Embassy by its diplomatic plates. In broad daylight, they pulled spray-paint cans and covered

Figure 2.2. Scrawled during broad daylight on a parked sport utility vehicle with U.S. embassy license plates, Rimi and Pero's graffiti reads: Against War Politics! *Photo by author.*

four sides of the vehicle in antiwar slogans (see figure 2.2). Their "Sabotage the War" stencil could be seen across the city center.

Finally, when an international bicycle caravan passed through Zagreb on its way to protests against the EU summit in Thessaloniki, Greece—which many activists decided later to attend—Rimi, Jadranka, and Pero helped organize local support and coordinate direct actions with them, including the "critical mass" described in the introduction. The primary focus of the caravan, made up largely of Western European activists, was the EU's restrictive migration policies, but these concerns were combined with an antiwar message for the May 8 Critical Mass through Zagreb's Lower Town. By this point, as Jadranka expressed it, "We have to continue to offer resistance even if it's futile, even if it's just to show that we're living according to our beliefs." Rimi added that "business as usual" could not continue while the victims of the war mounted: "We will use our bodies as wrenches in the works."

On this occasion, Pero did not appear to have been singled out for arrest; police only seized him when he attempted physically to "unarrest" a German cyclist being dragged by his dreadlocks toward a waiting prisoner van. Pero's subsequent interrogation confirmed his and Rimi's suspicion that they were under close surveillance. His interrogation also revealed a shared and, given earlier positive activist views, surprising understanding with the police regarding the nature of civil society. The detective's questions—about foreign funding, party affiliation, and professional staff rather than volunteers—and Pero's response, "It was like they thought I was one of those fucking NGOniks," reveal some of these common assumptions. (I return to this apparent understanding and the deeper political differences it masks below.) Zagreb's radical activists were feeling beleaguered, isolated, and targeted by mid-May. Pero, as usual, remained characteristically whimsical about this— even brushing off the police beating he received in detention as a "couple of smacks." Rimi, on the other hand, was angry, and not only at the police. "We had the chance with the antiwar campaign," he said,

> to reach a much wider public than usual. We had a rare chance to organize confrontational direct action against the state with wide public and wide media support. You saw how even those snobs (*šminkeri*) joined our march on Ilica. How the media ate up the theater of our protests. Reporters understood that these protests linked us to a much larger resistance to the war. Even they wanted to be part of that. Then those fucking "peace police" worried about appearing respectable, worried about looking like legitimate partners for the ruling coalition. They distanced themselves from us. Criminalized us! I mean, come on, let's be clear, some of them were worried about pissing off their funders. So they sold us out. They made it clear that we could be excluded, that we were beyond the pale. Not only did those NGOniks tolerate the police targeting us, they called for it themselves.

Jadranka was similarly disheartened about the role of Enough Wars! in "criminalizing" more "autonomous forms of actions"—in part seeing this as a personal failure. She explained that one of the reasons she had persisted in Enough Wars! was so that anarchists of her generation would have a "voice" in that forum and because she thought that her presence would make the marginalization of radicals less possible. Jadranka also articulated a broader sense of despair for participants in the alterglobalization movement, a despair precipitated by the invasion of Iraq and the wider War on Terror. "Look," she declared,

> on the one hand we should be proud of what we've accomplished. We [in the movement] built an infrastructure of communication, of collaboration, that

was able to generate the largest day of protest in history. We did this without centralized parties or labor unions. Or at least they were not dominant. . . .

On the other hand it couldn't be clearer that public opinion can just be ignored. Polite protest can just be ignored. Global public opinion is as irrelevant as Croatian [opinion] is. Polite protest is useless and anything more than polite protest is criminalized.

Pero, Rimi, and Jadranka's palpable anger would inform their decisions, along with another dozen Croatian activists, to make the 750-mile trip to Greece to attend the late-June protests.

NGO-nik Perspectives on Zagreb Anarchists

My primary field research, conducted among Zagreb's direct activists—including during the Enough Wars! campaign—positioned me in ways that inevitably color the descriptions above, tingeing them with the stark moral contrasts of the highly critical anarchist perspectives on civil-society organizations and actors. In an effort to complicate this overly simplistic opposition between civil and uncivil political engagement, I often spoke with representatives of various NGOs during my fieldwork. The two conversations below, with prominent civil-society figures, still bear the traces of my positioning, not least in the ways they both perceived me to be aligned in certain regards with Zagreb's anarchists. After all, by this time I had served as one of the rotating spokespeople for Enough Wars! (along with dozens of others) and had often been seen socializing and marching with radicals. Only a few weeks before my conversation with Goran, described below, my video footage of Pero's arrest had been used as evidence of police abuses against activists and had been shown extensively in the media. These two conversations, with very different NGO leaders, provide critical glimpses of the nature of civil society's relations with anarchists by spring of 2003.

Civil Scene: Encounter One

We are running late when we turn off Vukovarska Avenue and onto Savska Road and then into a maze of back streets, finally ending up at the rear of an eight-story apartment tower dating from the early 1970s. Only when we reach the fourth floor are we able to escape the unseasonable early June heat for the air-conditioned office. We are welcomed by Snježana, the wife of the director of this small but high-profile domestic human-rights NGO, which I will call CHR. Tihana, a moderate Enough Wars! activist from the city of Karlovac, accompanies me because she says she has followed CHR's work for years and has never "had an excuse to meet Goran." On the steaming tram ride to the office, Tihana explained that Snježana and Goran, the director, lost their faculty positions at the Electrical Engineering Faculty in the early 1990s as part of a politically motivated purge.

Inside the office, two aging Istrian hounds lounge on a well-worn couch. They are shooed away to make room for us. Alongside photos of Goran, posters from various civil-society campaigns around the former Yugoslavia adorn the walls.

While we wait for Goran to return, Tihana asks about the history of CHR and Snježana prints out a brief biography of Goran for each of us. She lets us peruse a half-dozen large binders with different CHR campaigns labeled on their spines, each binder stuffed with press clippings. She describes CHR's current humanitarian and legal work in Kordun, a region in the former Habsburg Military Frontier or *vojna krajina* that was the scene of reciprocal Serbian and Croatian ethnic cleansing in the early 1990s. Tihana, who grew up not far from this area and who is herself Serbian, listens intently. One CHR project involves buying goats for local residents, mostly elderly and impoverished Serbs who did not flee when Croatian forces retook the area. This project involves money from the Ministry of Agriculture being transferred to local municipalities where it is specifically earmarked for this project. With right-wing parties in control of the local municipalities, this arrangement has proven difficult, Snježana complains: "We depend on intervention by [the center-left parties in power] at the national level to overcome the resistance of local administrators hostile to the Serbian population."

When Goran arrives, Snježana serves us glasses of water, and a few minutes later she puts ginger snap cookies on the low coffee table between us. I explain to Goran that I am researching the Square of the Victims of Fascism as an example through which to show larger ideological changes, especially the shift in attitudes toward the antifascist struggle. Snježana fetches CHR's extensive archive from the Committee for the Square of the Victims of Fascism. The files include news clippings related to the renaming of the square as Square of Great Croats and the annual protests organized to return the name to Square of the Victims of Fascism, as well as a mix of fliers and posters. There is also correspondence: to various government ministries, the Sabor, President Tuđman, as well as to and from international organizations such as the Simon Wiesenthal Center. Goran, who has always been very publicly associated with the campaign to restore the communist-era name, appears pleased with this line of inquiry and we speak at some length about the campaign, including the vicious media attacks and anonymous threats he endured.

I then broach the second reason for my visit. I say that during my field-work in Croatia I have witnessed an emerging pattern of police pressure on leftist activists, a pattern that has intensified over the past year. I describe the case of Jure's involvement with last year's anti-NATO campaign. Jure, an an-archist in his late twenties who drove a forklift in a distribution warehouse for several years for Metro, a large international retailer, was terminated when he began to talk to coworkers about unionization. In September of 2002, he helped organize an "Anti-NATO Street Party" that gathered a few hundred people for Food Not Bombs, anti-militarist street theater, and music from live DJs. He was one of two organizers listed on the application to the police for a protest permit, a legal requirement for all public gatherings of more than fif-teen people. The event passed without incident.

Six weeks later, three plainclothes detectives showed up at his front door. They brought him to the central police headquarters on Petrinja Street for sev-eral hours of questioning. The police demanded to know who among Zagreb's activists was planning to attend protests against NATO's eastward expansion at the November NATO summit in Prague. The police told Jure that in the interest of "international cooperation" they would be sharing this informa-tion with their Czech counterparts so the authorities would know who to ban from entering the country. When Jure insisted he did not know people's plans, the police told him that his name and all those known to have participated in any Croatian anti-NATO activities would be listed. Jure, in fear that he would be turned back at the Czech border—or worse—decided to stay home.

I describe to Goran other "informational conversations" (*informativni razgovori*), as they have been known since the socialist era, in which activists were confronted with thick police dossiers that included pictures of them in public and private settings, employment and educational records, lists of or-ganizations with which they were associated, as well as the names of those in their closest social circles. I describe the developing pattern of arrests, such as those at the Philosophical Faculty antiwar march, where people were ar-rested, held for twelve hours, and released without being charged. I describe to Goran the arrests, only a few weeks earlier, of bicycle caravan participants on their way to Thessaloniki.

I ask Goran if he believes that these incidents constitute a violation of ac-tivists' rights. Goran responds by discussing police excesses prior to the cen-ter-left electoral victory in 2000, the right-wing culture of the police, and their lack of proper training. Sidestepping my question, he says, "The police force is characterized by a disproportionate presence of military combat veterans. The police have a desire to identify themselves, especially internationally, with the war against terrorism. But they are unwilling to address local far-right terrorism."

Goran, who had been quite animated earlier, especially when we discussed the Square of the Victims of Fascism, now speaks with a tone of fatigue, avoids eye contact, and stares down at his hands. "I never, even as a young man," he continues, "felt drawn to radical action." He intimates that these anarchists may be "violent" and that, though he worked with Antifascist Action on the protests for the Square of the Victims of Fascism, he does not know what kind of elements there may be among them. "The left in Croatia also has some dangerous tendencies to see the ends as justifying the means," Goran concludes, reversing the anarchists declared commitment to means over ends.

"But," I respond, "there are no examples of violence on the part of these activists—or for that matter any leftist element—in the twelve years since Croatian independence. These activists seem to be targeted solely for their political views, such as those against NATO." I say that the only stories of violence by leftists in Croatia I have heard in the course of my research were related to fights with skinheads. I do not mention what I have seen or heard of anarchist participation in confrontational alterglobalization protests internationally.

"In any case things were much worse before. And some of those groups," Goran insists, "may include violent individuals. Don't misunderstand me; I have no objections to physically defending oneself from skinheads. I wanted to beat them up myself after they attacked that Gypsy woman," he adds, surprising me by using the pejorative *ciganka* rather than the politically correct *romkinja*. "And anyway, the police have, back in the 1990s, confronted me with lots of things in my own dossier, such as the time I met with an American researcher writing his dissertation on NGOs."

I am not certain if this last remark is directly addressed to me or simply meant to indicate that one should not take too seriously such police attention. When I glance over at Tihana, I worry that she may be regretting her decision to meet Goran with me rather than waiting for another opportunity.

"But it seems to me," I insist, though I can feel myself faltering a bit, "that the police pressure comes from the highest levels. It is always the *interventna policija,* or special police, that monitor activist gatherings."

"It was so good to have the Minister of the Interior, Lučin, come to the Gay Pride protest last year," Goran responds, apparently returning to the theme of relative improvement. "That would have been unimaginable in the past. He is such a decent fellow."

Disheartened, I ask, "Who might be interested in dealing with this issue?"

"Do you mean which journalists might cover it?"

"No, I am wondering which human-rights organizations might be interested," I persist.

"You could tell them to come to talk to me," Goran says, shrugging.

When we are back out on the street waiting for a tram, Tihana says she does not know which way to read Goran, cynically or pragmatically. "Pragmatically, I think he just wants to keep the right out of power in Croatia because he knows how dangerous they are. With this in mind, he doesn't want to give the new government any trouble because this will only strengthen the right. But, cynically, I think . . . he just wants his goat money."

While I had long been impressed by the work of the CHR, especially during the Tuđman years—and believe it would be very reductive to see the organization as primarily driven by funding concerns—I had not expected an enthusiastic response from Goran to my questions about anarchists. In an earlier conversation with me, Jadranka had named him as one of the "civil society patriarchs." The extent to which the mistrust was mutual nonetheless caught me off guard. The conversation at CHR made clear that the organization embodied the kind of NGO politics that Jadranka had worked to resist within Enough Wars!, and to which Rimi and Pero had been so allergic that they had been unwilling to participate in the initiative at all. The CHR was built around a single prominent public figure—precisely the kind of leadership that anarchists' nonhierarchical practices sought to prevent or disrupt if it should emerge. The CHR also took funds from both USAID and the Croatian government, violating the anarchist commitment to autonomous forms of organizing and self-financing. In a related vein, anarchists were often troubled by the professionalization of activism that NGOs brought with them, in which some—Goran, Snježana, and one administrative assistant in this case—made their livelihood from the organization undermining the voluntaristic spirit that had animated many initiatives in their early years. What is more, both in their style and in the content of their critique of Croatian and global politics, the CHR crafted an image of itself as the embodiment of responsibility, moderation, and civility. To be sure, many of these differences were also generational, both in the sense that one's age defined one's specific historic experiences, and in the sense that youth, as a specific period of life, is impactful, as will become more evident below.

Civil Scene: Encounter Two

A few days after my visit to CHR, I contact Vjera, hungry for a perspective that might bridge the growing chasm between the NGO and anarchist scenes. Upon exchanging a few emails, we agree to meet at her attic apartment in the eaves of a 1920s working-class row house not far from Maksimir Stadium in Zagreb's east. I had rented a room from Vjera in this very flat in 1996, when I first did research in Croatia. She was under regular police surveillance at the time because the alternative biweekly she edited, *ARKzin,* developed out of the antiwar movement of the early 1990s, had published an investigative report on the personal wealth that Franjo Tuđman accumulated as Croatia's first president. Her landline would crackle and pop when I picked up the phone receiver. Sometimes one actually heard the police station in the background, behind the static. The point, Vjera explained patiently to me, was intimidation, not surveillance. Today I was turning to Vjera for her analysis, informed by her experience of moving from self-consciously anarchist initiatives to more formal NGO organizations. After participating in some of the earliest actions of the Zagreb Anarchist Movement in the late 1980s, Vjera helped to found a series of important and highly political Croatian NGOs, including the Antiwar Movement of Croatia (ARK), *ARKzin,* and then the Alternative Factory of Culture (Attack), the cultural center that hosts most of the concerts Rimi promotes. Finally, Vjera helped to found and run GONG (*Građani organizirano nadgledaju glasanje,* or Citizens Organized for the Monitoring of Voting), a key voting-rights organization that helped unseat the HDZ from power during the election of 2000.

We sit in the dormer near the only windows in her modest but cozy apartment, clutching mugs of tea made from the loose chamomile her parents gather near their home in Slavonia. In her midforties, with close-cropped hair and steel-rimmed glasses, Vjera can appear severe—and she is deadly serious when she talks Croatian politics. Once we catch up, I turn to the question of activist-civil society relations. Vjera is quick to preface her remarks with her enthusiasm for the younger generation of radical activists. "They've had a different experience than us. I'd even say I'm envious of them . . . They're not as burdened by the stifling inhibitions we felt having lived through and been active during the war and the 'years of lead.'" After a long silence, Vjera continues, "And, you know, they raise a lot of questions that we were certainly aware of but, because of the extreme urgencies of our reality in the 1990s, didn't dwell on." I ask her if she means questions around professionalization and formalization of civil society. She first speaks of the organizations of civil society in terms of their political legitimacy, the standing they had both among local progressives and with Western supporters. But it was also a matter of personal survival for many to be involved with these organizations, which represented one of the few sources of secure incomes for activists in very difficult times. Vjera also criticizes at length, however, what she calls, using an Anglicism, NGOization. Incidentally, in the longer passage of this discussion excerpted below, Vjera curses at precisely those moments when she understands that a moral compromise of some sort was unavoidable given the historic conditions she and other activists of her generation faced. "Look, now I'll be very, very honest," she begins.

> I was one of the first people who, in the middle of the 1990s, started to scream against NGOization because I thought that what was happening was a closing off, a loss of the spirit of initiative, the creation of some kind of semi-bureaucratic structures. [. . .] It seemed to me that through that relationship to funders you were caught in that circle of writing applications, getting money, justifying your activities, accommodating your activities with the immediate politics of foreign foundations. That seemed like something very problematic that we needed to be conscious of and to develop some strategy about how to negotiate.
>
> On the other hand, I have to say, I was twenty-seven years old when the war started. At that time I was unemployed and I had relatively little chances of getting a job in the system. And not just that I didn't have a chance, I didn't even want to work in the system. I didn't want institutional work; that's why it seemed terribly important to me to form alternative structures.
>
> We are a country that doesn't have social assistance in the way that exists in Germany or the Netherlands, where you can be unemployed your whole life, have social assistance, not sell yourself, be involved in various forms of radical action and be politically clean. Fuck it, that's not an option here. Here you have a choice: either you'll be unemployed, and that means your parents have to support you, or you have to, fuck it, go into institutions. For me, the formation of NGOs that could pay people was a terribly important escape.

I see NGOs, in the end, as what has allowed me to live and work on the scene. OK, sometimes you don't have money. Other times you do. But NGOs are what enabled me to remain what I am, to go on, to expand my thinking, to develop in this whole narrative. So in some way I see these fights about NGOization as a generational story. [...] I mean I really respect it if someone says: music is my life. But fuck it. I have to live from something! I don't have a patron. I don't have rich parents. [...]

Many activists are critical of any involvement with civil society. But when I decided to organize with GONG and try to finally get rid of Tuđman in 1999, I believed we had to do it however we could because he was just too fucking dangerous. I was even willing to work through elections, which, in principle, I'm opposed to. The institutions of civil society were the only ones we could deploy against him.

Vjera's remarks again delineate two distinct generational perspectives: the perspective of those who came of age during the antiwar movement of the 1990s and the perspective of those who became involved in activism in the 2000s. She also makes clear that some in the older generation were aware of political compromises they made—and believe they were necessary given the historical conditions they faced.

Beyond Civil Society

Bearing in mind the divisive history of Enough Wars!, what are we to make of Pero's interrogation? What does the detective's fundamental misunderstanding of anarchist politics—including its hostility to the state, its emphasis on decentralization, and its commitment to leaderless forms of decision making—tell us about the distinctive political imaginary that emerged during the alterglobalization movement of the early 2000s? How, on the other hand, should we understand Pero and the officer's implicit understanding, especially about "those fucking NGOniks"? Is this an instance of the apparent alliance between the far left and the far right in attacking the civil scene? Are these strange bedfellows evidence that—as is often asserted—the left and right meet at the extremes?

While police hostility to NGOs was not remarkable, anarchist antagonism toward civil society was almost unknown to Vjera's generation of activists, people who were only a few years older than Rimi, Pero, and Jadranka. To be sure, this new critical attitude toward NGOs reflected changes within the anarchist scene, not least the younger generation's vivid sense of participating in an ascendant global movement, a sense that was confirmed in the extensive links of Enough Wars! to the global antiwar movement. Such links—seen also in their other transnational collaborations—made it possible for activists in Zagreb to imagine that "another world is possible," an inconceivably optimistic ambition during the militarized, authoritarian, and repressive climate of 1990s Croatia. Anarchist attitudes also reflected changes well beyond activist networks: they point to the shifting historical ground beneath civil society as a concept and the specific set of organizations associated with it in Croatia. The precipitous decline in the global standing of the U.S.—long associated with the political ideals as well as the direct funding of civil society organizations—was especially dramatic in Croatia, which came under intense U.S. pressure to cooperate with the ICTY and join the Coalition of the Willing, even as it was forced to sign bilateral agreements that it would not send U.S. soldiers accused of war crimes to the ICC. The U.S.'s earlier promotion of humanitarianism and human rights, however opportunistic, was shunted aside to focus on security generally and the War on Terror specifically. Furthermore, in Croatian national politics, a center-left coalition came to power in alliance with many prominent NGOs, unsettling the longstanding association of civil society with opposition to state power (cf. Stubbs 2012:21). Finally, Croatia was undergoing broad economic changes during this period—in particular rising social inequality—challenges that NGOs seemed unwilling or unable to address. In this swirl of change, civil society, long associated with its autonomy from the state, was coming to be associated with dependence on state funding, proximity to official policy, and efforts to seek recognition from state officials—all positions fundamentally at odds with anarchist political principles. Rather than relishing confrontation with the state, NGOs sought a seat at the table and sought, at most, to return Croatia to the path of proper liberal democratization. These changes indicate, first, as Comaroff and Comaroff have argued in the African context, the aspirations of civil society have been "downsized, localized, tailored to the neoliberal era . . . [they are] purged, in short, of large historical visions and transformative schemes" (Comaroff and Comaroff 1999:vii). Second, the fluid political meaning of civil society—seen over the past three decades of Croatian history and dramatized during the Enough Wars! campaign—proves that, in contrast to the normative and ahistorical theorizations of civil society so common in political science (Tocqueville 1994 [1835]; Almond and Verba 1989; Putnam et al. 1993), civil society must always be understood in its specific political and social context.

Clarifying the reasons for anarchist alienation from civil society—including civil society's increasing association with the state—also allows us to distinguish the different motivations behind the apparent coalition between the police (often associated with the nationalist right in Croatia) and anarchists. To be sure, both anarchists and the police viewed civil society as lacking independence: both objected to NGO reliance on funding from foreign embassies and foundations and the inevitable political influence that came with it. But the police were defending the body politic from foreign influence, defending recently won Croatian sovereignty from "foreign mercenaries." The anarchists, on the contrary, did not object to the representatives of civil society as foreign mercenaries working against Croatia's national interest. They were fundamentally committed to transnational political practices, tactics, alliances, and collaboration. Their acceptance of, even demand for, my participation is one indication of this commitment. They did not posit the national state as an organism endangered by foreign objects within. Anarchists were not defending national sovereignty but the autonomy of self-organization that they feared was compromised by those who did not operate in a non-hierarchical, self-organized fashion.

This analysis, however, with its heavy focus on the state, perhaps misses one of the most important dimensions of the struggles around the Enough Wars! campaign and plays into the more moralistic and Manichean anarchist political tendencies: to see the state as a concrete thing and a mortal enemy. In this analysis, anarchists must keep the state at bay, external to their organizations—and if they do so, they will be free. This preoccupation implies a reified view of the state as an actual domineering force out there, a preoccupation which sometimes pervades anarchist scholarship as well as activism.[35] Throughout the Enough Wars! campaign, however, activist attention was not only on relations to the state as a centralized and sovereign power but also, and perhaps even more, on relations internal to the campaign, relations with one another. Activists objected to seating arrangements, to a deferential attitude toward expertise, to a creeping professionalism. They objected to styles of public engagement that were polite, civil, that they associated with notions of propriety—notions made explicit by Pilsel's attacks on forms of protest he deemed "uncivilized" and "barbaric." Activists were, in other words, attentive not only to the macro-power of the state but also to what Foucault has termed the "microphysics of power," those "subtle arrangements, apparently innocent, but profoundly suspicious" that structure power in everyday relations (1977: 139). We can see in these struggles an effort to cultivate particular kinds of relationships and particular kinds of political subjects—unruly, rebellious, in a word, uncivil—as well as a struggle to forge an autonomous sphere of politics beyond state power.

These efforts to work on themselves and their fellow activists, to develop other political sensibilities and desires, are further developed in later chapters, but first we will see how activists came to channel their deep frustration with the internal dynamics of Enough Wars! and their sense that, as Rimi summarized it, "No amount of polite protest will stop their wars. You have to be willing to use your body as a wrench in the works."

CHAPTER THREE

"FEELING THE STATE ON YOUR OWN SKIN": DIRECT CONFRONTATION AND THE PRODUCTION OF MILITANT SUBJECTS

This type of situation is doubly misleading. All at once the state reveals its repressive side, one that is more or less diluted in daily life. But now it has to make a show of force. To do so it sends in the police force with all kinds of gear and contraptions you didn't know existed. Fine. For the demonstrator the state appears like a vision, like the Virgin Mary at Fatima. It's a revelation. In extreme cases someone has the power to decide which side of the street you can walk on. And if you don't listen to kick you back into line. So the thing that forces you to get back into line is the state. But if you do force it to step back it's the state that steps back.

—CHRIS MARKER, *A GRIN WITHOUT A CAT* (1978)

Despite all their efforts to prevent it, you taste your own power. You see what you are capable of doing with others. . . . You never forget this. You're just not the person you used to be.

—JADRANKA

Messages ricochet—crossposted, forwarded, commented upon, glorified, mocked, deleted—through a vast interlocking web of listservs. Though virtual, these links provide one of the clearest infrastructural maps of the movement of movements, the network of networks. Zagreb activists' inboxes fill with calls to action, tactical debates, and news updates. Through the first half of 2003, we follow this flurry of electronic preparation for a "countersummit" against the meeting of EU member countries' heads of state in Thessaloniki as Greece takes over the rotating EU Presidency.[1] Activists in Zagreb take the pulse of the broader movement, decide whether to participate in this specific mobilization, and calibrate their expectations for the upcoming demonstrations based on the frequency of these electronic communications, the character of the actions planned, and the profiles of the networks involved. Some invitations, however, are delivered in person.[2] The International Bicycle Caravan itself, en route to Greece when it fell afoul of the Croatian police and Pero was arrested, represented a rolling, embodied invitation of sorts. A few weeks later, the lead singer of Czolgolsz—a Boston-based punk band named for President McKinley's anarchist assassin—exhorted the audience from the Attack stage to "join the marauding nomads."[3] The Greeks' invitation stands out, however, and because it was made using video—and centered on images of militant protesters confronting the police—it best sets the stage for the story I want to share in this chapter. This is a story of the images, experiences, and subjectivities generated when the activists clash with state authorities during large-scale direct action.

We gather in the large formal living room of Jadranka's squat—the space most reminiscent of Vila Viktorija's more prosperous past—to watch videos. Two activists from the Antiauthoritarian Movement,[4] one of the principal anarchist organizations in Greece, have carried these DVDs north as part of a hitchhiking tour of European "autonomous spaces." At their video screenings they solicit transnational participation in the coming Thessaloniki countersummit. A borrowed video projector layers incongruous images over the genteel-yet-faded green-and-gold-striped wallpaper: wave after wave of riot police, a blur of charging protesters, a fiery hailstorm of Molotov cocktails. The viewers in Zagreb sometimes cheer the protesters on. They sometimes whistle in disbelief. Pacho and I have our own anxious—if idiosyncratic—reactions to the videos. Our attention is drawn to brief glimpses of activists with cameras that the videos afford. They wear motorcycle helmets to protect themselves from police truncheons as well as a steady downpour of paving stones. In one sequence, a black-clad activist dodges between the waning flames of a shattered Molotov cocktail to her right and a car in full blaze to her left. She clutches a camera to her chest. I do not know if Rimi catches the worried look Pacho and I exchange, but as he pulls his black hoodie over his dreadlocks and prepares to head home he gently ribs me: "You did alright with the Croatian police [during the Bicycle Caravan], but are you ready for the Greeks?"

A week later, with these videos still fresh in my mind, I ask Andrej, a key collaborator in Ljubljana, if he plans to travel to Greece and his answer is swift: "No, I don't participate in actions when the organizers only share information related to medical and legal aid. You can imagine what kind of protests those will be."

*　*　*

Following the dramatic Seattle WTO protests, large protest mobilizations—usually in the form of countersummits against elite institutions' conclaves—became the most publicly recognizable face of the alterglobalization movement. These large transnationally organized demonstrations were conspicuous in the political imagination and social life of Zagreb anarchists. References to them appear in Rimi's songs and Pero's graffiti. Jadranka describes her first self-consciously political act as the small protest she organized in Zadar, her hometown, to express solidarity with protesters beaten and arrested in Genoa's G8 protests and outrage at the police killing of Carlo Giuliani. Activists in Zagreb regularly watched video dispatches, especially in the weekly self-education series *Subverzija*, from the frontlines of Seattle, Prague, Buenos Aires, Gothenburg, and Genoa. Furthermore, Zagreb's popular Enough Wars! campaign was organized through communications channels and collaborative networks first established for local protests tied to larger alterglobalization demonstrations.

I have resisted addressing these major transnational mobilizations earlier in this book, however, because I worry that these spectacular and relatively well-known events will overshadow other aspects of anarchist life in Croatia. Like many participants in the alterglobalization movement, I sometimes lamented the overwhelming media focus on mass protests—and dramatic and confrontational episodes in particular. Indeed, one of my early motivations for researching these movements ethnographically was so that I would be able to move beyond the now-familiar images of masked and anonymous activists hurling stones or building barricades in the streets, to provide a richer sense of individual activists and their daily lives. In this spirit, I have emphasized how physical confrontation during protest mobilizations is but one tactic in a spectrum of activities that make up an engaged and ethical life for my collaborators. The fact, however, that I did not first meet Croatian anarchists in Croatia—despite years in the region, collaborating and conducting research with various civil initiatives—but in Genoa, Italy, at the mass protests against the G8, is one indication of how central these protests were to my own research. My experiences in Genoa, Thessaloniki, Zagreb, and elsewhere convinced me that these mobilizations are crucially important. They are central to the reinvention of radical politics generally and, in particular, the subjective turn—the activist turn toward producing themselves as political subjects at odds with the dominant order.

These protests have generated vast scholarly and activist literatures[5]—including a rich ethnographic vein (Juris 2008; Maeckelbergh 2008; Graeber 2009; Razsa and Velez 2010).[6] I build on these ethnographies' key contributions, including the practices of antiauthoritarian organization and decision making (Maeckelbergh 2008), the dynamics of local and transnational networking (Juris 2008), and the ways the radical imaginary is both generated by and prefigured in collective action (Graeber 2009). My primary focus here, however, is on the experiential dimension of these mobilizations: the transformative effects of participating in dramatic confrontations with state security forces. Even before we departed for Thessaloniki, there was reason to believe, as Andrej concluded, that the protests in Greece would generate exceptionally intense confrontations.

Dynamics of Escalating Conflict

Andrej's critical assessment of the upcoming Thessaloniki demonstrations was not based only on the quality and quantity of invitations to Greece. He was also gauging local, regional, and transnational political dynamics when he concluded that physical confrontation was inevitable. First, many activists felt they had experienced the limits of "civil" protest when—despite protest mobilizations that were unprecedented in scale and global coordination—the "Coalition of the Willing" invaded Iraq. While some were furious that public sentiment was so easily disregarded, many anarchists argued that this only confirmed how fundamentally flawed and unrepresentative representative politics were in practice. Some activists pointed, furthermore, to a media dynamic around the wave of countersummits in the late 1990s and early 2000s that locked them into increasingly violent confrontation. Namely, if activists did not escalate their tactics at each successive summit, not least in terms of conflict with the authorities, there was a sense they would begin to decline, not least because they would be ignored by the media. As Rimi described it, "You have to outdo yourself each time if you want [mainstream journalists] to cover your actions." What is more, by the summer of 2003, the alterglobalization activists with whom I collaborated felt they were being swept up in the wave of state repression that followed their unexpectedly successful and disruptive direct actions at the 1999 WTO meetings in Seattle and the 2000 IMF and World Bank summits in Prague.

As scholars of protest and policing have noted (Della Porta and Reiter 2004; Tarrow 2005), this repression began in earnest in Genoa. In the days before the 2001 G8 summit—which gathered the political leaders of the world's wealthiest economies to make global economic policy—the Italian government closed the airport, railway stations, and harbor in Genoa. Italy's Minister of the Interior suspended the Schengen Agreement, reinstituting border controls with neighboring EU states. Fifteen thousand police and soldiers were mobilized, airspace was ceded to NATO-directed F-16 fighters, and batteries of rockets were placed around the port in a $115 million security operation (*CNN* July 18, 2001). Protest was prohibited in a vast "red zone" that encompassed the entirety of the historic city center. The Carabinieri, Italy's paramilitary police force, surrounded this zone with a twelve-foot steel wall and removed all residents they designated as security threats. Most ominously, Prime Minister Berlusconi made a public show of ordering two hundred "Vietnam War-style body bags" (*The Times* June 21, 2001).

Many activists decried this security operation as the "criminalization of the movement." However, this was a military rather than a law-enforcement approach akin to the ongoing U.S. "War on Drugs," or the worldwide "War on Terror" that would be declared only a few months later and would frame state responses to popular protest in the following years. Della Porta and Reiter describe Berlusconi's approach as nothing less than a "declaration of war" (2004). What is more, the militarized Genoa model was subsequently taken as a template and adopted elsewhere. Tarrow summarized this model:

> The Italian police were attempting to implement a new transnational strategy of protest policing, one that substitutes militarization for negotiation, truncheons for the provision of portapotties, and isolating protesters with chain-link fences for agreed-upon parade routes. We seem to be witnessing an international trend away from pacific protest policing to the militarization of police tactics. From Gothenburg to Prague, from Davos to Washington and Miami, police forces have been adopting harder and more punitive strategies toward protesters at international summits (2005:65).

Beginning on July 22 and continuing for seventy-two hours, Genoa witnessed full-scale assaults on public gatherings of any sort. Over five hundred were hospitalized (*The Guardian* August 1, 2001:2). Twenty-three-year-old Carlo Giuliani was shot in the head and killed by the Carabinieri.

Activists in Greece were clearly influenced by events in Genoa and the global dynamics of protest and policing it inaugurated—and there were constant references to Genoa in Greece—but activists were also responding to specifically local conditions. Several thousand Greek activists, including many from the growing anarchist movement, had themselves participated in the Genoa protests, becoming further radicalized by their experiences there (Giovanopoulos and Dalakoglou 2011). During the same period, Greek activists were confronting far-reaching urban redevelopment, especially in Athens, that sought to remove "undesirable elements" from the city center in preparation for the 2004 Olympics. These efforts included the eviction of anarchist-oriented social centers and squats, leaving many activists feeling targeted and setting the stage for a showdown in Thessaloniki (Giovanopoulos and Dalakoglou 2011). While local activists saw Thessaloniki as an opportunity to prove they could not be violently driven from public life, the Greek authorities viewed the EU summit as an occasion to demonstrate to the international community that they were capable of mounting a major security operation in the run-up to the games. Additionally, for a number of historically specific reasons, not least the legacies of resistance to the U.S.-backed dictatorship (1967–1974), Greek protest repertoires encompassed more militant tactics than in much of Europe—including, as international activists repeatedly noted, the embrace of Molotov cocktails.

"Summit Hopping"

Dozens of activists express interest in participating in the Thessaloniki mobilization, but many are unable, in the end, to secure funds for the long trip. Others, including activists affiliated with the Anarcho-Syndicalist Initiative in Serbia, are refused visas to Greece. Such constraints on activist mobility call to mind internal movement critiques of "summit hopping" and "riot tourism," especially concerns that transnational protest mobilization, as a mode of political engagement, favors the participation of the relatively privileged (Marco 2005; Juris 2008:157–159).[7] Some sixteen Croats, ten Slovenes, and two Macedonians make the trip to Greece. A few depart from Trieste by ferry. Others hitchhike to Belgrade where they catch free transportation on a Hungarian Social Forum bus. Jadranka, Pero, Rimi, Pacho, and I drive the 1100 kilometers across Croatia, Serbia, Macedonia, and Northern Greece, wedged into my 1990 Toyota Corolla. We travel mostly by night to avoid the scorching summer heat, stopping overnight in Belgrade and Skopje.[8] For Jadranka, Rimi, and Pero, like many activists, going to Thessaloniki seems to be as much about the trip as the destination. I do not mean to imply that the protests are a thinly veiled excuse for a vacation. The local activist-guided walking tour of Skopje, featuring its Albanian-Macedonian ethnic relations and punk hangouts, is as close as we come to traditional tourism. Jadranka, Rimi, and Pero do, however, eagerly anticipate visiting friends and comrades along our route, not least to compare their activism with the experiences of activists in other former Yugoslav republics.

In many ways, the trip through the former Yugoslavia is thus experienced as a personalization of existing electronic networks, a series of face-to-face visits with individuals usually encountered only as email addresses on the region's activist listservs, above all on the anarchist-oriented ex-yu-a-list. Throughout this trip, including during our time in Thessaloniki, activists stress the importance of conviviality, what Jadranka describes during the long drive south from Belgrade as "taking a little time to just be together as human beings." Rimi's written account of the summit—published in his zine *Borba* (The Struggle)—emphasizes socializing during our stops en route nearly as much as the dramatic events to come in Thessaloniki. He describes drinking cheap beer from plastic liter bottles with the anarchist punk Subwar Collective in Belgrade while dissecting nationalist Croat-Serb violence around recent water polo championships.[9] He writes of trading political fanzines, pins, and posters with anarchists in Macedonia, and, on the return trip, helping the Serbia-based Anarcho-Syndicalist Initiative put the final touch on an issue of *Direktna Akcija* before collapsing in exhaustion on the floor of their apartment. Eating, drinking, smoking, and dwelling closely together— often in trying conditions—are central to the bonds formed during these trips, as are the cycles of reciprocity initiated in such hospitality.[10]

This movement among activist nodes, including the series of international contacts and reunions that followed in Thessaloniki, make tangible the existence of new political collectivities, and the new forms of sociability that accompany them. The nodes through which activists travel are larger and relatively more permanent when they travel westward: squats in Austria, social centers in Italy, and Basque youth centers in Spain. When they travel south and east—as they do on their way to Greece—they find smaller, more informal, more secretive locations. Šibenik, on the Dalmatian coast, offered one of the most extreme examples, where we once found ourselves housed in a clandestinely squatted former Yugoslav army bunker, twenty meters underground (watch "Life Underground"). Such activist nodes structure patterns of movement and serve as familiar places that activists share with others.

When Jadranka meets international activists at an IndyMedia meeting in Thessaloniki—she is probably the most outgoing and effective networker of the group—she will find that they have both watched films at Rote Flora (a squatted theater in Hamburg), and have eaten (and cooked) at the Cucina Popolare at the Leoncavallo Social Center in Milan. In a manner analogous to how pathways of colonial travel and bureaucracy contributed to the emergence of national identification among colonial administrators in New Spain (Anderson 1991),[11] activist circuits of travel and reciprocal hospitality facilitate embodied lessons in common transnational belonging.

"Gathering of the Tribes"

We drive around in the bluish gray of early dawn, scouring the empty streets for someone who might direct us to Aristotle University. When we turn onto a broad avenue and see a five-story concrete building draped in a forty-meter "Smash Capitalism!" banner, we know we have arrived (see figure 3.1). We already know from listserv updates that various militant factions occupy the grounds of the university. Some, such as the Greek Social Forum (GSF), negotiated with the city for their space on this postwar modernist campus. Others, including several anarchist factions, IndyMedia, and some autonomist Marxists, have forcibly entered and squatted buildings. Though we read that the Law of the University—a constitutional legacy of the 1973 massacre of a left-wing student uprising against the junta—protects the campus from police incursions, we are nonetheless startled by the degree to which the campus feels like "liberated territory" as Rimi describes it.

Based on earlier reading and discussions—including with the two Greeks who visited Zagreb—the former Yugoslav contingent has decided to align itself with the Antiauthoritarian Movement (AM) while in Thessaloniki. We wander the campus in search of their encampment and find the anticlerical AM ensconced in the Theology Faculty. We will pitch camp on the lawn not far from their temporary infrastructure—vegan restaurant, stage, sleeping quarters, showers, first aid, and meeting hall—but for now we throw down our gear beside the International Bicycle Caravan's bike repair trailer and the aging Swiss tractor that has dragged it thousands of kilometers. Now we need to find our ex-Yugoslav comrades (*drugovi*) from Croatia and Slovenia, some of whom came earlier in the week to help squat buildings and plan events. Rimi immediately runs into Greg, the lead singer of Czolgosz, and a moment later Jernej, lead singer of Slovene anarchist punk band *Aktivna propaganda*

Figure 3.1. The occupied campus of Aristotle University, Thessaloniki, Greece, June 2003. *Photo by Francisco Ciavaglia.*

(Active Propaganda). Greg sketches the political geography of the campus for us and outlines the major events of the coming days. Wednesday there is an explicitly nonconfrontational immigrant-rights march against the "EU border regime" and the growing right-wing xenophobia in Greece. Thursday there are a series of actions planned against the fortified seaside luxury resort on the Halkidiki Peninsula in which the heads of state are meeting. Saturday is designated a general "day of direct actions" against state and corporate institutions within the city of Thessaloniki. "It's then everyone is expecting the most serious shit," adds Jernej. Greg and Jernej advise us to form an affinity group, especially for Saturday. "Anyway, you'll learn more at the spokescouncil meeting later today."

Despite the early hour—it is only now 6:30 AM—small groups gather among the tents, talking. Others, new arrivals like us, trickle in, picking their way among the scattered sleeping bag cocoons to claim open patches of grass. We have not slept since Skopje, but Jadranka is jittery, beaming. "All these little pockets of disobedience . . . from all the corners of Europe," she says. "It's a gathering of the tribes."

A few hours later, over a breakfast of bananas, bread, and boxed pineapple juice—food collectively "liberated" from a nearby grocery chain—Jernej fills us in on some of the factions present and on the organizational forms the AM has adopted to manage the political differences among these factions, the "gathered tribes." "Yeah, like Greg said, everyone who wants to participate in Antiauthoritarian Movement actions is being asked to form an affinity group, if they don't already have one. We've proposed having our people [the ex-Yugoslavs] form one. Then we can send a spoke [or spokesperson] to today's spokescouncil." The organizational form Jernej is describing was predominant among antiauthoritarian alterglobalization activists of this period (Maeckelbergh 2008:43–44), especially in the wake of what many saw as its dramatic success during the 1999 Seattle WTO protests.

While the term "affinity group" was often used loosely in Zagreb to refer to individuals who collaborated on a given initiative, such as Food Not Bombs or Green Action; more generally affinity groups are understood among direct-action-orientated activists as the basic building block of antiauthoritarian political organization. They typically consist of five to twenty people who have gathered around shared political causes and a common sense of what kinds of actions to pursue. Longstanding familiarity and trust within affinity groups is believed to prevent police infiltration and the decision-making process is typically egalitarian, participatory, deliberative, and consensual (Dupuis-Déri 2005). Such affinity groups can be traced from late-nineteenth- and early-twentieth-century Spanish anarchists, through U.S. and West German antinuclear movements during the 1970s and 1980s, to radical movements of the 1990s and 2000s.[12] A shared sense of what tactics are appropriate to a given event and what risks members view as acceptable is important so that quick decisions can be made in the dynamic conditions of ongoing actions.[13]

While intermediary forms are also sometimes utilized[14]—such as clusters of affinity groups—the spokescouncil is typically the largest, most overarching organizing structure in anarchist frameworks for coordinating mass action. Each affinity group (or cluster when clusters of affinity groups are used) empowers a spoke (spokesperson) to go to a spokescouncil meeting to decide important issues for planned actions—though it should be stressed that the spoke, unlike an elected representative in electoral democracy, conveys the affinity group's positions rather than deciding for those not present. In the context of a countersummit, spokescouncils often need to decide on legal and arrest strategy, possible tactical concerns, meeting places, and other logistics. A spokescouncil, it should be made clear, does not usurp an individual affinity group's autonomy; affinity groups make their own decisions about what they want to do on the streets (as long as it fits within action guidelines decided upon collectively). All decisions in spokescouncils are made on the basis of what affinity groups have authorized their spokes to endorse and by consensus, so that, ideally, all affinity groups have agreed, and are committed to, the mass direct action in question by the end of the process.

As mentioned above, in the wake of the Seattle WTO meetings[15]—especially the disruption of meetings and the collapse of the WTO's trade talks—these organizational forms were adopted to varying degrees throughout North America and Europe.[16] Of course not all participants in the Thessaloniki mobilization were anarchists or shared anarchist commitments to nonhierarchical organization. Those committed to network, egalitarian, and horizontal self-organization acted in relative degrees of coordination and antagonism with other constituencies, including not only Marxist-inspired revolutionary parties and nongovernmental organizations but also churches and labor unions. I will return to the ways that these various constituencies were coordinated despite profound differences. In any case, contrasting the militancy of the AM with some of the more moderate constituencies, Jernej concludes, "People seem to be expecting a real fight here."

While there is a growing concern—or anticipation, depending on one's attitude—that Thessaloniki is going to witness significant confrontations with the security forces, the experience of the countersummit is not primarily a violent, confrontational affair, even for the most militant protesters. We tour a pirate radio station in the occupied Law Faculty. We listen in on spokescouncil meetings. At the IndyMedia Center, we settle in at the open computer lab to check up on Croatian media coverage of the summit and countersummit. We stop to read posters and graffiti throughout the city, just as we would in Zagreb. When Pero finds that the large billboards surrounding the International Exposition of Thessaloniki read, "For a Europe for All Europeans," he intervenes with his always-at-hand heavy black permanent marker. The "corrected" text reads simply "For a Europe for All" (watch "Europe for All"). Ominously, Rimi finds a bloody medical stretcher on the street and delivers it to the Antiauthoritarian Movement's First Aid Center. We listen in on teachins and discussions about the political situation in Greece and the growing anarchist movement, much of which has emerged from a radical tradition of secondary and postsecondary school occupations against neoliberal educational reforms (see Giovanopoulos and Dalakoglou 2011). Most of our time is spent on the grounds of Aristotle University, exploring the activities of the numerous leftist groups, networks, forums, and movements that have occupied various faculties. We try to make sense of where we are, who is who, and what is planned for the coming days.

Thursday afternoon we join a six-mile march through the working-class and immigrant neighborhoods of Triandria and Ano Toumba in eastern Thessaloniki. The march is organized in solidarity with immigrants, mostly Albanian, former Soviet, and increasingly also African, who are widely perceived by participants as victims of EU migration restrictions.[17] A few years later, when the global economic crisis is felt with particular cruelty in Greece, migrant neighborhoods and businesses will become primary targets of neofascist Golden Dawn vigilante violence. During our Thursday march—because many migrants are undocumented—activists carefully avoid physical confrontation with police.

Late Thursday afternoon, Jadranka and I speak with Kostas, a local activist for IndyMedia Thessaloniki. He explains that there are sharp conflicts between various anarchist factions, especially between the Antiauthoritarian Movement, housed in the Theology Faculty, and what he refers to as the "Chaos Bloc," insurrectionist anarchist factions unwilling to affiliate with the Antiauthoritarian Movement. The Antiauthoritarians are nominally more tactically moderate, and hence are dubbed the "Sticks," while the mix of other anarchists—who occupy the neighboring Philosophy Faculty—are known as the "Molotovs."

One difference between the anarchist blocs—an especially contentious one in the setting of "campus life"—lies in their attitudes toward visual media, which epitomizes competing views among radicals. Some activists believe that radical politics, especially as enacted in spectacles of confrontation, can be disseminated through visual media. Others understand media, and visual media in particular, as intrinsically incompatible with radical action. Those associated with the AM are generally willing to collaborate with certain reporters from the mainstream Greek press—those they see as having a record of favorable reporting on the movement—and with members of the activist media, especially IndyMedia. The Molotovs, to the contrary, generally do not permit the presence of any video or photography, viewing cameras as an extension of the panopticon of the security apparatus. Early in the afternoon, Pero and I see two men rush a Greek journalist, beat him, and douse his camera with water when he dares to film near the Philosophy Faculty. A small crowd then rushes over from Theology Faculty, "Sticks" presumably, who attack the two men who assaulted the reporter. Needless to say, this approach to press relations does not put Pacho and me at ease. This situation prompts the activists traveling with us to plan to defend us and our cameras if we are attacked (watch "Protect the Camera").

What you ultimately experience in a countersummit like Thessaloniki—given the scale and diversity of these convergences, as remarkably varied activist traditions are brought together without any overarching authority—is highly contingent. In the end, how you feel about the countersummit, whether or not you ultimately judge it a "success," depends on which discussion circles you stumble upon, which local activists explain the domestic political context to you, which internationals you happen to camp beside, which bloc you choose to march with, even which alley you flee down when your bloc is shattered by tear gas, helicopters, fire hoses, and police charges.

A Militant March on a Luxury Resort

With physical conflicts over the presence of cameras—and hostile Greek network television crews reporting on the "terrorist threat" that anarchists pose—it is with some trepidation that Pacho and I prepare our video equipment for Friday's actions. We join thousands assembling to wait in line for busses, more than four hundred in total, to transport us to the Halkidiki Peninsula, some seventy miles east of Thessaloniki. Here, inside the walls of the luxury Porto Carras Grand Resort Hotel complex, the heads of state of the EU member countries are meeting. In the spectrum of the countersummit's militant direct actions, today's are planned to be somewhere between yesterday's nonviolent migrant rights protests and tomorrow's open attacks on a variety of corporate and state institutions back in Thessaloniki. Several activists remark that, because of tense political relations on the Greek left, common agreement among participating movements and organizations is more difficult to achieve, and more limited in scope, for this countersummit than for some others. In the weeks leading up to the countersummit, the agreement for today's actions was the subject of tense negotiation among delegates from the AM, GSF, the General Confederation of Greek Workers (the leading union federation), the Communist Party, and local community representatives, among others. Rimi outlines the agreement in *Borba*. He writes,

> At the coordinating meetings between blocs it was decided that while traveling to [Halkidiki] an agreement existed between all the groups, which included the communists and the social forum, that if the police stopped even one bus we would all stop and view that place as the Red Zone and begin the confrontation with the police.

A number of other baseline agreements were made among the various constituencies. For example, no Molotovs should be used today because the forested area is quite dry in summer and might easily catch fire, jeopardizing the homes and agricultural land of the small municipality of Neos Marmaras, which is formally hosting the protesters in opposition to the summit. The town council characterized the security operation as an "occupying army." Such baseline agreements are part of a framework developed in organizing previous transnational protests that make it possible for a variety of movements, from a diverse range of radical traditions, to converge rhizomatically and yet carry out common action. These agreements often include "diversity of tactics," allowing for the coordination of differing "blocs" of protesters prepared for different tactics, but nonetheless supporting one another in limited agreements. Agreeing to "diversity of tactics" means that those from one bloc will not publicly criticize the tactics adopted by others—though internal debate is welcome—and the organization of distinct blocs will allow each constituency to pursue its plans for direct action without interfering with others (see Juris 2008 for more on the tensions around diversity of tactics).[18]

Figure 3.2. Perhaps no image better captures the symbolic nature of militant action than this evocation of David and Goliath. Neos Marmaras, Greece. *Photo by Francisco Ciavaglia.*

Such blocs are often color-coded, though they are sometimes also known by the names of the respective organizations behind the blocs. Each bloc has, in theory, adopted a determined range of protest tactics to be practiced by that bloc. Activists and affinity groups are therefore able to choose the bloc in which they can make a maximal contribution and act in harmony with their political principles.[19] Blocs have most often been distributed geographically, with a distinct zone of the city reserved for their marches and direct actions.

In Neos Marmaras, however, because of the hilly geography, thick brushy forest of the area, and scale of the security operation, there is only one viable land approach to the resort complex, via the main access road, which is heavily defended at a bridge over a steep ravine. The beach is impassable because the military has stacked cargo containers two rows tall to form a seven-meter wall running into the sea. The sea is, in turn, guarded by a flotilla and destroyers, just offshore, train heavy guns on the marchers along the beach. After a few slingshot attacks on the Greek navy (see figure 3.2), we march to the access road, where some twenty meters from the turnoff there are hundreds of police blocking the bridge leading to the resort.

With only a single reasonable access point, any geographical distribution of the blocs is impossible, and the various constituencies have opted instead for the temporal distribution of blocs. This produces a situation in which the theatrical, perhaps even ritual, quality of direct action (Jordan 1998; Juris 2008:332) is more self-evident than it might be in other circumstances. In short, each bloc is forced to wait its turn to approach the single point of attack. Based on the participation of fifty local residents from surrounding villages in their bloc, the Social Forum is allotted the first time slot to engage the police. They adopt a White Overalls tactic—one created by Italian activists largely associated with the autonomist Marxist tradition—that has been common in antisummit protests and which thoroughly blurs lines between violent and nonviolent protest. A few hundred Social Forum activists wrapped in inner tubes, rubber matting, plastic bottles, swimming goggles, and hard hats charge the police. They bounced into the police lines with a padded thump before they are dispersed with a barrage of teargas (see figure 3.3). In the meantime, the bloc coordinated by the Antiauthoritarian Movement—hundreds of black-clad, motorcycle-helmeted participants wearing expired Soviet gas masks, clubs in hand—stands behind the SF, shuffling their feet as they wait impatiently for their turn in the hot sun. They step into the gulley to allow the gagging SFers to make their way back to the beach.

Figure 3.3. The Greek Social Forum was first in line to clash with the police, followed by the larger—and impatient—Antiauthoritarian Movement bloc. Pacho Velez and the author were trying to film from the slope visible in the rear. *Photo by Francisco Ciavaglia.*

The AM's earlier spokescouncil reached consensus that its bloc would initiate a frontal assault on the bridge and attempt to breach the police cordon. Pacho and I understood that this plan made the presence of cameras a potential risk for participants. Furthermore, we expected some activists, who would have no idea who we were, to be hostile to the presence of cameras, fearing that footage could later be used as evidence against them. We received mixed signals all morning, however. Many AM activists, not only the ex-Yugoslavs, had encouraged us to record. As we double-check our equipment and clean our lenses on the bus ride to Neos Marmaras, for example, two Greek women sitting ahead of us turn, unprompted, to say how important it was that "we make our own images. We know what theirs will be like." They closely echo the sentiment of an IndyMedia activist who pointed out yesterday that the police are using high-powered cameras both on the ground and from helicopters. "It's a shame we are ceding the war of images to the police and corporate media," he grumbled. "We should have our own self-representations." So as we exit our buses and the bloc begins to take form, Pacho and I film. Several activists gesture angrily, waving us away.

In an effort to find a balance between these conflicting demands and security assessments, Pacho and I modify our plan. We will record the march
from some distance, insuring that our footage will not reveal individual participants' actions, at least no more than police or media footage can. When
we see the terrain firsthand, however, it becomes clear we will be scurrying
up low stony hills covered in high grass, scrub brush, and terraces of olive
trees. To make matters worse, we are less mobile than usual because we need
our tripod for stability as we zoom in on the march from two hundred meters away. Just as the march grows close to the bridge, however, two dozen police in riot gear come out of the woods above us, sweeping down toward the
flank of the march. Having captured only a few shaky images, we scramble
out of the way. When we regroup, the march is already partially scattered, and
those who struggle near the bridge are shrouded in a cumulus of multihued
gasses. Soon additional police formations descend from a thick stand of trees,
and Pacho and I flee.

When we embark, a half-dozen activists gather at the rear of the bus to
see our footage. "We did not really get a chance to shoot," we try to explain.
As he watches the unsteady images we recorded, one Greek, his face caked
with tear-streaked white powder, asks us repeatedly, "This is all you got?"
"But people said we should only shoot from a distance," Pacho protests defensively. "*This* is not at all what it felt like," sighs another activist. Disappointed,
everyone turns back to their own discussions of the day's actions. Pacho's
pride as a cameraman is wounded; he mutters that this is all theater, enacted
so activists can perform militancy, then enjoy images of themselves.

Staging Performative Violence

Shortly before eight PM, our group of Slovene, Macedonian, and Croatian activists sit down in a tight circle among the tents. A few still visibly suffer from
the lingering effects of the chemical gasses and sprays the police dispensed in
Neos Marmaras. We discuss tactics for tomorrow's "Thessaloniki day of action." Activists speak a mix of South Slavic languages, most trying to approximate "Serbo-Croatian," the largest of what were three nominally equal national languages within socialist Yugoslavia. The Macedonians and Slovenes
are in their twenties, however, too young to have learned Serbo-Croatian in
primary school, before the collapse of Yugoslavia. Conversation proceeds fal-
teringly at times; a few resort to English.

Jadranka puts into words what many seem to have been worrying about:
"the atmosphere" is tense, suspicious, and at times outright hostile here on

campus. Last night, a fistfight between two Greek men broke out beside our tent, waking us at three AM. "It's not like normal," Jadranka continues, "when people gather and they're happy to see each other, happy to be together." She no longer expresses the buoyancy she did three days earlier when she first observed the "gathering of the tribes." "Everyone feels it," she frets, "the atmosphere is catastrophic." Indeed, in Genoa two summers earlier, I had been struck by the strong sense of camaraderie, even fierce joy among the most militant protesters—though anger came to predominate following police assaults on protest marches, the beatings of hundreds of demonstrators, and especially the Giuliani shooting.

Several others express similar anxieties about the atmosphere on campus, an atmosphere that exacerbates concerns some already had about the tenor of anarchist politics in Greece. Tanja from Zagreb says, "I keep hearing that many people came here to avenge Carlo Giuliani. That's only possible in Greece. What if they provoke riots?" Jadranka observes that the demonstrations might not be as large as expected, in which case it is unlikely that there will be violent confrontations. "No, it's not like that here," responds Tanja, "Here every protest, party, and concert ends in Molotov cocktails." "Ask him, he's been living here for months," she adds, gesturing toward Nenad, a Croat now living in Athens who came north to Thessaloniki for these demonstrations.

Rimi indicates that the likelihood of riots is, in part, what brought him to Greece. Jadranka—who I have heard criticize Rimi in an anarcha-feminist vein as too preoccupied with riots, too eager for direct physical confrontation with the police, and too prone to romanticizing the destruction of banks and other symbols of corporate and state power—turns to face Rimi, "You would have three days of riots, eh?"

> **Rimi:** No, it's not rioting for the sake of rioting, but rather because of the need to bring this whole situation into crisis, to open a bunch of questions. So people [who see these protests] ask these questions. It is obvious that something is rotten. How many people said "no" to the war in Iraq and look how it ended up. Peaceful protest is not enough.
>
> **Pero:** Wait, the point of such an attack is to create damage? To smash as many cops as possible? To smash corporate property?
>
> **Rimi:** The police will stand there, understand? I mean the goal isn't to attack cops. . . . We will not attack cops because we're dying to attack cops but because those cops will defend fucking capitalism with their bodies and that's

why they are attacked. I don't have anything personal against cops, you know. . . . Anyway, we know, we know from our own experience, that they want to terrorize us, scare us off the streets forever. We must show them we are still here.

Jadranka: Look, you can look at this as three levels. At one level there is straight at the bosses, at their resort in Halkidiki. The second level is to go into the city in a focused way. That means banks, corporations, and similar. . . . And the third level, which I think is a real possibility here, that's just plain wilding. I mean, sure, fuck private property. But if you want to send any kind of message, you have to figure out those levels—first, second, and third. Because the third [level] means destroying the cars of people who are just paying for them on credit. Where was it, in Switzerland, you were there [indicating Tanja]. The police channeled the protests into poorer neighborhoods [in Geneva during G8 meetings a few weeks earlier] where some people destroyed things. [The police] prevented them from going to wealthier neighborhoods.

Rimi: But, you know, we can solve that on the spot when it comes up. Because when we were in Brussels [for an earlier EU Summit in 2001] we experienced those kinds of things. Some people from the demo wanted to destroy some things, we even protected things with our bodies, things that were not agreed-upon targets. . . . I mean some people just came to destroy things. How can we prevent them from coming? But at the demo we can demand that they respect collective decisions.

Jadranka: Fuck the demo where I have to police my fellow demonstrators!

Rimi: Hey, that's the way it is. How can we control who comes? And if we want to communicate that resistance is still here . . . If we want to inspire others to not give up hope, it's on us to create these productive conflicts.

These affinity-group discussions highlight several aspects of my collaborators' relationship to countersummits. First, it is obvious that these activists have significant personal experience within transnational mobilizations. Tanja participated in the earlier Evian-Geneva G8 protests. Rimi joined previous demonstrations against the meeting of the EU presidency in Brussels. Pero and I traveled together to Genoa on the "G8 Express" train from Trieste. While I marched with Andrej—one of the organizers of the Noborder Camp—and other Slovene activists alongside the White Overalls, Pero sought out anarchists and the Black Bloc.[20] In making sense of what was happening and how to participate in Thessaloniki, activists drew on these earlier experiences.

What is more, the affinity-group discussions illustrate that the militant actions planned for countersummits—contrary to how they are often perceived by nonparticipants, a question I return to—are a form of intentional political action, even a specific form of communication. Rimi argues that they must "communicate that resistance is still here," so as to demonstrate that "the movement" has not been frightened from the streets by police repression, that it is "still possible to express real dissent," that the liberal consensus that the EU represents for him does not go unchallenged. Jadranka also implies that she understands their protest as a form of communication and, as such, they must calibrate their direct actions so they do not alienate the broader Greek public. While I had known these activists long enough not to be surprised by their extensive discussions of tactics, a few years earlier I had a very different sense of militant protest, formed primarily in relation to media representations of "violent protesters" and without direct contact with activists like Rimi and Pero. I saw confrontational tactics like those of the Black Bloc—which targeted symbols of state and corporate power—as an expression of thoughtless rage, almost a leftist analogue to football hooliganism. It was in Genoa, two years earlier, when I saw Black Bloc tactics firsthand, and later when I began to spend much more time with militants during fieldwork, that I began to question my condemnation. I came to see that the styles adopted, the targets chosen, and the images generated were a form of carefully considered symbolic action.[21] To say that these "riots" had a communicative dimension is politically significant because—as my own earlier dismissal indicates—the classification of actions as "violent," "mindless," and "destructive" structures fundamentally how we understand such actions.[22] Indeed, as scholars of political violence have highlighted, the ability to define political violence and popular riots as "irrational expressions of collective emotion and incapacity for self-rule" is crucial for state authority (Coronil and Skurski 2006:4; see also Cole 2006). In Thessaloniki, in other words, it is clear that, as E. P. Thompson has stressed, riots should not be seen simply as an instinctual response to stimuli, but, rather, as the intentional action of self-consciously political agents (1971).

While the confrontational tactics—including clashes with police and the targeting of corporate symbols for destruction—are intentional as a form of communicative action, they are definitely not revolutionary violence, at least as traditionally conceived. These actions are not intended to rout state security forces; they are not intended to overthrow existing authorities or seize control of the state. This became clearer when I later asked Rimi about how he understood his participation in such actions. "I mean you put your life in danger, we know that from Genoa, but you're not really in an all-out fight. You're not in the midst of an armed insurrection that's on the verge of a revolution," Rimi insisted. "I mean this is fundamentally symbolic, right?" Rimi's words are reminiscent of the activist essay, "Blocs, Black and Otherwise," written shortly after Thessaloniki (CrimethInc. Ex-Workers Collective 2005).

> As crazy as things get, remember that the police have firearms, and there's rarely any reason to risk getting killed for an action. A street confrontation with better-armed police officers *is almost always going to be something more of a spectacle of confrontation than a no-holds-barred, life-or-death battle;* there's no shame in this fact, it's just important to take into account. The police are restricted in what they can do by what public opinion will decree about it; you are limited in what you can do by a similar question, for whenever you move up to a more confrontational tactic the police will immediately upgrade their tactics to a level higher than yours. In this sense, streetfighting is a matter of chivalry for us radicals: we always permit our opponents the more powerful tools, in order to keep the violence from getting too out of hand—and, of course, to show off how much more noble and courageous we are! If the papers read (as they have before) "Violence erupted when activists began throwing back tear gas canisters fired by the police," it will be clear to everyone what's going on (CrimethInc. Ex-Workers Collective 2005).

The planned attacks on corporate and state symbols of power in Thessaloniki, as activists understood them, are therefore examples of what Juris has called performative violence (2008:166). With the political risks of performative violence in mind—especially the ways it allows the police to justify both the escalation of their own methods and a broader repression of protest (Juris 2008:162)—I later asked Rimi about his statement that there was a "need to bring this whole situation into crisis, to open a bunch of questions. So people [who see these protests] ask these questions." Did he worry that the police and the media would misrepresent his actions? "I don't worry about it," Rimi scoffed.

> I *know* it will happen. What else would you expect from the corporate media? From the police? Of course we'll be vilified on TV. But you can also organize actions that cannot be fully packaged by the media. You know they'll focus on what they'll call our violence. You know they'll say, "Look at what the poor police had to deal with." But some people will still see those images and be in-

spired despite their lies. They'll think, "I want to be a part of that." That's how it was for me when I saw the first pictures from [anti-IMF and WB protests in] Prague, of people really showing that they didn't agree with this system. They showed with their bodies that they resist. . . . No amount of lies can completely overwhelm the power of those pictures of bodies resisting.

What Rimi describes here is the collective production of scenes of militant resistance that in some sense cannot be fully reframed, that exceed police and the media's efforts to stamp their own meaning on them.

So while activists are self-conscious about the communicative dimension of confrontational direct action, this is nonetheless a highly specific form of communication. This is not primarily about the transmission of an alternative political platform—though media attention sometimes creates small opportunities for sound-bite-length interventions. It is, rather, about staging dramatic action that *in itself* embodies a message. After all, anarchists, like those gathered in our affinity group, did not plan to hold a press conference. They did not wish to address the state with a list of demands, an approach contrary to the prefigurative ethics of direct action.

In these affinity-group discussions, militants like Rimi and Pero were also expressing a sense that they were locked in a pattern of continually escalating their tactics if they hoped to continue to capture prominent media attention and with it the ability to communicate beyond anarchist networks.[23] In other words, without a major confrontation, there would be no press coverage of the movement. There was a widespread belief that protests—unless the conflict was more dramatic than previous ones—would be ignored, that their actions had simply become routine and were no longer newsworthy. It was with a desire to puncture this media blockade that Rimi spoke of reaching people so that they "wonder why we are ready to go so far. So it is obvious that something is rotten." What is more, because the anarchist movement was extraordinarily robust and militant in Greece, many believed that an exceptional mobilization that could not be ignored was possible here.

Beyond these efforts to communicate a certain form of political hope through militant action—that resistance was still growing, that activists were not giving up—there were also signs of despair. Rimi's remarks sometimes indicated that he believed their actions were ultimately futile. Four days earlier, after the drive through southern Serbia in the grueling afternoon heat, it was just finally cooling when we crossed the Macedonian border. Rimi was driving and he just stared straight ahead as the sun went down. "I just don't want to think later," he said, "that I didn't do what I could to express my refusal. I don't want to think in ten years that I lost my nerve when this much violence was being committed to protect this system both [in Iraq] and against us when we try to protest their plans."

After the affinity-group meeting, several of us walked over to the Law Faculty, where IndyMedia Thessaloniki had established a temporary media center for activist journalists. Each night, IndyMedia had screened videos in the large open atrium. People sat close together on wide concrete steps that afforded a view of the expanse of whitewashed wall that served as a screen. Some videos were announced in English, some only in Greek. They were primarily a blur of street battles. One featured Clinton's 1999 visit to Athens. Another I recognized as the video that Greek anarchists showed in Zagreb to invite us to this first "international mobilization in Southeastern Europe." The video showed hundreds of helmeted Greek militants hurling Molotovs at the police who tried to hold them back from the Thessaloniki shopping mall that housed the U.S. consulate.

A Greek standing nearby translated a few of the Greek announcements and provided running commentary. He intoned sarcastically—though at times mixed with a distinct enthusiasm—that the "riot porn" we were watching was "incitement." "There won't be any cameras tomorrow," he said, looking me up and down and pausing at the heavy camera bag over my shoulder. "People are furious," he added. "Did you hear? Some news crew smuggled a camera into the spokescouncil meeting and recorded secretly. They broadcast the most militant speeches [which called for the torching of the European Bank of Reconstruction and Development and the American consulate]. Those ones were probably by agents provocateurs too."

Jadranka had been sitting beside me through several Greek videos, but at some point I looked over and she was gone. I found her a few hours later near a stage erected for speeches and music. She was with an unfamiliar group of men and women talking quietly among themselves in English following a larger meeting on the "persistence of patriarchy" in the anarchist camp. The meeting had been called to respond to several complaints about sexual harassment as well as the generally macho climate on the campus, which Jadranka had described as, "Full of testosterone-charged guys ready to fight the police." The small group interrupted their conversation midsentence when I arrived. After a brief, awkward silence—ended only by Jadranka's reassurance that I was "OK"—there were hasty introductions.

Soon, Jadranka and I were walking back toward our encampment beside the International Bicycle Caravan. She told me that she had found a new group of anarchists with whom she would march tomorrow for the direct actions against major EU, corporate, and government institutions in the center of Thessaloniki. Jadranka spoke quickly and with an intensity I had not observed before. "They are insurrectionists," she told me. When I expressed incredulity that she would align herself with perhaps the most combative faction present, she smiled at me as if to say, "You *really* don't know me as well as you think."

I would only later—looking back over interview transcripts and recalling earlier conversations that had not made such an impression at the time—realize that I had failed to recognize a significant transformation of Jadranka's political outlook. Again, I had first met her only nine months earlier on the bus to the relatively moderate European Social Forum in Florence, Italy. She had been critical of the ESF and the WSF, but she nonetheless participated in planning sessions and networking with those present. In hindsight, her challenges to Rimi in the affinity group earlier tonight seemed as much the result of a now habitual personal conflict with him as some fundamental objection to directly confrontational tactics per se, as I had understood them a few hours earlier. I remembered our conversation a month earlier when we discussed Rimi's anticipated negative attitude toward her joining us for the trip to Thessaloniki. "Have you told Rimi I'd be traveling with you?" she asked. "I can imagine what he'd say since he thinks I'm an NGOnik. . . . He thinks that only real men can fight the police," she said sharply, "but he's never seen girls in action" (watch "Only Real Men").

As we arrived at our camping area, I asked her about her earlier participation in the Social Forums. She again looked at me as if I was quite naïve. "There is only so long I could let them use me," she said, speaking of the self-appointed leaders of the World Social Forum. "They use us, then turn on us, just like the NGOniks around Enough Wars! used us."[24]

Jadranka added that she'd just come from the basement of the Philosophy building (the building occupied by the "Molotovs") and she said that there was, fittingly, an assembly line for Molotovs.

"You will not be able to film tomorrow," she apologized. "I asked and no one felt comfortable with it in my affinity group. Even I'm not sure it's a good idea that there be a video record of this, especially after Gothenburg," she added, referring to incidents in which activists' video footage was seized by the Swedish police and used in the prosecution of activists involved in direct actions against the 2001 EU summit. "This, we'll have to do for ourselves."

Jadranka's comments indicate, again, that she felt activists had reached the limits of polite, legal, and strictly nonviolent protest during the campaign against the invasion of Iraq. What is more, the Enough Wars! campaign left her bitterly suspicious of those who spoke in the name of official NGOs. Her claim that "this, we'll have to do for ourselves" indicated a declaration of independence from these organizations, but also, perhaps, a claim that these actions were being carried out not for some larger agenda but "for ourselves," for what these actions would mean for the participants themselves—for their subjective stakes.

Saturday: The Limits of Confrontational Protest?

Pacho and I film the preparations: Rimi building tire-rubber armor, Pero cleaning Soviet-era gas masks, Jadranka checking eye rinse, goggles, gloves (watch "Hit Me With a Stick"). As the ex-Yugoslavs leave campus with the AM to form a Black Bloc on Egnatias Street, Pacho and I rush up the stairs of the Theology Faculty, hoping to film the assembly from the roof. We pick our way over several large barricades of classroom furniture—defenses should police attempt to storm the building. When we arrive at the ladder to the rooftop, we are met by two women in balaclavas. "Police helicopter coming down to watch us. And police filming from that roof," one says with a heavy German accent, gesturing to a building across the avenue. "Cover your face," she orders. This sets up the first image—and the absence of other images— which frame my participation and lack of participation in Saturday's actions. These images also reveal something of the political character of these protests. In this first image, a photo, Pacho and I are on the rooftop, crouched low, gas masks at the ready, lashed to our belts (see figure 3.4). As instructed, our T-shirts are wrapped around our heads to cover our faces. Something about the saturated colors of the photo, with the cityscape below us, calls to mind 1970s militants in the midst of an urban insurrection.[25] One has to look twice to see that it is a video camera, not a sniper's rifle or a mortar, at our feet. If this image is dramatic, snapped impatiently by one of the women in balaclavas, our footage is not. The camera, again on a tripod, frames faceless figures gathering in Black Bloc formation seven stories below. Tiny bodies lock arms around the periphery for security—to prevent police from splitting the march or pulling out individuals for arrest. It is distant, static, nearly

Figure 3.4. Pacho Velez and the author filming from the roof of the Theology Faculty, Aristotle University, Thessaloniki, Greece. *Photo by anonymous.*

soundless except for the circling helicopters above. When the march—some five thousand strong—has left our line of sight, we are warned that police and armored vehicles are grouping nearby. Everyone not prepared to defend the campus physically from police assault should leave.

In the end, Pacho and I decide not to participate in the Saturday action. We are concerned—tactically, ethically, simply for our own safety—about the level of force that many plan to use. We are worried that if we film our "characters," the footage might at some point be used as evidence against them. What is more, given the open hostility of some camera skeptics, it seems too dangerous to bring video equipment to the front lines. But, again, it is "an atmosphere" as much as anything else that makes us hesitate to join the planned direct actions—the rancorous climate that Jadranka alluded to in the affinity group meeting. Sian Sullivan, another activist scholar present in Thessaloniki, is scathing in her description of why she chose not to participate in what anarchists were claiming would be "the biggest riots Thessaloniki has ever seen." She wrote,

> Overwhelmed by a swaggering machismo and a palpable hatred of the police—matched by an intention to do physical injury—I left the campus before the

protest was due to begin, feeling confused and alienated by the calculated pre-paredness for violence amongst the protesters, and an obvious antipathy to in-tellectual reflection (Sullivan 2004:12).

While I recognize in Sullivan's description the Thessaloniki I experienced, I am less willing to render moral judgment with such conviction.

The last image that frames my (lack of) participation is another cityscape, shot from the city's northern hills. The video might also be a photograph but for a slight wispy movement in the frame. Clouds of tear gas puff first here, then rise there, tracing what Pacho and I anxiously imagine to be Rimi, Jadranka, and Pero's progress down the broad central avenue, down side streets, regrouping here and then there. A steady wind pushes the dissipat-ing bursts out toward the Thermaic Gulf (watch "Smoke Signals"). Like the footage of the Black Bloc gathering far below us on the rooftop, these tripod-shot images have all the humanity of a security-camera recording. There is nothing of the embodied, jostling drama of the Australian Noborder foot-age that inspired the re-enactment of the activist attack on the detention center. That footage jumps from one camera angle to another, from one ac-tivist position in the crowd to another, inserting the viewer into the intensity of the struggle. As participation and documentation merge in the Austra-lian footage, the viewer finds her consciousness suffused in the crowd. This echoes the ways Manoukian has described video making during the 2009 Iranian protests (2010). There is a "new social type in the street character-ized by the simultaneous engagement in a multiplicity of tasks. . . . This inex-tricable combination of action and mediation establishes new spatio-tempo-ral coordinates. Protests and their media become intertwining aspects of the same event" (Manoukian 2010:248). Image making is no longer the work of a semiprofessional clique of media specialists—whether a political or artis-tic vanguard—as it was for earlier movements,[26] but has become immanent to activist networks. In this respect, contemporary video practice mirrors the antiauthoritarian practices that typify other spheres of activist politics. But not today, not in our footage—and it turns out that Pacho and I were not alone in deciding not to film in Thessaloniki.

In the coming months, I try to track down footage of the protests that we might use in our film, corresponding with activists from IndyMedia Thessa-loniki and broader networks of European video activists. All will report that no one recorded during the Saturday confrontations. This contrasts sharply with other major mobilizations, such as the 1999 Seattle protests, when the

Figure 3.5. Many activists came to see cameras, even those held by other activists, as potential extensions of state surveillance. During Saturday's actions, security cameras were targeted for destruction wherever possible. Neos Marmaras, Greece. *Photo by Francisco Ciavaglia.*

first IndyMedia center was organized and activist filmmakers were able to draw on footage from more than 120 activists to produce *This is What Democracy Looks Like* (Friedberg and Rowley 2000). To fill this void in our own film, we are eventually forced to purchase footage from Reuters. No one but the police and the "corporate media," shooting from behind police lines, seems to have recorded the Saturday protests.

* * *

Later that night, I wait in the hills above the city. With Carlo Giuliani on my mind, I am already apprehensive when a text message arrives from Pero: "Me, Rimi OK. Jadranka arrested."

We speak with Rimi in person at one AM, some fifteen blocks from campus, at a prearranged spot where we could find one another if the police stormed campus after today's clashes. The Croats, like many other internationals, were skeptical when our Greek hosts assured us that the autonomy of universities would be respected despite the militancy of the actions planned for the day. While pitched battles were fought right up to the gates of Aristotle University, the police never entered campus.

Even now, the smell of teargas hangs in the air, five hours after the last barrages were fired.

> **Rimi:** The police just stopped me down below, when I was leaving the campus.
> **Maple:** Get in, have a seat. Is everyone okay?
> **[When Rimi gets into our car, the smell of teargas and gasoline is much sharper. The image shudders as Pacho sneezes. "It's the teargas," he apologizes.]**
> **Maple:** Any news from Jadranka?
> **Rimi:** Jadranka has been arrested. We're waiting to hear from the legal team to see what will happen to those arrested.
> **Maple:** Shit, what happened down there?
> **Rimi:** It was chaos, total chaos. I've never seen so many Molotov cocktails. I don't think that many of them were thrown in Genoa. . . . Molotovs flew at the communists [when they blocked our escape route] . . . Civilians on fire . . . it was horrible.

"And Jadranka?" I ask. She was with the small affinity group she met two nights earlier, Rimi explains, mostly international insurrectionists. Her group was close behind the ex-Yugoslav affinity group when a large formation of police charged. They successfully split the march, hewing Jadranka's group from Rimi's side of the march. The last time he saw her, Rimi says, Jadranka was crouched in a doorway midway down the block behind them, huddled with six or seven other activists. Police lines were closing in from both sides.

Rimi and I spoke for half an hour about various aspects of the day's actions, but his overall assessment of the protests was unsparing:

> **Rimi:** I don't know, I had such a good impression [of the organization for this], I thought we were going to do something, that this action would be successful since for the first time I experienced [spokescouncil] meetings where everyone seemed aware that it doesn't make any sense to attack just whatever. I thought it was good that there was an effort to organize a demonstration that could attack defined goals and which would at the same time be able to provide protection while such an action was being done—that everyone would be able to act together—so there wouldn't be arrests. But . . . some people, it seems, didn't share that view and they smashed everything. And inadequate equipment [against the police gasses] played a role. So this demonstration burst, there was nothing in the end. There was just useless destruction. With the slogan "we will avenge Carlo," pizzerias and kebab stands fell (watch "Kebab Stands on Fire").

Rimi, like most of the other activists I interviewed, said that their actions sparked rioting and looting by working-class and migrant youth who had their own grievances and who had not been party to any of the anarchists' collective decisions. As Rimi put it concisely, "They saw a chance to express their own rage and frustration at the system, in their own way."

Reflections on Limits

The subtleties of these dynamics aside, for many European militants, Thessaloniki marked the denouement of the cycle of mobilization around countersummits. After five years of continuously growing demonstrations and escalating tactics, the intensity and frequency of what Tarrow (2005) calls "megaprotests" began to diminish. In part, this reflects the limits of constant tactical escalation that, as Rimi articulated, necessitated that each new summit mobilization be more dramatic than the last to gain media attention and sustain a sense of a growing movement. Many also complained that countersummit direct action—despite the promise that accompanied its emergence in the 1990s of a return of creativity and spontaneity to left politics—was becoming predictable, even routine. Some grumbled that countersummits were always reactive; they were always organized in response to the plans of government and international organizations. Finally, there was also a strong historical consciousness—especially evident among some activist strands, such as Italian autonomists, who were tightly linked to my Slovene collaborators—that the experience of the 1970s, in which elements of the movement embarked on a clandestine urban guerilla struggle, must be avoided at all costs. Indeed, throughout the series of alterglobalization protests, there were efforts to find creative forms of direct action that were confrontational, which opened public conflicts with what were viewed as illegitimate authorities, while nonetheless trying to avoid being dragged by state violence into reciprocating.[27] In Thessaloniki, activists seemed to press up against the fraying edges of this creative direct action experimentation.

If not for the question of what befell Jadranka, this chapter might be concluded here. The methodological limits of my participatory research—especially as it involved shooting video—on the one hand, and the tactical limits of the escalating militancy of the alterglobalization summit protests, on the other, dovetail; both perhaps point to the political limits of this particular form of confrontational direct action. In terms of video, the Thessaloniki protests would not be shared with activists elsewhere as previous mobilizations had been—there would be almost no images recorded from within the movement to inspire further action. In terms of the trajectory of escalating confrontation, Thessaloniki seemed to indicate that only low-intensity warfare lay further along this trajectory. When I spoke with Jadranka years later about Thessaloniki, I said, "Many see Thessaloniki as a failure. Do you?" "No," she replied, "I see it as an endpoint of that period of protest." "Of those big demonstrations?" "Yes."

To be sure, as we will see, activists in Zagreb changed their emphasis in subtle and evolving ways in the months after Thessaloniki, turning their energies especially to the squatting of a community center and "Free Store." They sometimes described this new initiative as addressing the shortcomings of militant protest, especially insofar as it allowed them to reach out to a broader public, engaging their neighbors in viable alternatives rather than primarily expressing their refusal of the existing system and authorities. This shift in emphasis also seems to reinforce the sense that a certain limit had been reached—and perhaps it had in this cycle of global protest. I am nonetheless uneasy, at a number of levels, about making such conclusions too quickly. First, I am troubled that in the above narrative it seems that Thessaloniki only confirmed my initial views of which tactics were appropriate and which were too extreme. I knew better, it would seem, than to participate in such ill-fated and ethically questionable actions and so I withdrew to the hills. Such a self-congratulatory narrative establishes the ethnographer as arbiter of which actions are appropriate—even ethical—and which are not. This narrative would imply that I knew all along that violence only begets violence: I knew that Jadranka, Pero, and Rimi should never have been so naïve as to expect their acts of radical insubordination to achieve anything but an aimless riot. I am anxious because such a narrative would position me as precisely the kind of "judge" Herbert Marcuse (2007) argued so forcefully against in his refutation of intellectuals who condemned the radical movements of the 1960s. He wrote that,

> Law and order are always and everywhere the law and order which protect the established hierarchy; it is nonsensical to invoke the absolute authority of this law and this order against those who suffer from it and struggle against it—not for personal advantage and revenge, but for their share of humanity. There is no other judge over them than the constituted authorities, the police and their own conscience. If they use violence, they do not start a new chain of violence but try to break an established one. Since they will be punished, they know the risk, and when they are willing to take it, no third person, and least of all the educator and intellectual, has the right to preach them abstention (Marcuse 2007:55).

Maeckelbergh makes a similar point to Marcuse's, if more specifically related to the dynamics of protest mobilizations and tactical debates. Discourses on violence, she argues, are frequently middle-class discourses. When some activists criticize acts of property destruction, of self-defense, or attacks on the police because of the danger that they will alienate the broader public, they are thinking of a middle-class, white, relatively privileged public. Migrant youth, the urban poor, and the marginalized are more likely to come out and join the protests when they can relate to them and from Maeckelbergh's observations, and in the case of Thessaloniki, this seems to be more common when protests are confrontational (personal communication).

In any case, by the time I arrived in Thessaloniki, I was considerably more confused about the implications of these now predictably confrontational encounters than I had once been; I was far from certain that I should be acting as judge of my collaborators' militancy. My decision not to participate was made not with ethical clarity but from within a murky fog of fear and confusion, as well as a failure to see any role for my ethnographic methods in the specific political context that was Thessaloniki.

Beyond even these dangers of an all-too-easy moralistic conclusion regarding Thessaloniki, I worry about what will be overlooked if we consider Rimi and Jadranka's militant direct actions there only in terms of tactical and ethical debates around the question of violence. In part, I probably also imagine a middle-class audience considering my collaborators' participation and worry that the ferocity of the protests will repel them, make it too difficult for readers to remain open to Jadranka and Rimi's experiences (watch "Reflections on Images of Militancy"). In other words, I am concerned that a preoccupation with the external political efficacy or ethical justification of confrontational tactics will obscure what I came to see as one of the most important outcomes of these protests: their subjective effects, the ways they fundamentally changed those who participated in them. It is not that Jadranka and, even more so, Rimi did not understand the dramatic tactical failings of the Thessaloniki demonstrations. They clearly did. But their descriptions of events also indicate that something else, in addition to explicit political goals and forms of communication, was at stake in these actions. Their feelings about Thessaloniki were by no means one-dimensional. There was a mobilization of affect that mirrored the mobilization of bodies for protest. Rimi and Jadranka each found aspects of the confrontation emotionally exhilarating.

What is often glossed simply as violence opens to a multiplicity of social connections and subjective stakes. As Coronil and Skurski have argued, the connections forged in violence link physical and psychological force, individual and structural harm, pain and pleasure, degradation and liberation, the violent and the nonviolent (Coronil and Skurski 2006:5). The experiential and subjective stakes become clearer when I eventually speak with Jadranka—and clearer still in her political development, especially her wholehearted participation in subsequent militant action across Europe and beyond.

Experiences of Direct Confrontation

Jadranka arrives at the car only an hour after Rimi told of her arrest. She describes herself as *komirano,* in a coma, but she appears highly animated, even effervescent, to me. "It was good," she says. "What are these rumors? I was never arrested." Her face, like Rimi's, is flush from the sun and the gases, but also, from the thrill of what she has experienced. She acknowledges that the protests quickly got out of hand, losing all focus. "It was true what Kostas from IndyMedia said," she smiles.

> A Greek can't hold a Molotov in his hand for more than two minutes. . . .[28] People destroyed everything, not just what we had agreed upon as targets [worry passes briefly over her face], even bus stations, little shoe repair stores. Also our actions created an opportunity for local youths, including a lot of migrants, to express their rage. But I found real teamwork, real camaraderie like I've wanted for years. . . .

"It was, ahh, beyond words!" she continues. "We moved like clockwork. We were one unit. When anyone slipped, we had them up on their feet in a second. We were inseparable. I could feel our power, our potential. I don't know how else to say it. I was in love."[29] On the drive back to Zagreb, she adds, "When you've been through something like that together, you have a different kind of bond. You never feel the same again about those people, or yourself."

In *Borba*, Rimi describes his own experiences in the midst of the near-urban warfare in Thessaloniki. At times the sheer drama of events displaces the sense of strategic failure that he emphasized in our conversation immediately following the protests.

> At one moment the police tried to cut the demo from both sides, so now we were fighting on three fronts. While I was taking shelter in a nearby street, a special police unit arrived that wanted to divide our main bloc. But as soon as they came up the street a rain of Molotovs fell on them and they retreated. We pressed deep into that street and built a barricade of cars in the middle of the block. Later, as we started to retreat, the barricades were lit on fire. In one moment we found ourselves between fires. On one side and the other of this narrow street there were cars in flames and we were between them waiting to see the police's next move. At that moment it seemed to me that we were standing between two bombs. If those cars exploded I was going to die. . . . If we didn't fight together, we were not going to make it out of this alive.

This description, like Jadranka's, runs against the grain of Rimi's critical assessment of Thessaloniki, raising questions about the experiential and emotional dimensions of militant protest—and the ways that such actions are also implicated in efforts to recreate dramatic experiences, and images, of resistance.

*   *   *

Only a few years earlier, I had been absolutely certain of my ethical opposition to what I then dismissed simply as "activist violence." The videos I remember most vividly were shown at the first Noborder Camp, projected on a sheet stretched taut between two volleyball poles. The audience was scattered on and among the picnic tables and benches of a neglected socialist campground. I was shocked, even morally outraged, as I watched the scenes of protesters and police battling at the 2000 Prague IMF meetings. The pitched battle at Nuselsky Bridge was especially revolting. In the flickering images, cobblestones are piled high, forming barricades that hold the police's armored vehicles at bay. Masked and helmeted protesters hurl shattered pavement and Molotovs toward the police lines. Had anyone asked me, I would have been quick to condemn such actions.

In retrospect, I have come to realize that my certainty about the tactical inappropriateness, even moral bankruptcy of confrontational protest like I saw in those videos, was grounded in my experience of the outbreak of war in Yugoslavia. Nonviolence was the lesson I took to heart, having witnessed the downward spiral of reciprocal hostilities in the name of Serbs and Croats that destroyed Yugoslavia as a unified state. In this sense I shared the imprint of the war experience, if much less personally and directly, with the activist generation in Zagreb who formed the Antiwar Campaign of Croatia to oppose ethnic hostility. As emerged clearly during the Croatian movement against the U.S.-led invasion of Iraq, this older generation was quite critical of what they perceived as some younger activists' ambiguous relationship to political violence. The older generation was almost universally committed to strictly nonviolent principles.

My own moral certainty was first unsettled only a week after watching those Noborder Camp videos, when I found myself filming near the frontlines of the White Overalls march in Genoa. We were suddenly, without warning, the target of a massive coordinated assault by the Carabinieri. The memories are somatic; I feel them as much as I see them. Even now, when I watch the footage from those three days, my heart races. The images I shot during the beginning of the assault wobble as the camera dips to follow the arc of the falling tear-gas canister dropping into the crowd a few rows in front of me. Then I still *feel* what another viewer would only see: the crowd begins to jostle around me. Soon the recorded images are only backs and backpacks, glimpses of pavement, feet. There is a lot of screaming in Italian that only one of my Slovene traveling companions understands. They are shooting from the rooftops, he says. Tear-gas canisters are raining down from the helicopter that has been following us along the protest route. They also seem to be coming from the roof of the six-story building on our left. In a few moments, we see that police on the raised railroad trestle to our right are also firing tear gas from grenade launchers mounted on their rifles. Gases—yellow, white, and dark gray—arc into the crowd. Some hundred meters ahead of us armored personnel carriers block the forward progress of our heavily padded procession (watch "Genova Libera"). We scramble to the left side and try to go between two buildings, but there is a large wrought-iron fence, and in a moment Tomaž is vomiting from the gas. Though I am only breathing through a wet T-shirt, the gas bothers me less than him for some reason, so I have a hand on his shoulder to guide him. I struggle to keep him on his feet because I have seen several people nearby disappear beneath the trampling legs of the panicked.

*   *   *

More than these images, it is the footage from the next day's march that really makes my adrenaline flow, that I still feel in my stomach when I watch it even a decade later. We are walking near the rear of the Saturday march— the march that brought an estimated three hundred thousand onto the streets of this gritty port, the march that many read as popular defiance in the face of "low level state terror" (Juris 2008). Suddenly the loose crowd behind us begins to run forward in fear, for no apparent reason. Through three days of constant marches, and countless police attacks, we have grown accustomed to such collective panics—sometimes warranted, sometimes not. We follow the lead of nearby marchers and raise our arms and yell, "Calma!" A few bursts of tear gas are visible at the rear, where a police phalanx follows the tail end of the march, but nothing so obviously unusual as to justify the scale of the stampede coming toward us. Only when a police siren is audibly on the other side of us—that is further along the route of the march than we are—does it become clear that the fleeing Italians are screaming that we will soon be encircled: police units are speeding along a parallel street so they can sever the rear section from the rest of the march. We will soon be trapped in the middle of this block with police on both sides. My companions realize what is happening a moment before I do. By the time I begin to run forward along the protest's route—three armored personnel carriers slide into the intersection ahead of me, wheels locked in full skid. The doors are already open. Armed

Carabinieri in battle gear land running on the pavement before the vehicles have even stopped their forward motion. Activists running alongside me try to squeeze between the officers before they fully close the intersection. I am among the last few to slip by unharmed. I hear bone-crunching blows just to my left and just behind me.

I do not realize that I have not turned the camera off. There is almost nothing recognizable on the tape after I begin to flee and the camera drops to my side. As I run it twirls, first clockwise, then counterclockwise as the straps wind and unwind. The images are just a kaleidoscope of sprinting legs, sky, patches of clothing. The soundtrack is pounding feet, approaching sirens, screams, and the thumps of clubs on flesh (watch "Reflections on Images of Militancy").

Later that same night, I am with a small group of Slovene and Croat activists. We are trying to reach Carlini Stadium, where we left our sleeping bags that morning. We work our way through small side streets in the foothills to avoid the police checkpoints at major intersections. Police and military helicopters fly low over the city. Twice they follow us with blinding spotlights, hovering so close that we cannot see for the swirling dust and litter. Tomaž is only half-joking when he comments—referring to Pinochet's rightist crackdown at the outset of the Chilean military dictatorship in 1973—that we were granted space to camp at the stadium to save the trouble of having to round us up after the demonstrations. I find it uncanny that he mentions Chile because the military checkpoints, burned-out cars, and armed police patrols of the last two days keep calling to mind images from the Costa-Gavras's film *Missing* (1982), a fictional account of the Chilean coup, including scenes of union organizers, youth leaders, intellectuals, and critical journalists imprisoned in a soccer-stadium-cum-concentration-camp. In the face of Italian state repression, there is only a hint of irony from Željko—an experienced Antiwar Campaign of Croatia organizer and a longtime advocate of nonviolence—when he says he is ready to take up arms and head into the hills. We find Pero back at the stadium, after a day with the Black Bloc. There is not a glimmer of his usual deadpan humor. "I only feel safe," he says, "when I'm in a group large enough to defend itself." We all know what he means. This sense of a collective need—but also a collective capacity—to defend ourselves will stay with all of us.

Theoretician and activist Brian Holmes writes of his experience at the "Carnival Against Capitalism," a countersummit to the 2001 Free Trade Area

Figure 3.6. In the moment of direct confrontation between protesters and police, participants have the starkest sense of the state as a tangible enemy, even as an immediate threat to their physical integrity. Neos Marmaras, Greece. *Photo by Francisco Ciavaglia.*

of the Americas (FTAA) meetings in Quebec, in terms that resonate with my field notes from Genoa as well as activists' descriptions of their experiences. Holmes (2003) writes of the emotional experience and subjective transformation catalyzed by encounters with state security forces. He writes that subjectivities of resistance are forged in the heat of direct confrontations with the police—and as such have two faces.

The first face comes into view when you encounter state security forces. Holmes argues,

> You touch the concrete limits of your rights: you face the police, the gas, the fence, you feel the worst of the system in your own body, and you need that. Touch the state and be radicalized. It's a way to get beyond the cool media screen, to verify what oppression is, to better imagine how it works far away (2003:96).

Indeed, there is something transformative about seeing and feeling the array of equipment the state always has in reserve directed at you personally, not someone else far away on television. Some equipment only becomes visible during social unrest: armored vehicles, military helicopters, water canons, grenade launchers, an array of gases, sprays, dusts, projectiles, ordnance. You feel you are learning something essential about your relationship to the state. Several years after Thessaloniki, I ask Rimi what he felt protesters learned from such encounters. He says, "The state is, to its core, a violent institution, but that's hidden from most people in everyday life. We [anarchists] may talk about it a lot in the abstract, but when you face the police in a demo, you know this in a different way. You feel the state on your own skin."[30]

If the repressive visage of the state is the first face that contributes to one's radicalization, the other is reflected back at demonstrators in the polished visors of riot police helmets and the gleaming Plexiglas shields. Participants become acutely aware of *themselves* as a collectivity, their seriousness of purpose, as well as their potentiality, at the very moment of the state's attack on them. Holmes writes that,

> Solidarity, mutual support, we're all here to help each other, with almost nothing on our backs, no armor, no hierarchies, and when someone has the courage to throw the tear gas canister back at the police, you love that someone. Love on the barricades. You can talk to anyone in the crowd, say things you never said for years to your colleagues or even your friends. You can act collectively in simple but essential ways (2003:96–97).

Such feelings of having violated the political order publicly, with a clear sense of purpose, and in concert with thousands of others, are remarkably potent. Jadranka would say that her Thessaloniki experience—what she, too, described as "falling in love"—sustained her for years, inspiring her to participate in further militant actions during the Paris riots of 2005, in defense of Palestinian homes before Israeli bulldozers in 2007 with the International Solidarity Movement, and again in Greece during the dramatic uprisings of December 2008 that followed the police killing of Alexandros Grigoropoulos. While I did not embark on the same militant trajectory Jadranka did, I, too, was transformed by these encounters. I, too, felt the collective power of the multitude acting in common, not least its power to create the very kind of encounters that transformed participants, which crystalized new senses of individual and collective subjectivity.[31] Had I not also experienced the subjective stakes of protest firsthand, I might not have been alerted to how my collaborators engaged in efforts, sometimes more consciously, sometimes less, to remake themselves through direct action. Given my participation in these actions with a camera in hand, I was especially attuned to the ways activists drew on the emotional, embodied, and sensory qualities of these confrontations through their engagement with and deployment of images of conflict, with "riot porn."

Before turning to the key role of video in cultivating militant subjectivities, it is worth pausing to consider the ways activists anticipated—and perhaps even purposefully coopted—state violence. To be sure, the declaration of war on social movement mobilizations that began in Genoa and continued at other countersummits, from the Free Trade Area of the Americas meeting in Miami to Thessaloniki, succeeded in scaring many away from protest. The police assaults frightened, even terrorized, many participants. For months after Genoa, for example, I flinched at the sight of police, the sound of sirens, or the smell of smoke. But for some activists, especially those who became radicalized by these experiences, confrontation with the police became an anticipated aspect of the countersummit experience. There were many signs that activists were cognizant of what awaited them, that they went knowingly into these confrontations. They watched videos of past confrontations with the police to prepare. They secured gas masks, built body armor from old tires, and openly discussed the police repression to come in their affinity-group meetings.

Video and the Production of Unruly Political Subjects

While I had already noticed, and been puzzled by, activists' preoccupation with riot porn, the full significance of this preoccupation only began to dawn on me when I noticed my own bodily, sensory, and emotional responses to such footage after Genoa. Images of confrontation with the police—and not only recordings of the events in which I myself had participated—triggered intense reactions in me, like those I describe above. Images from Seattle or Prague, images that had not moved me earlier, left me with clammy hands and a pounding heart after Genoa. I felt a striking emotional proximity to, and identification with, the bodies of protesters subjected to police violence.[32]

Were it not for my own experiences of both protest and video images of protest, I would not have thought to ask my collaborators about their reactions to video images, reactions which indicate that video, especially the footage activists sometimes described as riot porn, offers a unique point of entry into the experience of direct confrontation. Activists return to these experiences to transform themselves. Shortly after Thessaloniki, I asked Rimi how he felt watching protest footage. "Speaking only for myself," he began,

"I can say that each time I watch a video of street blockades or protesters be-ing beaten by the police or activists banding together and fighting back, I have a strong physical reaction. It's like I feel myself running again from the police in Genoa, in Brussels, and in Thessaloniki." Barbara, a twenty-seven-year-old Slovene activist who helped organize both Slovene Noborder Camps, echoed my experience of adrenaline when watching videos of rioting, not as intense, she said, as when she watches the actual footage of the pitched street battles of Genoa, where she participated, but similar. Pero, always a bit skep-tical of my need to be so explicit about everything, simply said, "It puts you right back there in the thick of things, of course." And when I followed up, he added, rolling his eyes at my insistence, "You also remember they are out for your scalp!"

To be sure, variously positioned activists used the term "riot porn"[33] in distinct ways.[34] Sometimes the term was used to criticize, in a feminist reg-ister, the fetishization of violence among activists; that is, as part of a critique of how images of political violence valorized hegemonic notions of mascu-linity associated with ideals of physical strength, courage, emotional pas-sivity, and competiveness (Connell 2005; cf. Sian 2005; Razsa 2014).[35] These feminist inflections of riot porn were echoed in some of Jadranka's disputes with Rimi. As a term, however, riot porn also highlights the activist aware-ness that such videos worked on and through the body, that they belonged to what film theorist Linda Williams calls body genres (1991). Williams has in mind those fictional films that work on the body: melodrama that makes viewers cry, erotic films that arouse, and horror films that provoke screams (1991). More than how activists speak of video, however, it is the practices they developed around video that offer a revealing point of entry into the mo-bilization and deployment of the experience—affective, bodily, and sensory—of radical protest. For example, activists watched hours of riot porn the night before the most militant actions in Thessaloniki, as they had two years in ear-lier in Genoa. In less dramatic contexts, activists also watched and rewatched the most stirring scenes from these videos, immersing themselves in these images of open conflict with security forces. Such viewings, when read in re-lation to activist experiences in Thessaloniki and Genoa, provide a glimpse of the ways that activists are changed, both by taking part in such direct action and by watching videos of these actions. With these uses in mind, we can per-haps more clearly understand how the Woomera Noborder video catalyzed the European activists' reenactment of the assault on the migrant detention center. It is worth returning to this example for what it reveals of the political stakes of such videos, the political and subjective implications of video as it has come to suffuse activist movements—and what might be jeopardized when, as in Thessaloniki, it is no longer possible to film.

With the concept of "political mimesis," Jane Gaines (1999) provides an initial way to think beyond the more educational and realist activist uses of video, a way to glimpse what is at stake in the repetitive, sometimes almost compulsive, viewing of militant video by activists. The power of *Holiday Camp,* the Noborder Camp video from Australia, to inspire a similar intervention by those gathered at the Slovene-Hungarian border did not lie only in the transmission of an idea—the dissemination of direct assault on detention centers as one possible tactic. Nor perhaps is the historical argument about the subjugated place of African and Asian immigrants in Australian White settler colonialism the most potent aspect of the film, especially for activists in very different historical circumstances. Instead, according to Gaines (1999), films like *Holiday Camp* appeal directly to the bodies of those who watch. In such images of confrontation, viewers come to identify with the disobedient bodies on the screen, those who push the police lines back despite the blows of the truncheons, those who pry the bars apart, those who embrace strangers even as the police encircle them. It is in this sense that *Holiday Camp* is analogous to Linda Williams's body genres. Riot porn can be seen as belonging to such body genres in that it is experienced viscerally and—as Gaines describes the affects of an earlier generation of activist videos—produces bodily swelling, the "enlargement of the body politic, the ranks" (1999:98).[36]

The recognition of riot porn as a body genre provides a crucial opening, directing us to the key place of the body—the common link between sensual images of bodies, the bodies of viewers, and the bodily reenactment of direct action—within political mimesis. Nonetheless, Gaines's notion of political mimesis potentially leads to a relatively thin and uncontextualized understanding of how such reproduction is possible, how activists might spark action and even subjective change with such videos. What Gaines describes as political mimesis risks being understood reductively as a kind of hydraulic response to images, a monkey-see-monkey-do model of filmic influence. In such a reading, activists who watched earlier riots in Thessaloniki would be swept along, almost against their will, by the force of bodily suggestion.[37] These images are better understood, however, not primarily for some intrinsic transhistorical quality of the image but for their effects in specific social contexts. After all, we can imagine audiences for whom the very same footage activists refer to as riot porn would be experienced as riot horror. We must attend, therefore, to the social life of these images, to the specific conditions in which they are circulated, screened, and viewed; we must take up ethnographic methods to understand their place in social practice (Ginsburg, et al. 2002; Hirschkind 2006; Larkin 2008). In this spirit, it is crucial to situate the specific communities of viewers gathered to watch video in Genoa, Thessaloniki, or the Slovene Noborder Camp and they ways they engage with militant video.

First, in all these cases—Genoa, Thessaloniki, and Goričko—activists were already participating in what they understood to be a project of radical social transformation: these viewers were engaged in, or poised for, political action. Indeed, in the case of the Noborder Camp's participants, activists watched *Holiday Camp* at the end of their own camp's week of lectures, trainings, and discussions, a week during which many had already expressed frustration that they had not found a way to take action against the "border regime."[38]

Further distinguishing politicized viewers from the alterglobalization movement was the fact that the majority had had prior violent encounters with the state. In other words, these viewers, as they described, had specific—and highly charged—responses to this footage. For them, viewing video was a bodily experience, sensually linked to the elicitation of embodied memories of earlier confrontations. The experience of the confrontation on screen and the viewers' embodied memories of other confrontations reinforce and invigorate one another—giving a particular emotional charge to the question, posed by the young woman in Goričko: "What will we do about the detention camps in our midst?" What comes into view around militant video practice is not mimicry in any simple sense, but a tangle of mimetic processes, some of them self-consciously cultivated by activists to produce new actions, even to produce in themselves new desires and hence new subjectivities. As such we can speculate that these militant videos help to bring about what Rancière has described as new distributions of the sensible—that is, new modes to redefine what is perceivable, what is visible and invisible, audible and inaudible (2006). Video is uniquely suited to such a task because, unlike text, it is a sensory medium; it is experienced through the senses of its viewers/listeners. Vision and hearing are, of course, themselves already guided by cultural and personal interests, but sensory perception is also the mechanism by which these interests are supplemented or altered (MacDougall 2006:10).[39]

What stronger affirmation of common struggle—of insurrectionary intimacy—could one find than the bodily inhabiting of images of others? Mi-

mesis carries us bodily into alterity (Taussig 1992:24; Benjamin 1968) because through our imitative faculties, "we learn to inhabit what we see" of
others (MacDougall 2006:7). One takes up the same chants, the same tactics,
the same physical poses; one attempts to recreate with one's body the same
scenes. One is subjected to the same tear gas and clubs.

The ways activists use video make clear that they at least implicitly understand the technology's role in this chain of political mimesis. When activists
gather to watch videos, they valorize precisely these confrontational scenes;
they affirm Zapatista leader Subcomandante Marcos's pronouncement
that "in these images of people under attack, we see dignity and rebellion"
(2001:131). This is most explicit when videos are screened before demonstrations, as in Goričko or Thessaloniki. On these occasions, and many others,
video is screened to embolden activists directly—as a means of physical and
affective attunement—to give them the courage to carry out actions they may
already see as politically justified, such as the assault on the detention center,
but for which they may still lack the bodily resolve to initiate (cf. Hirschkind 2006). This is not an individual experience alone, and it is more than
a process of individual transformation, though it is also that. When activists watch these videos, they see that they are part of a larger collective ready
to take militant action. As I began to consider these aspects of video, I asked
Jadranka what she thought of the technology's role in affective and bodily
training. After saying she had not thought of video in precisely these terms,
she added that this side of video touched on "one of the most fundamental
tasks" for activists. "Many of us know a lot of things are wrong in the world,"
she said. "The question is, how do you turn this vague sense into action?"

Militant video, and the cluster of practices developed around it, with
their sensory, bodily, and affective dimensions, serve to cultivate activists prepared to take action. In seeking out such encounters with militant video, activists create the social conditions that structure this encounter, but they are
by no means fully in control of these encounters. After all, "affects are not
feelings," as Deleuze has argued, "they are becomings that go beyond those
who live through them (they become other)" (quoted in Thrift 2000:219). This
condition of both possessing and being possessed by videos of militant confrontation may account for some of the anxieties that surround their production, circulation, and consumption.[40]

Radical activists embraced video for a number of uses, many of which
were grounded in a realist understanding of the medium, on the belief that
the technology is uniquely suited to forms of truth telling such as witness-

ing, documenting, reporting, and educating, not least because of the notion that seeing is believing (McLagan 2003). In this regard, they share much with the boom in video activism within human-rights networks of the same period (McLagan 2003; Gregory 2007). In militant videos—unlike in human-rights contexts—suffering bodies were not represented as helpless victims. On the contrary, activists sought out, watched repeatedly, even valorized, unruly and insubordinate bodies, especially those confronting state violence. Activists came to use video images, in other words, as a kind of "affective pedagogy" (Allen 2009:170) to facilitate emotional relationships with activists elsewhere, to steel themselves for physical confrontation, and to cultivate new desires and therefore to become new political subjects. So direct confrontation, whether through coopting state violence to foster experiences of militant resistance or through the materialization and deployment of these experiences in video images, becomes another technology for the production of new selves. These are not only individual quests for self-realization; they are collective efforts to achieve autonomous control over the kinds of people activists might become in struggle together.

The Effects and Limits of Mass Mobilization

As in the earlier countersummits of the late 1990s and early 2000s, the mobilization for Thessaloniki reactivated, intensified, and personalized networks that activists more commonly experienced electronically. Participants ate, traveled, and dwelled closely together in difficult and politically charged circumstances, initiating new cycles of reciprocal hospitality. Despite the sometimes acute factionalism that marred Thessaloniki, militant formations with different traditions, tactics, and styles were arrayed together. As they formed a multiheaded hydra moving through the city or a vast swarm charging the Red Zone, they made concrete for participants the irreducible complexity of the "movement of movements" as well as some of its many commonalities. These were not only commonalities of the lowest common denominator—of the "no" shouted at those gathered inside the red zone—though the discovery of a common enemy was by no means insignificant. Activists were also aware that they organized these convergences without any overarching sovereign power, without recourse to any centralized authority. Their encounters with other political traditions and approaches, the unexpected intersections of forms of organization, sensibilities, tactics, references—intersecting here, diverging there—helped to produce a concrete awareness of a collective subject that exceeded the sum of its parts.

By 2003, however, there were also signs that the alterglobalization movement was in crisis. State security forces—which had been caught off guard by the decentralization, pluralism, and militancy of the first globalization protests in Seattle and Prague—launched militarized attacks on subsequent demonstrations in Gothenburg, Genoa, Evian, Miami, and Thessaloniki. State violence against demonstrations, the struggle for media attention, as well as activists' anger with the invasion of Iraq despite protests of historic size, among other factors, generated a dynamic of increasing physical confrontations at later countersummits. Many European activists felt this dynamic reached its apotheosis in Thessaloniki. The movement's crisis was palpable in the atmosphere of fear and suspicion that pervaded Aristotle University's campus. The crisis was also evident in the eclipse of the innovative video practices that had characterized earlier mobilizations. In such circumstances, my participatory research—especially as it involved video recording—also became impossible in Greece. Indeed, I did not ask the details of what my collaborators did during the Saturday actions—for fear of incriminating them—and they did not tell.

Ironically, however, if the near impossibility of shooting video was one indicator of the crisis, the ways the technology was and was not used in Greece also offer a revealing point of entry for understanding activists' experience there—as well as how such emotionally charged, sensory, and embodied experiences are materialized, circulated, deployed, and reanimated by activists. Sometimes such uses are part of a self-conscious effort to intervene in activists' emotional states, in activists' formation as political subjects. Attending to how video was or was not taken up in Thessaloniki also highlights a series of significant ambiguous subjective effects generated by the trajectory of intensifying confrontations. For example, the impossibility of shooting video was one sign—like a canary falling silent—of the vulnerability of activists' subjective efforts to engage state violence.

While state violence obviated activist video production and frightened many away from participating in countersummits, activists' ways of watching and discussing videos, both before and during Thessaloniki, show that direct confrontations with the state became an anticipated, and for some even a relished, aspect of these encounters. This is clear in the way the AM used video to recruit activists to participate, or the ways activists watched videos prior to their collective action as a means to embolden themselves. In this respect, despite the risks, and despite the potentially damaging consequences for the movement, some activists coopted aspects of state violence for their own ends. They traveled to Thessaloniki with the intention to, as Rimi put it, "feel the state on their own skin." Activists, especially anarchists, sought to confirm for themselves the latent violence of the state and experience the limits of their political freedom within the current order. In such encounters, emotional lessons were written onto the bodies of participants through a violence that substantiates both the enmity of the state and a lived sense of contributing to a militant political movement.

The direct confrontation with the state, which imprinted on participants a tangible sense of belonging to a larger militant and transnational movement—as well as of facing off with an enemy bent on destroying that movement—nonetheless had contradictory consequences. To be sure, activists felt love—and hate—at the barricades. As conditions approached those of an urban uprising, of low-intensity warfare, however, the open cooperation, including horizontal forms of organizing and decision making—perhaps the most important political innovations of the alterglobalization movement—were eroded by suspicion and mistrust.

What is more, the apparent self-evidence—and emotional extremity—of Thessaloniki's us-versus-them political lessons reinforced the more rigid and identitarian anarchist tendencies. In these conditions calls to openness, to work with others quite different from themselves, appeared very dangerous. Zagreb anarchists' proclivity to work within their own small subculture—with those who were similar to themselves—was exacerbated. In short, nothing confirmed anarchists' sometimes Manichean worldview, their understanding of themselves as the embattled few keeping the flame of liberty alight in a darkening world, more than actual experiences of being an embattled few targeted by hostile and overwhelming state security forces. In these ways, and at the very moment when the movement was most palpable for participants, the movement may also have been fundamentally at risk.

Finally, if activists like Jadranka described their encounters in Thessaloniki as transformative—altering their sense of self and energizing them politically for years to come—their emotions in the wake of these transformations were never straightforward. To be sure, when I spoke with Jadranka about Thessaloniki years later, she said that her participation in militant collective action there gave her a very rare sense of being the author of her own life. She described this as one of the most empowering experiences of her life. But she was quick to add that it left a "gaping hole in me that I find difficult to fill." Relative to Thessaloniki, much of her life felt "bleached out, desiccated."

Tasting "momentary liberation," she said, made it all the more clear how little control she had of her life most of the time.

This did not mean, however, that this experience of "momentary liberation," as well as its limits, left activists only craving, and seeking to reproduce, such dramatic confrontations. Critical reflections about what went wrong in Thessaloniki—as well as a need to model other possibilities rather than only reacting to existing authorities—led Zagreb activists to turn to new forms of community organizing after their return home. There were many ways, they argued, to assert control over their living conditions and even the constitution of their desires.

CHAPTER FOUR

"STRUGGLING FOR WHAT IS NOT YET": THE RIGHT TO THE CITY IN ZAGREB

As we approached the shuttered printing complex, I asked Pero if he thought this "night action" was risky. "Yes," he responded bluntly. He then went ahead with Rimi and three others to force open the front door of *Tiskara znanje* (Knowledge Press), a shuttered factory that has not been in operation for several years. Pacho and I recorded from the car until Pero signaled that they were in. We rushed to join them. When I listen to the footage later, I am immediately back inside Knowledge—and I say listen because once inside we filmed in near darkness so our camera lights would not draw attention to their night action (watch "High Voltage").

Everyone races to tape large faded sheets of drafting paper over the windows, especially those facing busy Zagrebačka Street, so passersby will not detect that the activists inside are busy repurposing the space. Pacho and I grope around. We try to take advantage of available light—the glow of the neighboring supermarket parking lot filtered through dusty panes—to shoot a few impressionistic images before the windows are completely covered. When I hear a slight scraping at my shoulder, I turn and find an exposed medusa-head—the severed end of an industrial cable dangling from the ceiling. I peer at a handwritten note taped to its shredded rubber sheathing.

Me: What does "*pod naponom*" mean?
(Silence)
Me: *Pod naponom?*

Rimi: What?

Me: *Pod naponom,* what does that mean?

Rimi: Oh, that means "high voltage."

When I initially asked Pero about risk, I had in mind the police, or perhaps the neighborhood's right-wing soccer hooligans—the Bad Blue Boys. Ten days will pass before we know more about these dangers, but electricity at least—we now know—has been cut off.

The whiff of the absurd clings to our break-in—almost as distinct as the dank odor of Knowledge's oily, ink-stained floors—but this night action nevertheless marks the beginning of an intensive period of collective effort by several dozen activists. They throw themselves into founding a community center in Knowledge—the Network of Social Solidarity. Inspired by neighborhood barter systems established in the wake of the 2001 financial collapse in Argentina and a squatted Dutch "Give-Away Shop,"[1] the Network's first initiative will be a Free Store. Their flier describes the Free Store as a "place where used belongings can be collected and exchanged without any cash changing hands." Rimi acknowledges that the turn toward a local, neighborhood-centered initiative after a period of dramatic transnational mobilizations—and especially after the confrontational demonstrations in Thessaloniki—marks something of a departure. "Of course, international demonstrations have their place," he says,

> and will be needed soon enough again, but they also cut us off from what's going on here in Zagreb. After Thessaloniki [where Rimi feels things went amiss, especially when participants damaged local businesses] I don't want to put so much of my energy into refusing the existing system. I want to demonstrate an alternative . . . in a way that responds to the frustrations we all experience in Zagreb every day.

Jadranka's words echo Rimi's. "In this city it seems like you either ruthlessly compete with people or you try to sell them something. I want to show that it's possible to relate to those around us in a different way."[2]

Activists' commitment to direct action—interventions against existing social relations in a manner that models, or prefigures, an alternative to those relations (cf. Graeber 2002)—is seen in efforts ranging from their opposition to the dominant local politics of ethnic hatred and exclusion to their participation in transnational protests against global inequality. Direct action also includes their interventions in Zagreb's rapidly commercializing urban landscape. They brought this direct-action ethic into their everyday lives in the city—into how they clothed, fed, and housed themselves—as well as into their efforts to found and defend the Free Store. From the initial breaking and entering in a facility to which they had no legal title, through the opening of a cashless exchange for personal belongings, to the management and defense of Knowledge by an open and expanding network of participants rather than a single owner, the Free Store was in conflict with taken-for-granted Western legal notions of private property. In contrast to these dominant assumptions about property, the very ones that were foundational for the wave of privatization that accompanied the transition to a market economy in Croatia, and all of postsocialist Europe for that matter (Verdery and Humphrey 2004), the network's interventions make clear that the nature of property cannot be assumed in advance; it is, rather, a terrain of struggle (Verdery 2003). Subsequent articulations of the Free Store's importance also made clear that activists had a keen sense of the intertwining of the personal and political—what I have been calling the subjective—stakes of their struggles over property. Jadranka put it most succinctly when, looking back on the Free Store later, she said that the effort was nothing less than the "struggle to try to be the kind of people we wanted to be." Activists' words and actions around the Free Store point to an awareness of a fundamental link between particular notions of property and specific forms of personhood, a link that anthropologists have also highlighted (Strathern 1996).[3] Activists' struggle for the Free Store as a collectively managed, or common (Jeffrey et al. 2011), resource was a self-conscious effort to promote alternative ways of being together with others.

From the beginning, however, the survival of the Free Store was in doubt. Previous squats had been violently evicted by city bulldozers, riot police, armed owners, and Molotov-cocktail-hurling skinheads.

The Urban Landscape

Two weeks earlier, I had joined a small "scouting expedition" of eight activists as they toured the west side of Zagreb searching for the optimal site for the Network of Social Solidarity. We all pile onto a creaking East German-built tram at Ban Jelačić Square and—because they never pay for tickets—watch carefully for the periodic *kontrola*. Pero and Rimi review the possibilities, drawing on their careful observations of the city over recent months. They point to evidence that particular structures are no longer in use and therefore potentially available to squat. Klara—the Network's "legal team"—will be asked to put on her most respectable clothes and check the municipal property register for the status of the buildings where Rimi and Pero note accumulating mail; wax stamps (those telltale signs that properties have been sealed by court order); or trash and leaves collecting in doorways. After we climb around an estate's grounds, the scouting party declares the beautiful villa in the foothills above Zagreb's Upper Town too remote for its purposes. They also dismiss a former medical-device manufacturing facility in the Trešnjevka neighborhood, deciding it is more appropriate as a squat dedicated to larger public events, like the concerts that Rimi organizes and promotes. Knowledge—one of several unused industrial spaces identified for squatting by student-activists at the Faculty of Architecture—is the last address on our list to check, and dusk is already upon us.

After circling the facility, climbing its fences and walls to explore the larger compound, and peering through the crusted windows, everyone confers in a rear alley (watch "Location, Location, Location").

> **Rimi:** It's busy around here so it will be easier to get in contact with people, easier to get them involved. I mean it's not the center of town, but I think it's okay. The trams run right by here.
> **Pero:** It's a good neighborhood for this kind of thing.
> **Rimi:** Yeah, there's a homeless shelter nearby. We can scavenge for food at the farmers' market.
> **Pero:** There's a social-work center here.
> **Rimi:** Yeah, we could maybe speak to them. The space needs a lot of work, but that's true everywhere.

When they share their findings with a meeting of the wider Network, Jadranka emphasizes an "unexpected plus" associated with Knowledge as a site: its location is adjacent to the international discount grocery chain Billa. She stresses that this will reveal the "clear contrast" between "our values and theirs," perhaps even leading to a direct public confrontation with the firm over the use of the space. Alluding to neighborhood rumors that the Austrian conglomerate hopes to knock down Knowledge for additional parking, Jadranka adds, "It'll be an opportunity to open a public discussion about what's of more value: another parking lot, another space to buy more trash, or a space for supporting our neighbors and coming together on our own terms."

The Free Store tells us much about activists' practices, values, and hopes for the future, but, like other episodes in the recent history of squatting in Zagreb, the initiative also reveals much about the dramatic transformation of

Zagreb's urban landscape (Vuković 2005)—and the forms of personhood encouraged by that landscape. In 1994, for example, when he was only fourteen, Pero helped squat Kuglana (Bowling Alley) in a derelict train factory.[4] Activists organized a concert hall, social club, and an infoshop (a small library of anarchist materials) before the city ordered the facility condemned and bulldozed in a matter of weeks—a record for Zagreb municipal efficiency. Four years later, activists occupied the large Taxi-Remont complex, which had produced replacement parts for the ubiquitous domestic automobile, the Yugo. In the massive empty halls young punks built a skateboarding park and concert hall. Eventually, some thirty neo-Nazi skinheads armed themselves with Molotov cocktails (with police encouragement, Pero insisted) and burned the skate park and concert hall, rendering them beyond repair.[5] While much could be said about these squats—both in terms of activists' commitment to securing a space for alternative culture, their violent evictions, and their relation to broader European squatting traditions[6]—they highlight that by the time activists squatted Knowledge, the city was littered with empty industrial complexes.[7] The deindustrialization that the U.S. has experienced since the late 1950s, epitomized in the public mind by the decline and near collapse of Detroit, swept Croatia much more rapidly—primarily in the first decade after its independence in 1991. This rapid transformation has been particularly disorienting in Croatia because manufacturing facilities were the pride of socialist Yugoslavia—symbols of the country's rapid modernization and, because of the relatively high living standards they supported, a primary source of the regime's moral legitimacy. Today they are darkened, decaying, and boarded-up hulks that, as one forty-year resident of the surrounding Voltino neighborhood expressed to Pero when he was distributing Free Store flyers, "make our neighborhood feel more dead than alive."

Getting By in a Changing City

The suspicion that my unusual presence generated—as an American who spoke Croatian and followed radical politics in Zagreb with great interest—never wore off completely. This was perhaps to be expected, especially in the tense period around the U.S.-led invasion of Iraq and among activists who knew that they were closely surveilled by state security forces. Even after our experience traveling the length of the Balkans to the demonstrations in Thessaloniki, Rimi, for example, would make comments that implied lingering suspicion. He was relaxing with a joint after a physically exhausting day of emptying Knowledge's cluttered storerooms when he remarked only half-jokingly, "The CIA must now have an extensive video archive on the Balkan anarchist scene."

Over the course of my months in Zagreb, however, many other activists came to share their daily lives with me, revealing that their politics did not end with their more public forums, protests, and direct actions—like the Free Store—but extended into everyday life. This was especially true of Jadranka. Unlike Pero, who had inherited his grandmother's rundown apartment when she passed away, or Rimi, who lived with his mother in the apartment where she had raised him, as was common in Croatia until marriage, and sometimes after, Jadranka was not originally from Zagreb and faced what she called "existential difficulties" as a consequence. Understanding better how activists like Jadranka survived in a city they experienced as quite hostile is crucial to understanding why they cared so deeply about the Free Store, why they saw it as part of wider struggle to "be the kinds of people we want to be."

In the months prior to the squatting of the Free Store, Jadranka was featured in several media accounts of alternative lifestyles and politics, including an episode of the popular Direkt documentary series. "The role of anarchist poster-child," she said with a wry smile, "is not one I was trained for from an early age." Indeed, Jadranka was raised in a conservative Catholic family in famously right-wing Zadar. The coastal city drew criticism from across Europe when local officials mounted a three-by-four-meter banner at the main entrance to the historic walled center depicting Ante Gotovina—a Croatian General and international fugitive wanted for the murder of 324 Serbian civilians—with the slogan "A Hero, Not a Criminal."[8]

With a mixture of bitterness and black humor, Jadranka recalls stories of her family's hypocrisy and intolerance. As a child, they forbade her to socialize with Serbian schoolmates, asking her on numerous occasions, "Who would you rather marry, a Serb or a Black with no legs?" "In a rare victory for antiracism in my family," Jadranka said sarcastically, "it was supposed to be obvious that you answer: a Black." No one repeats the family joke to her youngest sister, however, because in 1992 Jadranka's father stepped on a landmine while fighting Serb paramilitaries in Zadar's hinterland and lost part of his own right leg. Jadranka left Zadar as soon as she completed secondary school, and when she does return it is usually to visit her grandmother, with whom she lived on the nearby island of Ugljan during the heaviest shelling of Zadar by Serbian forces (watch "A Tree Far From the Boys").

Unwilling and unable to draw on family support, especially once she moved to Zagreb to study, Jadranka was forced to develop an array of survival strategies. Much of her food, for example, came from "dumpster diving," as seen in a scavenging expedition we filmed shortly after returning from Greece (watch "Perfectly Good Cheese"). In this footage, we hide our bikes in the scruffy grass along the far side of the parking lot and make our way through a gap in the chain-link fence. We navigate among the high green walls of empty beer cases until we are in the loading zone behind Billa, by coincidence a different location of the same ubiquitous chain that is adjacent to Knowledge.

Two of Jadranka's squat-mates rifle through the garbage. Kata climbs into the massive steel dumpster. Ivo balances on his stomach across its lip—legs outstretched behind him for equilibrium—as he grasps for something just out of reach. Jadranka and the fourth squatter, Toni, clamber up onto the loading dock where a sympathetic employee left out a cardboard box of dented and past-due canned goods, leaking cooking oil, torn bags of rice and pasta, and a broken Thermos. Jadranka and her friends later express relief that Zagreb supermarkets do not splash ammonia or rat poison into their trash, a common Western European practice used to prevent dumpster diving or, as it is sometimes known, freeganism (Shantz 2005).[9]

Jadranka's dumpster diving, her occasional shoplifting forays, as well as the Billa parking lot encroaching on the Free Store, direct our attention to what was supplanting industrial capacity across the city. By the mid 2000s, Zagreb was ringed by an archipelago of big box stores, the kinds activists invariably called *hipermarketi* (hypermarkets), many exceeding ten thousand square meters. There were local chains, such as Getro and Super Konzum, but they were modeled on the prolific international megastores, like Italy's Ipercoop, Germany's Lidl, and, of course, Austria's Billa. The transformation of the city during these years was so conspicuous that a collection of short stories—titled *Horror and Huge Expenses (Užas i veliki troškovi)*—was marketed as "Stories from the Time When Megastores Sprouted Like Mushrooms" (Perišić 2002). Billa alone built some 210 supermarkets across formerly socialist Europe between 1995 and 2004.

While most literature on the former Yugoslavia has, understandably, focused on nationalism and ethnic conflict, in fact the region has gone through fundamental economic changes similar to other postsocialist economies, though there are also specifically post-Yugoslav characteristics. In this context, we find that market transition and nation-state formation—contrary to common assumptions that the state and market are locked in a zero-sum struggle—mutually reinforce each other in a variety of ways. First, the "Croatian nation" was represented as essentially Western and capitalist; indeed, this was an early argument for secession from the "imposed" communism of "Eastern" or "Balkan" Yugoslavia. Later, the privatization of socially owned firms was carried out with the express intent of building a *national* economic elite, epitomized by Tuđman's "200 families program," which envisioned the creation of national economic elite (200 families was the stated goal)[10] in whose hands the country's wealth would be concentrated. For Tuđman, the privatization of companies to those close to his HDZ was not solely a matter of nepotism. For him the national interest and the interest of his party, which led Croatia to independence, were nearly one and the same (Bellamy 2003). Finally, criticism of privatization was often portrayed as retrograde at best, "anti-Croatian" at worst. Even the purchasing of international or Western products had a nationalist dimension because, again, Croatians were seen as essentially Western. Given this framework for Croatia's "national liberation," it is easy to see how antinationalism and anticapitalism were understood as complementary for Zagreb's radical activists.

Squatting Life

Dumpster diving, however, was not Jadranka's only survival strategy—and Knowledge was not her first squatting experience. The time I spent in Vila Viktorija, her residential squat, helped me understand a great deal: how she was able to dedicate so much time to activism; why her survival strategies in the city were central to her sense of personal "self-determination," a self-determination she linked closely to the Free Store; and, finally, as we will see, what forces proved decisive when the Network of Social Solidarity was threatened with eviction from Knowledge. Nestled among ten-story socialist-era high rises near the Sava River—and not far from a major thoroughfare studded with hipermarketi—Vila Viktorija nonetheless seemed to exist outside the normal bustle of daily life, surrounded by large overgrown gardens and brush. Traveling German carpenters had recently reinforced the old villa's grand mansard-topped tower. When I teased Jadranka for having said her room was a mess—and therefore not suitable for a filmed tour (watch "Jelena's Mess")—she responded with a wink, "Your apartment can be a mess, but this is a squat. It should be nice." The property was the subject of a long-running legal dispute over the title—between the descendants of the wealthy family that built the villa in the 1920s and the poorer families who settled there when the property was nationalized and subdivided in 1945. One of the families was Serbian and now living in exile in Malmö, Sweden; they gave Jadranka and the others permission to stay while the case made its circuitous way through the courts.

Within this collective squat, which housed a relatively stable dozen residents and another half-dozen periodic guests, Jadranka was adept at bridging the differences between those residents who shared her political commitments and others, usually referred to as the "hippies," whose politics were limited to avoiding engagement with mainstream society. In general, she played what could be seen as a feminine role, keeping the house in order both physically and emotionally. Jadranka was, however, often away from home, traveling to gatherings such as the World Social Forum in Porto Alegre, Brazil, and antinuclear protests in Germany.

Jadranka saw Vila Viktorija, the scavenging she did at farmers' markets and behind hipermarketi, and her other freegan practices as the basis for a declaration of independence from both her parents and the life of consumerism she saw as overtaking Croatian society. It was through these tactics— and a small state scholarship to study sociology—that she was able to avoid financial dependence on her parents and the loss of control she felt certain this would engender. In these ways, she also managed to avoid what she called "wage slavery," employment in the "flexible" employment sector that increasingly typifies Croatia's labor market, and which had pulled some activists into its orbit.

Her daily practices, which were experienced as humiliating by many of the Croats forced to resort to them,[11] were nothing less, she claimed, than a means to autonomy and self-determination—core values of anarchism. But for Jadranka this meant more than sheer material survival. The changing landscape of the city—especially the "relentless marketing and rise of hipermarketi"—was not only experienced in material ways, whether as new physical presences in the landscape or as potential resources to sustain her. The stakes were more intimate. "It's a struggle," she said, for "my desires, hopes, and fears." "They tell us repeatedly," she continued,

> that now we are free, that in socialism we were oppressed by an imposed system. Don't get me wrong, I'm not nostalgic for communism, but how free am I if I don't even have the liberty to decide what I want, if a whole sophisti-

Figure 4.1. Façades along major thoroughfares or at busy intersections were often covered by multistory advertisements. This one for Renault reads, "Tune out the TV. Tune in to life!" *Photo by author.*

cated system of marketing, "proper behavior," and society's idea of success is creating in me desires that are not my own. You can't move in this town any more without [marketers] trying to whisper in your ear. Every surface is covered with ads and they find ever more sinister ways to insinuate their way into my psyche!

And at an early planning meeting, even before Knowledge was selected as a site, Jadranka argued that the Free Store must be understood in relation to the "creeping of the hipermarketi into our souls."

> The problem is not just that this is a new enclosure movement [many European activists referred to privatization during this period as "enclosure," referencing the historical process of fencing in the medieval commons in England, converting them to private property]. This is not just a problem of them taking away our last public spaces.
>
> It's also making us more private people, closing us off from the people around us. When all the city is dedicated only to shopping, when there's no-

where social left to go, you become a more private person. You only think about what you can buy, what you can sell, about your individual needs. You only think about yourself. That's why we need [the Free Store] so desperately in Zagreb.

Jadranka made clear that for her the new archipelago of hipermarketi was not only closing the city off as a material resource; the commercialization of the landscape was closing off other ways of being human.[12]

A Right to the City?

I have screened *Bastards of Utopia*, the documentary film we made about Jadranka, Pero, and Rimi's activism, in a variety of settings—film festivals, anthropology classes, independent cinemas, academic conferences, activist gatherings, even anarchist book fairs. A common reaction from some viewers is to identify the perceived ethical and political contradictions between my collaborators' ideals and their actions. How can Rimi oppose the war in Iraq, even militarism more generally, while simultaneously embracing militant tactics, rhetoric, and images? Why does Pero oppose the EU and then lament the very borders that continue to separate Croatia from the EU, borders that persist precisely because Croatia is not a member of the European Union? How can Jadranka oppose state authority in the name of her anarchist politics and nonetheless accept a state scholarship to study at Zagreb University? Pero, Rimi, and Jadranka would surely have their own responses to these criticisms. Jadranka for her part would also sometimes simply acknowledge these tensions, saying that activists must accept that "there is no way to escape the contradictions that come with trying to live according to your ethics in a world that's hostile to your ethics."[13]

One scene of the remodeling of Knowledge often provoked such "gotcha" responses. The reasons that viewers perceived the scene as embodying activist hypocrisies are worth dwelling on; they reveal much about the way activists imagined and practiced their politics—as well as how they are understood by others. The extended montage begins with Pero placing a scratched record on an ancient turntable inside Knowledge (watch "Take It or Leave It"). As a socialist-era anthem plays—its refrain, "We work in harmony, we build anew," evoking the voluntary work brigades that rebuilt Yugoslav infrastructure in the years after World War II—we see a series of shots of the labor being invested in Knowledge. Activists discard the chemical- and ink-soaked floorboards, clean the walls, repair the toilet, reconnect to the power grid, and rewire the circuit board, paint a "Take-it-or-leave-it" sign, distribute fliers in the neighborhood, and sort and display donated clothes.

Intercut with these other efforts is a series of shots of the front locks being swapped out for a new spring bolt and door handle—and it is to the images of the lock that viewers often react. As the music fades and the montage ends, we see Pero turn the key in the front door and walk away. Some viewers ask how my collaborators reconcile their criticisms of the privatization of state-owned firms and public spaces—even their criticism of private property itself—with their own privatization of Knowledge, epitomized by the installation of their locks. This question leads to others for me. Does locking the space mark its privatization? Who had access to the space and how was this decided? In other words, was the Network of Social Solidarity private? Finally, is space either public or private, as we often assume? Or are there other possibilities?

The first meeting inside Knowledge, held only two days after the break-in, illustrates how the ideas and practices of the Network of Social Solidarity confound commonsense understandings of private property. Seventeen activists sit around a large table in the space off the main hall once used by factory workers for their own meals and gatherings. The assembly lasts nearly three hours—"confirming the saying," as Jadranka puts it ruefully, "that the revolution will be an endless meeting."[14] Activists discuss decision-making process; alliance building, including why and why not to work with NGOs; staffing the free store; security in the face of soccer hooligans and skinheads; whether or not to allow overnight sleeping, alcohol, or soft drugs; the priorities and schedule for rehabilitating the space; as well as tangents on the previous evening's raucous anarcho-punk show—by Anger is Beautiful—and an impassioned debate on the best place for dumpster diving for pastries.

At the outset, Jadranka, who is moderating, reminds everyone of the decision-making process adopted at previous meetings of the Network:

We've committed to direct democracy—so we won't delegate our decisions to anyone else. All of us who care about the fate of the Network and the Free Store will manage it together. And all these decisions will be made by consensus, not by majority voting. This means making decisions only after hearing everyone's concerns and alternate proposals. Remember, this means it's important to be very cautious about blocking [consensus]. Nothing can move forward without [consensus]. So if it appears that most people are leaning in one direction after full discussion, you shouldn't block the decision unless you have a serious ethical problem with that decision. . . . The Network and its meeting are open to all who wish to be involved. You gain full rights to participate in decisions at your second meeting. Any questions?

"Yeah," scoffs Ante, a wiry, tattooed punk who recently moved to Zagreb from the small city of Požega and who is attending his first Network assembly, "since when do we have to be so fucking formal? Don't we always more or less decide by consensus?" "Well, since new people *who haven't been to meetings before,*" Jadranka replies pointedly, "will come and they will not be familiar with our decision making, we want to be clear. But, really," she adds, softening her tone, "if we are successful, this will be more than the usual suspects. There will be a lot of people who don't have experience with nonhierarchical decision making." "Also," Rimi interjects, "if we are asking each other and our new neighbors to risk confrontation with the police, and possible arrest, we've all got to be onboard. This can't be something you drag people into without their genuine consent."

While they might not express themselves as profanely as Ante, many readers would likely share his impatience with anarchists' emphasis on the formalities of the decision-making process. As seen in the Thessaloniki mobilization, anarchist principles, including direct democracy, antiauthoritarianism, consensus, and autonomy, are understood to be embodied in organization and decision-making as much as in any long-term political goals.[15] What Rimi and Jadranka emphasized in the context of the Free Store, however, was different from the demonstrations in Greece. They were self-consciously trying to facilitate the involvement of the wider neighborhood in the Network, rather than coordinating action among those who were already radicalized. The Network of Social Solidarity was not envisioned as closed or private but, rather, open to all who committed to its initiatives. One gained the right to participate fully through involvement, by investing energy in the Free Store. In other words, far from being closed, or hoping to limit access to Knowledge, activists intended to develop a space that was broadly open and participatory. The Network was trying to bring to life a new political community—a new collective subject—involving those who recognized in the Free Store a necessary and worthwhile intervention in their city.

Following the reminder of decision-making protocol, Jadranka calls for "report backs" by those who committed to tasks at the previous meeting. There are brief reports on the history of Knowledge, the former book publisher, and Billa, the grocery chain next door. The report from the "legal team" is a bit more involved. By legal team, everyone meant Klara, who is in her eighth and—"this time I swear it"—final year at the Faculty of Law. Klara is better versed in these issues than most law students, however; she works for an NGO that is assisting Serbs displaced during the war, many of whom had ethnic Croats move into their homes. This other, darker, and vastly larger history of property seizure—justified with ethnic animosities and carried out at gunpoint—makes clear that squatting as such does not have a uniform political significance. One must carefully consider squatting's motivations, methods, and social consequences in order to evaluate it.[16]

In any case, Klara, expanding on her earlier reports, advises that property law is quite clear with regard to premises being used as a place of residence:

> Once you have slept in a space, you acquire use rights if those holding legal title do not order you to leave within forty-eight hours. This means you can no longer be evicted from Knowledge without a court order. Well [glancing at her watch], since it has only been forty-five hours, you could still be evicted if the owners show up in the next three hours! After that, they'll need a court order.

Klara reports that she has called the Zagreb municipal court and established that the current backlog for such cases is nearly four months. Furthermore, the ownership of Knowledge is contested, already the subject of a long-running lawsuit between the City of Zagreb and the court-appointed trustee of a now bankrupt firm that was close to the long-ruling right-wing HDZ party. If either party is sufficiently motivated to pursue the matter of legally evicting the Network, Klara advises, it should be possible to further delay any court order to vacate the premises by challenging that party's standing in the matter because of a lack of clear title.

During the next report back, when Pero and Ante share their draft of the Free Store flyer, the meeting bogs down. The text is to serve as something of a manifesto for the Network, to be distributed to neighbors, other activist networks, and journalists with a record of sympathetic writing on anarchist initiatives. As such, it is parsed with great care; each line is read aloud, commented upon, critiqued, and rewritten. Several people object to the fourth line, "They've expropriated the working class's labor and abandoned them to starvation." Rimi, often the most dogmatic and incendiary in his rhetoric—at this very meeting he is wearing a T-shirt he silkscreened with the common slogan "No war between nations, no peace between classes"—surprises me with his moderation. "In this flier," he insists, "we should avoid class analysis, at least in those terms." Ante, who usually sees eye to eye with Rimi, who even belongs to a clique of young men that some women refer to as "Rimi's boys," protests, "Why not call it what it is? This is class warfare from above." "Of course it is," retorts Rimi,

> but this Free Store will succeed or fail not only because of our fierceness, you know, but also on whether it has the support of the wider community. I mean, of course, class war is really what's going on, but you know how allergic people are to anything that reminds them of the former [communist] regime (*bivši režim*). We need to explain our motivations in the language of our neighbors.

"Yeah," adds Ivo,

> we need something more like the RAI [Rijeka Anarchist Initiative] Mani-festo,[17] which reminds people of whose work built these factories, whose work is the source of this wealth that has suddenly, in the most shady fucking ways, been transferred to Tuđman cronies. It's obvious the Social Democrats won't dare to confront them or their two hundred families.

"Exactly, exactly," Rimi agrees with Ivo, reading from the back of an envelope,

> I jotted down something similar to their manifesto. The industrial symbols of our city, the ones we grew up with and lived with, are turning into ruins along with those who created them. The generations before us, those who created what we have today, are progressively deprived of that which should never be denied them: the product of their own labor and their dignity as human be-ings. All the years of sacrifice by workers are either allowed to rust or seized for private gains by a few tycoons.

Two aspects of the "report backs" and the lengthy discussion of how best to represent the Network and its Free Store, further illuminate the Network's relationship to private property: the Free Store relationship to the history of ownership in the region and the Network's emphasis on the public defense of the Free Store.

Given that Knowledge was sold off under what Klara described as "murky" circumstances, it is not surprising that activists referenced the widely perceived corruption of the privatization process, in which, in the fog of war, the ruling HDZ sold off many firms to those close to the party (Bičanić 2001). Beyond the explicit critique of how privatization was carried out, activists also framed factories like Knowledge as the product of past generations' labor and therefore part of a common heritage, echoing the socialist history of ownership of this and most other factories.[18] Much of Socialist Yugoslavia's productive capacity, rather than being state owned, belonged to a third category of *social property,* to be self-managed by the workers associated with the relevant firm. The promise of economic democracy and autonomous workers' power that such an arrangement implies was far from fulfilled—the party retained ultimate power over important decisions. Nonetheless, and though Rimi was correct that explicit uses of class analysis were taboo in public discourse, the socialist understanding of productive capacity, which was developed rapidly in the years following WWII and the establishment of communist rule—as collectively produced and owned—continued to resonate. There was a widespread belief that the wealth of the country was the product of earlier collective effort (such as the volunteer work brigades that the song "We Work in Harmony" called to mind). If it was no longer possible in contemporary Croatia to discuss collective ownership explicitly, it was still possible to make moral claims about how this inheritance should serve the public good in ways that are difficult to imagine in a U.S. context, where underlying collective effort is obscured by longstanding and wholly naturalized relationships based on private property.

Beyond the broad, if relatively diffuse appeal to a history of social ownership, activists carefully framed the Free Store in a way that would appeal to a wide audience; they saw the Free Store as dependent on public support. A heated exchange, following Ante's repeated insistence that they be more explicit in their class analysis, drove this point home. Rimi, raises his voice,

> Look, like I said, this Free Store will survive, or not, depending on the public legitimacy we have. It's not just a matter of how militant and committed we are. It's a matter of whether the politicians who will order in the police will be afraid of the public price they'll pay for that. That's why we're squatting now, during the [parliamentary] election season, during that rare period when they pretend to give a fuck about what people think.

Even the legal tactics Klara outlines are not intended simply to give the collective more time to use the Knowledge facility, but, rather, more time to build a public profile and develop support among neighbors and sympathetic journalists. Ironically, when I think back now to the editing of the montage of the rehabilitation of Knowledge, the scene that for some viewers epitomized activists' privatization of the space, I realize that the very existence of this scene points to activists' concern from the outset with the wider appeal of this project. The reason Pacho and I had worked so hard to document the labor being invested in the decrepit structure—that is, the reason we had an editing bin full of footage depicting work inside Knowledge, including the changing of the locks—was because Rimi had insisted upon it. As he put it, "Our improvement of the space, the sweat we've put into it, will be an important part of our public argument that *we* are better for the neighborhood than [the current owners]. . . . And we'll show our neighbors that we haven't just stolen this space; we've made it what it is."[19]

So within days of the break-in—through the formulation of an inclusive and participatory collective, the claim to serve a broader social good, the appeal to common inheritance, the concern with the wider legitimacy and public support for their initiative, and preoccupation with participatory and collective labor—the Network can be seen to be operating in, perhaps even creating, distinctive property relations. While clearly not public—that is, administered by the state in the name of its citizens—it was certainly not private either, as traditionally understood: "belonging to or for the use of one particular person or group of people only" (*Oxford American Dictionary* 2009). Politically engaged scholars and activists have in recent years developed *the common*[20] (Blomley 2008; Harvey 2008; Jeffrey et al. 2011; McCarthy 2005; Hardt and Negri 2009) as an alternative concept for such property. The common evokes the precapitalist tradition of the commons, most familiar in North America in the form of the town commons on which residents had shared rights to graze their cattle. Though the Zagreb activists did speak of a "new enclosure movement" to describe privatization, they did not explicitly use the language of the common themselves, at least not to the degree that my informants in Ljubljana did. But, then again, the Slovene activists were translating Hardt and Negri's *Commonwealth* (2009) into Slovene at the time. In Zagreb activists' practices around the Free Store, we, nonetheless, can make out the contours of what one such common might look like. Theorists stress that the common does not refer only to material resources that are collectively administered—in this case Knowledge. Just as important are the kinds of social relationships, new ideas, even emotions, generated around the common (Hardt and Negri 2009), as indeed they were around Knowledge. That said, we should not forget that the Network was also deeply dependent on Knowledge, inextricably linked to physical space in the city for its existence. The Network was formed to seek just such a space, and all of its activities now revolved around or took place within Knowledge.

During the hectic week of rehabilitating Knowledge for the public launch of the Free Store, however, there is little time for theoretical reflection. When

I finally have a chance to talk to Jadranka in calmer circumstances—over a beer at a neighborhood café, halfway through the rehabbing of Knowledge— I ask her how she would respond to those critics who are sure to ask how she justifies taking control of property that does not belong to her.

> The anarchist values of mutual aid, autonomy and, you know, self-realization can't just be some ideas I cling to in my head. And I can't create them through some kind of self-sacrifice. If they can be expressed in more than just an individual guilty conscience, I mean, if they are to be modeled as a way of life here and now, we need to have the ability to access the resources for realizing these values. And this includes the city around us . . . We have the right to at least try to be the kinds of people we want to be, and this means being able to use the city in the ways we think matter most.

Rimi is, characteristically, more blunt: "This is my city as much as it is theirs, those fucking war profiteers and HDZ tycoons who own everything now. I have every right to resist what they are doing to my city. I have every right to fight for the kind of city I want to live in." Jadranka and Rimi both speak in ways that echo recent articulations of a "right to the city," a language for laying claim to the common in urban settings (Harvey 2008; Jeffrey et al. 2011; Mitchell 2003).[21] Again, the right to the city is not just the right to access urban resources, though it is that as well. As Rimi and Jadranka make clear, the right to the city is also a right to participate in the creation of the kind of city one wants to live in, and through this to become the person one wants to be. If the common is to become a meaningful concept in urban settings, it would seem to depend on such a right to the city. Such a right is not, of course, only individual; as is seen in the Free Store, it is asserted by struggling together with others to create the conditions that make such self-creation possible.[22]

The Brief Life of the Free Store

While Zagreb anarchists' criticism of and direct actions against Croatian nationalism often served to isolate them from the broader public,[23] the brief life of the Free Store is different. No sooner have they distributed fliers in the neighborhood and thrown open the front doors than a steady stream of visitors begins to make their way through Knowledge. Given the cashless free-store model—and the poverty of many neighboring residents—it is perhaps not surprising that many from the surrounding Voltino neighborhood and beyond come for free clothes, shoes, and household goods (watch "The Regular"). But there are also enough donations to keep pace with the needs of these "customers"; from the outset, supply often exceeded demand and the piles of clothing climbed higher each day.

The shop fills up with initial anarchist deliveries, but with donations from neighbors as well. Many, including a prosperous middle-aged couple who arrive on the fourth day of the Free Store's operation, seem to grasp the underlying principles and the larger significance of the store rather than seeing it as simply a clearinghouse for used goods (watch "Donations"). After receiving their substantial delivery of kitchenware, a pink-haired and pierced Ivana asks if they need anything themselves, gesturing to the piles. "I think we have too much stuff as it is," answers the wife. Ivana nods, "Well, you know where we are now." Obviously a bit uneasy in the rough surroundings of the raw industrial space with its unusual occupants, the older woman waves good-bye, saying, "You never know, tomorrow, the day after. You never know when you'll need help." A moment later she pokes her head back through the door to add, "I congratulate you on your courage here. We need to watch out for each other and we need to take our city back."

The (En)Closure of Knowledge

2:30 PM

We have been doing a brisk business all afternoon when the police arrive (watch "Forget the Bed"). They step in the front door, look around in disbelief, and turn to Pero:

> **Police officer #1:** Who's in charge here? What's going on?
>
> **Pero:** In the context of revitalizing abandoned spaces in the city of Zagreb—
>
> **Police officer #2 (interrupting, his face an expression of bewilderment and rising anger):** This building belongs to this man (pointing to the middle-aged man accompanying them, who we will learn claims to be the owner).
>
> **Police officer #1 (more perplexed than angry):** Do you have any documents? A rental contract?
>
> **Me (in English, as it is almost always safer to speak with Croatian police in English):** Have you given them the flier?
>
> **Pero (looking at me and shrugging):** Yeah, I just gave it to them.
>
> **Police officer #2 (holding out his hand):** Who has a passport? Who has ID here?
>
> **Police officer #1 (as both officers gather IDs):** Who gave you permission to be here?

Pero (heeding Klara's legal advice): We have a bed here—

Police officer #1 (interrupting): Forget the bed! Who gave you permission to be here? How did you get a key?!

Pero: The space was open—

Police Officer #2 (interrupting and pointing to the owner): It's his, understand?

Owner: I will demolish this building.

When they step outside to call for backup, Pero locks the front door from inside and tells the police they do not have his permission to reenter Knowledge.

3:15 PM

Initially the complex is relatively porous because not enough officers are present to secure the large perimeter. Jadranka, for example, is en route to the Free Store when the police arrive, but she manages to climb in a rear window. Several Dutch squatters, who are in town to give a public lecture—"The Social Benefits of Software Piracy"—scramble in behind her to join the standoff.[24] Pero, who thought we had exhausted our small collection of vinyl, remembers that he has another record in his backpack. The album sleeve reads "Boney M, making disco a threat again."

5:30 PM

Now a dozen more officers have arrived. Several are milling around in the alley, effectively closing our rear (window) entrance and sealing us off from the outside. There are a number of tense exchanges. In particular, the police are not pleased when Pero chastises them for scaring people away from the Free Store. "We can't work like this," he intones. At his shoulder, Ivana only manages a strained smile.

7:00 PM

Jure and Ivana try to prepare dinner with the scavenged ingredients we have on hand: vegetable oil, beets, lemons, and Swiss chard.

Jadranka makes the rounds, gently encouraging the more anxious occupiers.

11:45 PM

Hour nine of the standoff. A special tactical unit (*interventna policija* or "intervention police") has arrived in armored Land Rovers. Most of these officers are already familiar to us from earlier direct actions. They arrested Pero, for example, during the Bicycle Caravan in May. They are often deployed for politically sensitive operations, and most recently I saw them on television at violent nationalist protests. Veterans of the war for Croatian independence were blocking a highway in defense of accused war criminals facing deportation to the International Tribunal in The Hague.

12:30 AM

One of the members of the *interventna policija* recognizes Jadranka from previous protests and her recent television appearance on Direkt. He calls her over to a window that opens onto Zagrebačka Street. "If you make me come in and drag you dirty fucking shits out in front of the cameras," he snorts, nodding toward the television crew that has just arrived in response to activists' urgent calls, "you'll never sleep in peace again in that old house of yours on Horvačanska. You have my word." Her residential squat under direct threat, Jadranka retreats without responding to the officer, visibly shaken.

12:45 AM

Shortly after Jadranka's exchange about Vila Viktorija, the ranking officer on the scene informs us that we have five minutes to leave the building voluntarily or police will enter by force. "If you make this necessary," he adds, "you will face much more serious charges." Two of the largest "RoboCops," as activists call them, lug a battering ram toward the front door, apparently intent on shattering Rimi's handiwork.

For the past hour, Ivana has been pulling people aside, trying urgently to convince them that we should leave immediately and not risk further incensing the police. We gather in a tight circle among the piles of clothes to decide how we will respond to police demands (watch "Riot Cops"):

> **Ivana (discomposed, walks up and interrupts the ongoing discussion):** Guys, what will we do? There are two simple questions. Are we going now or . . .
> **Vjeran:** Wait, we are discussing things!
> **Ivana:** I'm sorry . . .
> **Jadranka:** Will we say we are staying?
> **Pero:** We should say we are willing to be arrested.
> **Ivana (now seated within the circle, groans as Pero speaks and interrupts again):** They will arrest us in any case!
> **(several people speak simultaneously)**

Jure: One by one, please!

Ivana (raising her voice but straining to sound calm): We should leave now, then go tomorrow to the city administration and file as an official association.

Jure (impatiently): We have our collective. We don't need an official association [NGO status]! Anyway, the city hasn't given any NGOs space.

Ivana: Then we stay in here until they enter by force and arrest us? Is that how we'll do it, come what may? Or do we all leave together?

Jadranka (eyes flitting from one face to another): So?

Eviction

As Pero would say later, with some bitterness, "Now we don't know what would have happened if we'd stayed. And now we'll never know." While we would certainly never *know*, from inside the standoff it seems relatively clear what awaits us if we refuse to exit willingly into police custody. In the end, Pero is the only local willing to face arrest—along with the Dutch squatters, and Pacho and me, who say we will record what happens if those who remain want us to.

A number of circumstances conspire to undermine the collective's resolve in the face of the police's apparent willingness to brush aside legal procedures requiring a court order and forcefully remove them. First, because the police arrived unexpectedly and sealed the premises, forbidding anyone to enter, those who happen to be at the Free Store are not necessarily those most committed to the Free Store, or most prepared to resist police pressure. Second, Rimi, who can be relied on for just such a willingness—as well as rabble-rousing language—and might have helped rally the occupiers in the face of the authorities, is home in bed with the flu. Third, Jadranka, who is well respected by the activists present, initially appeared the best prepared to organize resistance within the surrounded Free Store. While she never calls for the abandonment of Knowledge in the last tense meeting before we exit, she no longer argues for holding out either, saying that personally she will choose to leave rather than place her and her squatmates' home at risk. Given the (gendered) role she plays in sustaining collective life in Viktorija—both the physical labor of cleaning and upkeep as well as affective labor in managing different individuals' needs—she may be particularly susceptible to these threats.

Pero, on the other hand, insists that they tell the police, "We are staying and they will have to arrest us." But he has a well-deserved reputation for disobeying police orders regardless of consequences. This leaves me in an unexpectedly awkward position. Though I generally participate as fully as possible in activist life, I try to remove myself from decisions that involve significant risk. This is not because I think it is possible, or even preferable, for me to be neutral or objective. Rather, I try not to influence my collaborators' decisions when they are, I believe, in much more vulnerable positions than I am. They are unable to hide behind the privilege of U.S. citizenship or the status of international researcher from an elite university. Most already possess extensive police records. Observation—and filming in particular—is always a form of participation, however. On this occasion, I worry that our presence with a camera might make Pero more likely to stay to the bitter end, might pressure him to perform for the imagined future audience of the film. I find myself discouraging him from staying. I remind him that everyone else who is willing to face arrest can later leave Croatia and not deal with the potential fallout of a larger conflict with the police and extended legal difficulties. In the end, he reluctantly agrees to depart with everyone else.

Ironically, given how concerned I have been about my collaborators, in the end I am the only person involved in the standoff whom the police do not release after (extensive) questioning. I am unaware that my residence visa expired three days earlier. I am held overnight for an immigration hearing (watch "Not Cool").

The Struggle for the Means Of Producing Subjects

Not much reminds the well-heeled shoppers who stream daily into Kaptol Centar, Zagreb's most elite shopping mall, that they are entering the remodeled shell of what was a textile factory. They rarely read the small plaque beside the entrance to the mall's multiplex cinema, which reads, "On September 8, 1950 the work collective 'F. Gorjup' took over the management of this factory. They realized this action with the slogan of the workers' movement, 'Factories to the Workers!'" This neglected marble panel commemorates the struggle that defined Croatian politics for much of the Twentieth Century, the struggle of its workers—or at least the party that claimed to represent them—for control of the means of industrial production. Zagreb anarchists' survival strategies, as well as their political interventions in the urban landscape, point to a dramatically changed terrain of struggle. The industrial production that defined socialist modernization lies in ruin, increasingly supplanted by spaces of consumption and entertainment.

While the Free Store was ill-fated—perhaps even quixotic in light of the repeated eviction of earlier squats—Zagreb activists nonetheless modeled very different urban possibilities during its brief existence. First, they opened a space for the free exchange of goods, based on the core anarchist principle of "mutual aid" (Kropotkin 1902), in stark contrast to the international discount supermarket chain next door. What is more, rather than express nostalgia for the dwindling number of public spaces in the city, spaces lost in the rapid privatization of this period, they created a form of collective property that was outside the assumed binary of private-public. In creating a space open to all who recognized its importance, especially as a way of serving a wider social good, collectively managed through direct democracy, invested with collective labor, and dependent on the support of the wider neighborhood and city for its survival, they offer one example of what has come to be theorized as a common (Jeffrey et al. 2011). In asserting a right to make such interventions in the city around them, a "right to the city," they were not only laying claim to Knowledge as a space, however. They were asserting, again, what they perceived as a fundamental right to self-determination, the right to have a say in the kinds of people they would be. Because they understood urban space to be a key means of producing social relationships and political desires, they understood Knowledge as a means of producing the kinds of individual and collective subjects they were struggling to become.

* * *

In the final few days after my release, and before my return to the U.S., I made an effort to film an interview with each of my collaborators about the demise of the Free Store. "Depressed," as she put it, and perhaps a bit embarrassed that she had caved to police pressure, Jadranka refused to appear on camera. Rimi, on the other hand, was not angry but, instead, uncharacteristically philosophical—perhaps because he had not endured the humiliating surrender into police custody followed by hours of questioning. This was an "important experience" for the collective, he insisted, and what you have to be prepared for when you are "struggling for what is not yet." Rimi may have focused on the experience rather than the frustrations of defeat because he felt from the outset that the Free Store was an ultimately doomed endeavor, at least in the sense that holding onto Knowledge was unlikely. After all, he had participated in many earlier squats that were violently dislodged.

When I consider Pero's comment that "we'll never know" with the benefit of hindsight, I realize he might well have been speaking not only of the immediate strategic question of whether or not to remain barricaded within Knowledge, or even the loss of the Free Store itself. He might well have been referring to a less tangible sense of loss, related to the "experience" that Rimi cast in a positive light. "We won't know what would have become of us had we barricaded ourselves inside," he said. This question about what would have "become of us" strikes me as especially poignant looking back. When I consider the divergent paths of activist initiatives in Zagreb and Ljubljana, where I conducted parallel research with radical movements during the same period, I cannot help but speculate about foreclosed possibilities in Zagreb. To be sure, there are a variety of factors that set the two contexts apart, and by the mid-to-late 2000s both had entered what Jadranka would describe as a "quiet period where the old tactics that created this explosion no longer worked" (watch "A Quiet Period"). In other words, this was a quiet period in comparison to the dynamic large-scale globalization protests that marked the initial period of my fieldwork with Zagreb's anarchists. At a minimum, the sense of loss that Pero articulates points to having missed the opportunity to experience collective strength, to experience acting together in the face of state authority, "come what may." I do not necessarily have in mind the successful defense of Knowledge. An activist in Slovenia, for example—who participated in a collective effort to blockade the home of a debtor against eviction—described how, even though they were ultimately physically overpowered and arrested, "We had the experience that we could hold ranks, couldn't be intimidated, and were capable of publicly defying police orders. That will always stay with us."

There is also, of course, the loss of the space itself, a space that might have allowed for encounters with quite different experiences of the city—as activists originally envisioned the Network of Social Solidarity. This space, and these encounters, might have helped to generate other, expansive trajectories, rather than the relatively constrained and submerged efforts that characterized the next few years in Zagreb. The experience in Ljubljana, where activists squatted the former Rog bicycle factory eighteen months after the demise of the Free Store, gives a sense of these other possibilities. The Social Center founded within Rog became the central node of migrant community organizing in Ljubljana, generating experiences that ultimately contributed to the distinct—and unexpectedly dynamic—organizing that developed there during 2011, in the midst of the uprisings that spread rapidly from the Arab Spring, through Europe, to North America (Razsa and Kurnik 2012). In any case, after the lull that characterized the latter half of the 2000s, submerged organizing burst onto public squares around the world, including the occupation of the Ljubljana Stock Exchange. This new organizing can only be understood in relation to the experiences, shared sensibilities, and sense of a common purpose generated within the Rog Social Center. We turn next to these new claims for a right to city, and new forms of collective struggle emerging during the Occupy Movement.

CHAPTER FIVE

THE OCCUPY MOVEMENT: DIRECT DEMOCRACY AND A POLITICS OF BECOMING

"We Will Not Pay for Your Crisis"

Activists in Ljubljana, Slovenia, were already planning an encampment modeled on Occupy Wall Street (OWS) when they watched the YouTube video of Slavoj Žižek, their city's most famous son, addressing the protests in lower Manhattan on October 9, 2011. They were stunned. Perhaps, they speculated, the experience of hearing each line of his speech echo out through the "people's mic"—the collective repetition of a speaker's words, developed when police banned amplified sound—had swept Žižek up in the "exuberance of democratic self-fashioning" (Garces 2011). Slovene activists had not expected Žižek to support OWS because, his international reputation as a radical philosopher notwithstanding, his writings largely dismiss the possibility of political resistance to capitalism (e.g., Žižek 2007). Furthermore, as Barbara, an activist in her midthirties whose political experience stretches back to the globalization protests of the late 1990s and early 2000s, pointed out, as a member and theorist of the Liberal Democratic Party, Žižek had never supported the radical, migrant, and minority struggles out of which Ljubljana's own Occupy Movement grew. Even so, much of Žižek's speech, with its enthusiasm for Occupy, resonated with the wave of activism that was about to sweep through Ljubljana.[1]

Five days after watching the video, we were jostling with security guards at the headquarters of Slovenia's largest bank—Nova Ljubljanska Banka (NLB).[2] The guards insisted the space was private and barred our entry. Irfan, an activist from the Erased, the association of those who were stripped of permanent residence when Slovenia declared independence from Yugoslavia in 1991, retorted that NLB was state owned and therefore public property. Andrej, an experienced radical activist, political theorist, and one of my most important Slovene collaborators—whose experience and analysis are woven throughout this chapter—turned to the chief of security and went further: "You are making decisions here about the common wealth (*skupno bogastvo*) we've all produced and you are mismanaging that wealth. We will open a new public space here," he continued, "and we will speak about alternatives." Taking advantage of a moment of confusion, we surged past the guards to chant, "We will not pay for your crisis!" in the marble lobby. "No one represents us!" we shouted next, on the one hand a condemnation of Slovenia's political parties and European technocrats and, on the other, a declaration of autonomy. These chants, as well as activists' self-conscious decision to sidestep political institutions and directly confront financial ones, echoed Žižek's speech, which declared a general crisis of liberal democracy and denounced political representation as the outsourcing of political engagement (2011).

The activists who spoke at NLB understood their actions in precisely such terms; disavowing representation, they spoke of their own direct experiences of precarity, unemployment, and poverty. Sara, thirty, employed intermittently by research institutes and NGOs, described the failure of any legal status—student, employee, unemployed—to apply to the actual conditions of her life and, therefore, secure her what are still widely considered basic social rights in Slovenia: pension contributions, health insurance, and unemployment benefits. Armin, a twenty-eight-year-old Bosnian migrant and activist in the Invisible Workers of the World, an initiative at the forefront of much recent migrant political organizing, described living in twenty-two square meters with his wife and infant daughter. Romana, who had secured permanent employment (*zaposlitev za nedoločen čas*), listed her living expenses in relation to her pay, an accounting that showed that "if nothing goes wrong this month . . . 30€ [$38] remains for books, lessons, concerts, theater, clothes, shoes, etc." Whether speaking from personal experience, eschewing political parties, intervening directly against financial institutions, or deciding collectively in assemblies to take actions like this teach-in, Slovene activists described themselves as filling a vacuum created by the crisis of liberal democracy. When we tucked into a café to debrief after the teach-in, Barbara summarized that at "the center of our political practice here is a commitment to direct democracy, especially the local approach we've come to call the 'democracy of direct action'. . . It's about initiating a liberation movement in which our different struggles can converge and together we can seize back control of our lives."

As activists' viewing of the Žižek video already indicates, Occupy Slovenia's actions were part of a much wider European, even global, resurgence of protest in 2011. This resurgence surprised many observers, disrupting the years of relative quiet that followed the alterglobalization movements, which arguably peaked in Genoa in 2001 and, at least for my Zagreb collaborators, began to decline following the Thessaloniki protests. Beginning first in Tunisia in late 2010, before spreading to Egypt and much of the Middle East, the Arab Spring inspired further unrest. The *indignados* took up the torch in squares across Spain with their 15m movement—named for its May 15 launch—which in turn inspired New York-based activists to "Occupy Wall Street" on September 17. The contagion of this period reached Slovene activists not only via YouTube videos and other social media. Several activists who organized the NLB teach-in had traveled to Tunis and Barcelona a few weeks earlier to share activist experiences and coordinate protests transnationally. Following these meetings, activists back in Ljubljana decided, joining hundreds of other cities worldwide, to initiate Occupy Slovenia on the October 15 Global Day of Action.[3]

These "global uprisings" of 2011 erupted in response to a variety of social conditions—corruption, dictatorship, austerity, and wealth inequality, among others. If the targets of their protests—what they opposed—varied, their protests have almost universally affirmed two sets of practices, practices that are linked to the assertion of new forms of collective rights. First, movements asserted a "right to the city" by collectively occupying urban space. This right to the city echoes the Zagreb Network of Social Solidarity in certain regards, but it has generally expanded participation to include a much wider cross section of society. Second, in each of these spaces, activists have in various ways radicalized democracy by embracing direct democracy. This emphasis on direct democracy has led critical theorists—not only Slavoj Žižek (2011) but also Judith Butler (2011), Michael Hardt and Toni Negri (2012), and others—to frame these movements as responding to a fundamental crisis of representative politics and embodying an alternative to liberal democracy. Despite this recognition of the centrality of direct democracy to the uprisings, our knowledge of these concrete political experiments remains immature. Little description and analysis is available on the specific forms of directly democratic practice enacted in settings as distinct as the

Casbah in Tunis, Tahrir Square in Cairo, Syntagma Square in Athens, Puerta del Sol in Madrid, Tel Aviv's tent city, the Wisconsin statehouse, and the hundreds of encampments associated with the Occupy Movement. In the former Yugoslavia, like elsewhere, Occupy has presented both continuities and discontinuities with earlier struggles.

The emphasis that Barbara and others placed on direct democracy is not, of course, unprecedented. As we have already seen, whether in the acephalous and nonhierarchical organization of alterglobalization protests or in the consensus decision making that the Network of Social Solidarity adopted in its defense of the Free Store, direct democracy was central to the political imaginary and practice of regional efforts to reinvent the radical tradition after the demise of state socialism. In part there are continuties because activists like Andrej and Barbara were first politicized during the alterglobalization period and they have helped to transmit the practices and insights of earlier movements to a new generation of activists involved in Occupy. Over the past decade, while I was conducting research with the Zagreb activist scene, I carried out parallel research with activists in Ljubljana, two hours by train to the northwest of Zagreb. The two fieldsites often intersected. Andrej and Barbara, for example, were key organizers of the 2001 Noborder Camp, where I first met Croatian radicals, including Pero, the week before the Genoa G8 protests. I will return to anarchist life in Zagreb in the Conclusion, but the Occupy Movement in Slovenia during 2011 provides a revealing counterpoint to Rimi, Jadranka, and Pero's political engagement.

As a result of both the specificities of earlier struggles in Slovenia and new social and political conditions, not least the global financial crisis since 2008, there were clear discontinuities with previous regional practices and significant divergences from other uprisings of this period. Earlier campaigns in Slovenia—including those carried out in solidarity with minority and migrant activists during the 2000s—shaped the unusually decentralized and minoritarian character of the direct democracy adopted in Ljubljana, which set the democracy of direct action apart from practices developed elsewhere during 2011. In order to bring these continuities and discontinuities into relief, I trace the specific history and practices of Occupy Slovenia and contrast the democracy of direct action with the consensus-based decision making of OWS, about which much has been written to date (Gessen et al. 2011; Graeber 2011; Juris 2012). Understanding the specific and innovative nature of direct democratic practice in Slovenia provides a fresh critical vantage point from which to understand some of the potential limits of Pero, Jadranka, and

Rimi's anarchist politics from the early 2000s—and how later initiatives tried to overcome those limits.

I begin this chapter by giving a detailed account of the texture of the democracy of direct action as experienced in the daily assemblies of Occupy Slovenia. Of particular importance is the way that the democracy of direct action, with its empowerment of decentralized workshops rather than the central assembly, encouraged new initiatives, even initiatives that the majority of those at the assembly might not actively have supported.[4] I then turn to the recent history of social movements in Slovenia, because the practice of the democracy of direct action developed out of activists' experience and knowledge, produced through a series of migrant and minority campaigns during the 2000s.[5] Indeed, according to movement participants, experiences of liberal democracy as it is traditionally understood—as the rule of the majority—as well as the exclusion of non-Slovenes from national citizenship, an exclusion later confirmed by popular referenda against minority rights, led to the adoption of a minoritarian decision-making model within Occupy Slovenia. This decision-making process ensured a space, they claimed, for action by those who belonged to marginalized minorities or held minority political positions, and thereby also facilitated the expansion of the movement by encouraging participation, innovation, and initiative, what they often called *protagonizem,* perhaps best translated as "agency." Finally, I describe the Workshop for Direct Social Work as one example of the kinds of collective action grounded in personal experience facilitated by the democracy of direct action.[6] Direct Social Work created spaces for encounter and collaboration among those with distinct and even antagonistic positions—for instance, social workers and those officially called "users" (*uporabniki*) of social services. Central to its process of "rebuilding society from below" was mutual transformation, what one woman who was involved with Direct Social Work's activities described to me as a process of becoming-other-than-one-now-is (*postajajoč-drug-kot-si-sedaj*) through encounters with difference. This theme of becoming came up repeatedly around Occupy Slovenia.

In conclusion, I consider whether the direct democratic practices of Occupy Slovenia, especially the emphasis on becoming, might offer an opportunity to extend the ways that direct democracy and direct action have been theorized to date, including the ways I made sense of *direktna akcija* as practiced by Zagreb anarchists. Rather than emphasizing the prefigurative qualities of direct democracy—that is, *being* the change one wants to see in the world—I consider the shift toward the politics of *becoming*-other-than-one-now-is, toward forms of open-ended subject making that are embedded in and constitutive of collective struggle (Hardt and Negri 2009:367; cf. Biehl and Locke 2010). This politics of encounter and becoming offers a revealing contrast to the relative social isolation that Zagreb anarchists experienced as they strove to remain ethically pure and refused to work with those who did not share their political orientation.

The Democracy of Direct Action in the Daily Assemblies

Like Occupy Movement activists elsewhere, Ljubljana's radicals were surprised by the public response that their first general appeal elicited. A crowd of thousands joined the protests on Congress Square, leaving the small sound system utterly overwhelmed. When activists proposed a march to the Ljubljana Stock Exchange, the crowd roared enthusiastically. The assembly that gathered there promptly decided to establish an indefinite encampment in front of the stock exchange. As activists described their arrival at the stock exchange in a collective diary written during the first week of the movement,[7]

> In front of the stock exchange protest becomes resistance; demonstration becomes assembly. The letter "R" is knocked off *Borza* (Stock Exchange) and a "J" is inserted to spell *Boj za* (The Struggle for . . .). With television broadcasting live, the assembly decides to occupy. We have broken with the dictates of financial capitalism and representative politics. We are building a movement based on principles of direct democracy and direct action—horizontally, in network form. We will liberate our strivings, our desires (see figure 5.1) (*Večer* 2011).

Tents soon sprouted like mushrooms. The situation in those first weeks of Occupy Slovenia was disorienting for many activists—who, after years of organizing alongside migrant and minority groups in Slovenia, organizing that led to the marginalization of activism and even led, at times, to its public vilification—found suddenly that many embraced their radical activism. They understood this newfound public support in relation to a fundamental political disorientation in Slovenia. In the face of the deep economic and political crisis, the goals that had guided public life for two decades—economic liberalization, European integration, and democratic consolidation—had lost their self-evidence.

In light of past experiences, activists responded to their newfound popularity[8] with an insistence on a transnational rather than national framing.

Figure 5.1. After occupying the square in front of the Stock Exchange
(BORZA) activists held a renaming ceremony. BORZA became BOJ ZA
(the struggle for). This open-ended slogan hung over the encampment for
the seven months the occupation lasted. *Photo by 15o.*

Another passage of the activist diary captures this sentiment: "On the way
protests from abroad are heard: Madrid, Barcelona, Rome, New York, Tunis,
and Argentina are echoing in our chants. *Que non nos representan! Degagez!*
This is what democracy looks like! *Que se vayan todos!* And the Slovenian re-
frains. No one represents us! Money to people, not banks! We will not pay for
your crisis!" (*Večer* 2011). By stressing "No one represents us," "Real democracy now," and "Que se vayan todos" (They all must go), as well as bemoaning
the consequences of the "monopoly of 'democratic parties' over political life,"
activists positioned Occupy Slovenia as a response to a crisis of representative
democracy in Slovenia.

Daily assemblies quickly became the public forum of the movement in
Ljubljana. One assembly (*skupščina*) I attended in late November 2011 provides a sense of the dynamics of these gatherings, the decision-making process within the democracy of direct action, and the forms of political action
that came to define Occupy Slovenia. They also provide interesting similarities and differences with the direct democracy of the Free Store. Tjaša vol-

Figure 5.2. During the early days of occupation, evening assemblies were held outdoors among the tents of the 15o encampment. From mid-November onward, they moved into a large military tent. *Photo by 15o.*

unteers for the role of recorder (*zapisnikar*), who takes notes and posts them on 15o.si.[9] A voice from my left nominates Marko, thirty-one, to facilitate the proceedings by asking, "You've never been moderator, right?" Indeed, as he recites aloud the rules that structure the assembly—as is done at the beginning of each gathering—Marko struggles. The crowd of fifty, now in a tight circle, teases him when he forgets the second of only three agenda items considered at each assembly: camp logistics, workshop reports, and miscellaneous. Marko reminds everyone that the assembly does not decide the content of workshops (*delavnice*); that is the autonomous prerogative of the workshops themselves. When Marko pauses too long, others in our circle call out the rules: Raise your hand to speak, wait to be acknowledged by the moderator, respect the expression of others, and, if you have already spoken, defer to those who have not yet had a chance to express themselves.[10] Do not engage in dialogue with others, especially if this means criticizing the proposals of others, but instead propose your own action—and only an action that you yourself are willing to participate in and help organize. Be concrete. Propose the idea for a workshop and announce when and where it will meet. "So, in short," continues Marko, catching his stride, "it's direct democracy. Everyone present participates" (see figure 5.2).

Turning to camp logistics, participants discuss the kinds of issues that might arise among roommates or within the context of any extended camp-out: lost sweater, main tent opening hours, organization of night watch, how to handle late-night drunkenness, smoking in the main tent, and wet sleeping bags to be collected and hung to dry. Irfan, fifty-six, speaks next. With his graying mustache, it is easy to imagine him as the dignified yet surly socialist-era waiter he was until he was "erased" in 1991. He reports on Occupy Slovenia's finances: 26€ ($33) in donations, 18€ ($23) in outlays, leaving a total of 136€ ($172). There is a brief discussion of buying a higher grade of kerosene for the space heater so the walls of the main tent—as well as the lungs of those who spend time there—will not be covered in the kind of fine black soot that I blew from my nose last night with some consternation.[11]

A number of workshops report back to the assembly on their activities. Emil, fifty-one, a migrant worker from Bosnia, reports from the Workshop for the Workers Dormitory Rent Strike. He describes the difficulties former employees of Vegrad, a large construction firm that has been in bankruptcy for nearly eleven months, are having with the management of the company-owned dormitory.[12] Vegrad owes back pay of between 5,000€ ($6,340) and 15,000€ ($19,020) to these workers. These debts, unlike those of the company's creditors, Slovenia's major financial institutions, Emil explains, are not to be paid from the bankruptcy fund. What is more, the court-appointed trustee is insisting the workers continue to pay rent to the dormitory or face eviction. The workers have responded that they should be able to stay on, subtracting the rent from the back pay they are owed. They have declared a rent strike. If evicted, however, those with permanent residence risk losing social rights such as health insurance, and those with temporary residence face deportation.[13] "Do you have a workshop proposal?" Andrej asks. "Yes, please come to a meeting at the dormitory at 8PM on Tuesday," Emil appeals to assembly, "to plan action against the management."

Other announcements? "Yes," Andrej speaks up. "The Workshop against Precarity and for Common Welfare met on Sunday with families who have been, or are in the process of being, evicted from their homes by Raiffeissen [Bank]." Living in Slovenia's poorest region, Prekmurje, most have already paid back the loans with interest, Andrej explains, but they have not managed to pay off the high fees and penalties they received during periods when they were unable to make payments. Mostly impoverished peasants, many with a foot in wage labor of one kind or another, they contacted the workshop after seeing coverage of the teach-in at NLB on national television. Andrej describes planned direct actions, under the name Days of Indignation Against the Banks,[14] culminating in an action to move one family back into their home. "We will demand the writing off of their debts. This is a crucial turn in our struggle," he continues, "in which we can begin to open direct conflicts with financial institutions and begin to establish new relations of force."

"Any questions?" asks the moderator. "Yes," responds a clean-cut man in his midthirties. "These people should also take some responsibility for these loans. We should be avoiding these financial institutions, boycotting them instead of borrowing from them." "That's neither here nor there now," retorts Andrej, "and it's impossible in today's era to get ahead without credit. These people took relatively small loans for necessary expenses and they were forced to put up their homes as collateral." As the back and forth continues, with escalating intensity, the moderator intervenes to remind the two interlocutors that they should not be "dialoguing"; comments should be addressed to the assembly. "Anyway," the moderator continues, addressing the clean-cut man, "unless you have a fundamental ethical objection to what they're planning, you should just get involved in the workshop. Otherwise, propose your own damn workshop!"

The specific decision-making practices that constitute the democracy of direct action, as exhibited in this assembly, have a number of political implications. To clarify these practices, it is helpful to first contrast them with those of OWS—and by OWS, I am referring specifically to the encampment in Zuccotti Park in New York City, the first and best-known Occupy encampment. Movements in other U.S. cities have adopted varied models of organization. At first glance, the democracy of direct action, as embodied in the Ljubljana assembly, appears quite similar to those direct democratic practices adopted by OWS, comprising the constituent elements of general assemblies and working groups—or assemblies and workshops, as they have come to be known in Ljubljana. In fact, the relationship between workshops and the assembly is reversed, which shifts significantly how decisions are made—and where power lies. Whereas at OWS all decisions need to be approved by modified consensus at the general assembly—that is, at least 90 percent approval after all objections have been heard and addressed by facilitators (#OccupyWallStreet New York City General Assembly 2011)—the assembly in Ljubljana is not Occupy Slovenia's primary decision-making unit. Workshops, although they operate under the umbrella of Occupy Slovenia and report back to the assembly, have autonomy to organize themselves in any manner they see fit, implementing the internal forms of decision making they think most appropriate.[15] Working groups at OWS, by contrast, are empowered only to develop proposals, which have to be approved through modified consensus at the general assembly. Participants in the general assembly sometimes number in the thousands and proceedings lasted for many hours (Gessen et al. 2011),[16] whereas assemblies in Ljubljana typically last from thirty to forty-five minutes. My concern here is not primarily with efficiency, though it is not irrelevant, for, as Barbara quipped in late November, "It's too cold for consensus."[17] More importantly, when I asked activists about their impressions of the democracy-of-direct-action model, two themes came up repeatedly:

1) that the form empowered minorities and
2) that it unleashed energies that were otherwise dormant or even actively blocked in their daily lives.

Migrants from various backgrounds were an important constituency within Occupy Slovenia. I address some of the historical reasons for the heterogeneous composition of the movement below. Here I consider the ways that the democracy of direct action opened a space for minority participation, not only by ethnic or racial minorities (*manjšina*) but also by those with minority political positions or groups who had particular concerns that might not have any immediate urgency for the broader assembly, for example, those labeled mentally ill. When Andrej and I finally found time to sit down and discuss the implications of the democracy of direct action, I asked him why the practice was especially inviting for those who did not feel they belonged to the majority for one reason or another. He responded,

> Well, it's related to the same dynamic of empowering workshops and not requiring initiatives to seek majority endorsement. Emil, for example, can propose a workshop on his specific concerns at the workers dormitory without needing anyone's approval. Or I don't have to worry if that guy at the assembly doesn't fully understand our approach to addressing evictions. The emphasis is on action by anyone who feels a workshop addresses issues of real concern to them. That's the reason we ground these proposals in a willingness to participate in them, to take action. By design there is no overarching sovereign authority that would define the direction of this movement . . . And, hence, there is no authority that can determine that a minority's position doesn't represent

Occupy Slovenia as a whole. . . . No one can say, for example, as some have tried to say, 'Oh, don't let those homeless people speak in our name. They make us look bad.'

Activists' antipathy to majoritarian decision making, which, for some like Andrej, extended to sovereignty itself, had implications both for the dynamism of Occupy Slovenia's campaign and for the role of those who held minority positions. The historical experience that generated this hostility to "sovereignty" will become clearer below, in light of the history of recent Slovene activism.

Activists also often discussed the democracy of direct action's capacity to unleash creative energies. As Andrej explained it, "The movement here in Ljubljana is similar in composition to [the movements in] Tunisia and Spain—a highly educated generation whose capacities to produce, to network, to express themselves are completely blocked. What we envisioned, and what's taken shape to a degree we'd hardly let ourselves hope, is an open framework in which people can develop new demands, new social rights. That's why it's important that people be able to pursue the projects they propose, assuming it's an idea that can attract collaborators."

As I became more familiar with the democracy of direct action, two critical issues about its practice kept recurring to me, both related to the political coherence of Occupy Slovenia in light of its adoption of this model of organization. First, I pressed Andrej on the question of what the limits of political participation in Occupy Slovenia might be: within the framework of the democracy of direct action, with power residing in the workshops, what would prevent initiatives that are fundamentally hostile to the movement from co-opting it? "All workshops are to abide by the framing principles adopted when the encampment was declared on October 15," Andrej explained, "by organizations like the Invisible Workers of the World, the Union of Crane Operators, Social Center Rog, We are the University, and An Alternative Exists." These principles included opposition to financial bailouts and austerity, rejection of political representation, and contribution to the development of an autonomous movement and solidarity. When a leader of the Party of Youth-Greens (*SMS-Zeleni*), for example, tried to participate in the occupied Faculty of Arts Assembly as part of his party's preelection campaign, Andrej continued, he was booed into silence and told not to return as a party representative, though he was welcome as a human being. How would the movement respond to a populist anti-immigrant initiative? "Look, first, you've seen how many migrant initiatives are represented here, the Erased, Invisible Workers of the World, and the workers dormitory strike," Andrej responded, "so we've created a clear profile that is inhospitable to the politics of hate. But if force was needed to eject them from our midst . . ." In the final analysis, Andrej argued,

> What is important is that the democracy of direct action does not establish some kind of general will of the people but seeks to make beneficial encounters possible. The assembly is the space that searches for commonalities among different workshops, to produce new common notions that would compose an expanded collective subject, not by majority principle but by keeping processes of empowerment of everyone directed toward expansion . . . This means producing norms, like defense of minority positions, norms that ensure the process continues its expansive trajectory.

Second, I wondered what would prevent centrifugal forces from undoing Occupy Slovenia. Was there not a tendency for people to self-select into workshops of like-minded people? Was there not a danger, especially in light of the sectarian tensions that marred the alterglobalization movement in Slovenia and elsewhere, of groups spinning off from Occupy Slovenia and no longer returning to assemblies, no longer engaging with those who were different? "Well," Andrej admitted,

> this is a very real danger, and there have at times been signs of such centrifugal tendencies. We don't know where this will lead. For the moment, however, I'd say two elements counter this tendency. First, in creating a camp in front of the Stock Exchange, we've clearly defined a common enemy, an enemy that many of us can link directly to the conditions of our daily lives, the nature of our employment, the debts we can't pay. But second, that camp is also a common resource we are governing together. Not, of course, just the physical camp, though that is crucial. I mean we recently discussed the possibility of closing the camp because it's just so exhausting to sustain it in this [late December] weather, but many felt that it was what linked us in some fundamental ways. And, from the discussion, it was clear that the camp was the physical manifestation of the broader common resource of the movement, the profile we've built publicly, but also the new forms of social relations we've produced collectively around that camp.

So while the democracy of direct action was distinctly minoritarian, especially in comparison to the consensus decision making adopted in New

York, and this brought potential risks, activists remained committed to these practices. In order to explain the origins of these distinctive practices and commitments, I turn now to the ways that previous struggles alongside minority groups inform this minoritarian orientation, i.e., the ways earlier political experiences led activists to studiously resist both the rule of the majority and the delegation of power to representatives, principles, and practices that are at the heart of liberal democracy.

A Minoritarian History of Social Movements in Slovenia

Although many commentators on the Occupy Movement have noted its similarities to the alterglobalization movement (Klein 2011; Tarrow 2011), few have described the actual organizational and biographical threads tying these two periods together or the significant shifts in activist practice that separate them. In the Slovenian case, understanding the struggles that preceded Occupy Slovenia—their history and the political lessons gleaned from that history—is essential because earlier movements directly inform the democracy of direct action. As in other 2011 uprisings, some activists in Ljubljana were first politicized in the globalization campaigns of the early 2000s, especially the transnational mobilizations against elite summit meetings in Seattle, Prague, Gothenburg, and Genoa at which Pero, Rimi, and Jadranka were also radicalized. Indeed, in Slovenia there was a rapid succession of campaigns through the 2000s, beginning with alterglobalization protests and quickly followed by campaigns against the invasion of Iraq and Slovene membership in NATO—campaigns very similar to Croatian ones of the same period.[18] But struggles over citizenship and belonging (Beznec 2008, 2009; Kurnik 2008, 2009) came to dominate activist life from the mid-to-late 2000s, struggles that left their stamp on the decidedly minoritarian practices of the democracy of direct action.

   With EU membership and the highest per-capita income of formerly socialist states, Slovenia was often held up as a success story.[19] The struggles of Slovenia's minorities, primarily those from other former Yugoslav republics, cast its recently gained statehood in a different light, however. Following Yugoslavia's collapse, the formation of an independent and ethnically defined state (Hayden 2000), and accession to the European Union, citizenship, and migration, became the most politically charged issues in Slovenia, as they were in much of Western Europe. Between 2000 and the Occupy protests of 2011, public conflicts erupted around a series of migrant populations: pre-independence migrants from elsewhere in the former Yugoslavia protest-

Figure 5.3. The author shoots video as Andrej addresses striking dock-workers at Slovenia's container port. The August 2011 strike, the first to see broad cooperation between directly hired and outsourced migrant labor-ers, was successful, in part, because it was able to gather at and sometimes block the entrance to the port. As activists planned 15o, they frequently asked what space would give them similar power. *Photo by Dare Čekeliš.*

ing their removal from the register of permanent residents, displaced Bos-nians seeking official status as refugees, asylum seekers pushing for greater freedom of movement pending hearings, undocumented migrants denounc-ing their detention conditions, and workers on temporary visas objecting to labor abuses.

Slovenian popular discourse about migrants (Doupona-Horvat et al. 2001) in many ways paralleled the dominant scholarly frameworks, which either treat migrants as a threat to receiving countries (Hirsi Ali 2006; Hun-tington 2004; Ye'or 2005) or as helpless victims of human-rights abuses (cf. Cunningham 1995; Giordano 2008). Some migrants and activist allies in Lju-bljana, many of them veterans of the global justice movement of the early 2000s, insisted that a different approach was needed. Indeed, in many ways, the concept of "insurgent citizenship," developed to describe the informal practices of residents in Brazilian *favelas* that "created new spheres of partici-pation and understandings or rights" (Holston 2008:303), describes the creative ways migrants have managed to act politically even when they have none of the legal rights afforded to citizens (cf. Rosaldo 2009).

Among these migration struggles, the self-described Erased were the most contentious in Slovenia and perhaps illustrate most clearly the troubling qualities of ethnonationalist citizenship and liberal democracy grounded in the rule of the majority. As such, the experience of the Erased provides an important background against which the democracy of direct action was later developed. The 1992 removal, or "erasure" (*izbris*), of more than twenty-five thousand people—primarily those born in other Yugoslav republics—from the register of permanent residents was not controversial at the time. Though this act by the minister of internal affairs affected more than one percent of the overall population of two million, the public and many of those affected were unaware of the scale of erasure until the Association of the Erased was formed in 2002 and began to challenge their near total dispossession. The erasure was but one facet of the exclusionary definition of Slovene nationhood,[20] which entailed constitutionally defining Slovenia as the state of "Slovene people" (*slovenski narod*) and therefore the state of its ethnic majority (Hayden 2000). The ethnic character of Slovene citizenship was further evidenced, for example, in guaranteed citizenship for those born to ethnically Slovene emigrants abroad.

In the tradition of the Association of the Erased, who often used testimonials to dramatize the human consequences of the erasure, it is instructive to consider Asim's story. Activists first met Asim when he returned to Slovenia in 2007 and visited Social Center Rog. Housed in a former bicycle factory, the social center had been squatted by activists in 2006, becoming a central node for migrant organizing. Asim, in his late forties, came to the social center for legal advice about how to normalize his status in Slovenia. He told the story of his erasure from a country he had long considered home. He was born near Cazin, one of two Bosnian regions that provided much of the labor that fueled the rapid industrialization and modernization of Slovenia after World War II. After finishing primary school in the late 1970s, he moved to Slovenia, as did many of his peers, to attend a secondary school specializing in the building trades. After qualifying as a construction worker, he worked for several major Slovene firms, living in workers dormitories, a form of social housing for single workers coming from other parts of the federal state. Later he settled in Ljubljana, moving into a studio apartment, which he registered as his permanent residence. Following Slovenia's declaration of independence in 1991, he applied for citizenship, as was required by law for non-

Slovenes, but he received no official response. In early 1992, during the severe economic crisis that followed Slovene independence and loss of access to the wider Yugoslav market, Asim's firm laid him off. He went to visit his family in Bosnia for a few weeks just as armed conflict broke out. He tried to return to safety in Slovenia but was rejected at the border. Though he did not understand why at the time, he had been erased. Forced to remain in Bosnia, he was mobilized and sent to war.

The act of erasure transformed others into "illegal migrants" overnight in a territory where they had lived legally for decades or, in some cases, been born (Blitz 2006). Along with legal residence, the Erased lost medical care, work permits, pensions, even the ability to obtain a driver's license or to travel outside Slovenia. Because local clerks had a great deal of discretion regarding who would actually be purged from the register, ethnic Roma were targeted disproportionately in the erasure (Zorn 2005). With the exception of informal activist initiatives and a small number of formal NGOs, especially the Peace Institute, the Erased were vilified in the national media, portrayed as a dangerous fifth column disloyal to Slovenia (Zorn and Lipovec Čebron 2008). The Erased, like other politically active migrant groups, worked closely with a loose-knit web of allies, the more radical of whom gathered around Social Center Rog, a space that allowed varied migrant initiatives to socialize extensively and develop a sense of common struggle. The activists around the social center encouraged the active participation of migrants themselves, seeking ways to valorize what they called their *protagonizem*—that is, their agency— rather than emphasize their victimhood (Kurnik 2008).

And, indeed, despite the hostile atmosphere the Erased faced, their lack of legal rights, and personal experiences of dispossession, their association pursued claims in such venues as the Slovenian Constitutional Court, the European Parliament, and the European Court of Human Rights (Beznec 2008). The Erased also organized an international solidarity campaign, sometimes coordinated with migrant initiatives elsewhere in Europe, including the French *sans-papiers,* and continually worked to ensure that their predicament was at the center of public debate.

Their activism—which challenged what one Erased activist called "our ethnic cleansing by bureaucratic means"—provoked a virulent response. First, the right-wing Slovenian Democratic Party (SDS) organized a popular referendum on the Erased in 2004, which provided another opportunity for public attacks on Roma and "Southerners" (*južnjaki*), i.e., those born in other former Yugoslav republics. Although participation was low, some 95 percent

Figure 5.4. Irfan Beširević, one of the leaders of the Association of the Erased, speaks during the Workshop for Opposition to Increased Fares on Ljubljana Public Transportation. *Photo by 15o.*

voted against the Erased (Zorn 2005). Second, in this politically charged atmosphere, NGOs such as the Peace Institute, with its origins in the wave of activism in late 1980s Slovenia (Mastnak 1994), pursued a quite different approach than those associated with the Social Center Rog. They advocated *on behalf of* migrants, seeking to speak for them in public and legal settings and therefore to mediate their relationship with the state. As one longtime radical activist critical of the Peace Institute's approach lamented, "Many of our early efforts to build new forms of power with migrants were contested by civil society organizations, which always attempted to impose themselves as mediators for the marginalized, representing them as helpless victims rather than allowing them to articulate their own politics."

These experiences help to explain activists' deep skepticism of liberal democracy as traditionally conceived, i.e., as majority rule. To begin, the definition of the ethnic majority as sovereign in the new state—and the accompanying expulsion of the Erased from the political community at Slovenia's founding—dramatized for activists what Balibar has described as the always exclusionary character of national citizenship (2004). Next, this exclusion was affirmed through popular referendum—itself a form of direct democracy, though one based, again, on the will of the majority. In short, a majority of voters negated the rights of the minority. Furthermore, activists came to believe that forms of organization that sought to represent minority concerns *on behalf of* those affected by such discrimination—i.e., rather than encouraging the Erased to speak for themselves—further entrenched their status as victims and denied their *protagonizem* (see figure 5.4). Finally, activists came to be skeptical of exclusively national frameworks, insisting instead on a transnational orientation in alliance with movements elsewhere. These lessons would come to inform the innovative approach to direct democracy developed later within Occupy Slovenia.

To be clear, my earlier contrasting of the democracy of direct action with consensus models, like that adopted by OWS, was not meant to imply that consensus decision-making practices cannot protect the rights of minorities. Indeed, consensus, which typically requires the consent of those who hold minority positions, can be quite effective in protecting minority voices—though this is less true of modified consensus, where a supermajority can simply overrule a small minority no matter how adamantly it opposes a given decision. Within the framework of the democracy of direct action, however, it is possible to act, to take initiative from minority positions, even to take actions that may not be popular among the majority.

When I shared the above history of the development of a minoritarian orientation among Slovene activists with Andrej, he said it left him with the nagging sense I had neglected something essential about the quality of the democracy of direct action and what had motivated its development. To be sure, the above history demonstrates why activists would be decidedly ambivalent about majoritarian and populist articulations of the Occupy Movement. So, even though the slogan "We are the 99%" was sometimes heard in Ljubljana, it always had a strange ring for those activists who spent years working alongside Slovenia's 1 percent—the Erased.[21] Similarly, statements like those OWS issued in the name of "the people, united" (#OccupyWallStreet New York General Assembly 2011) grated at the ears of some Slovene activists. For Andrej, invoking the *narod,* which includes both "the people" and "the nation" in Slovene, always called to mind the foundational exclusion of Slovenia's declaration of independence.

But all this, Andrej complained, makes the democracy of direct action sound as if it is only a reaction against the dangers of sovereignty—hard lessons learned from discrimination. "For us, however," Andrej added, the democracy of direct action "is also a positive affirmation not only of the marginalized and the minority but also of minoritarian politics as the organization that will be expansive and ever more inclusive rather than disciplining or normalizing those who participate." In other words, for a movement that was becoming increasingly diverse—including radicals and vilified minorities like the Erased but also those facing eviction, migrant laborers, and the precariously employed, unemployed, and homeless—an organization that was affirmatively minoritarian had a positive value beyond safeguarding the rights of minority activists from being trampled by the majority. First, even those who held minority views could take initiative without seeking the support of the majority. Second, the movement did need not to be limited to a national frame, it could both appeal to migrants within Slovenia and actively link with struggles based elsewhere. "At the center of this organization," as Andrej articulated the matter in a typically theoretical flourish, "is the figure of the minoritarian as a universal figure, in the Deleuzian sense of becoming everybody and everything."[22]

But what was to prevent this diverse assemblage of constituencies from remaining utterly incoherent and fractured? What was to prevent the development of parallel struggles that were in no way in dialogue with one another? In the next section, I turn to one example of how the democracy of direct action facilitated spaces for sustained encounter and mutual transformation, leaving many who participated fundamentally other than they once were.

Workshops and the Politics of Becoming

By late November, a multitude of workshops were meeting around Slovenia—the cities of Maribor and Koper, the Faculty of Arts, the Faculty of Social Sciences, and the Faculty of Social Work in addition to the original Boj za encampment. There were individual workshops on the "Bible and Social Criticism," "For a Better Old Age," "For Media Relations," "For Improving the Camp," "For the Blockade of the Humanities Faculty," and "For Action against the Detention and Treatment of People against Their Will." Activists argued that the relative autonomy of workshops, especially as compared to the OWS model, and the emphasis on the proposer being prepared to contribute to his or her proposals, encouraged action, innovation, and diversity. Of course, as Barbara was quick to point out, "Many initiatives wither on the vine. The workshops that captured people's imaginations," she elaborated, "but that could also be put into action, were the ones that grew." I turn now to the description of one workshop to provide a sense of the kinds of concrete activities that were taking place in these forums.

I heard much praise for the Workshop on Direct Social Work—especially the participants' "Occupy Psychiatry" action, in which they invited patients to speak in front of the Ljubljana Psychiatric Clinic about the violence and humiliation they had endured while institutionalized there. The core of those involved in Direct Social Work are professors, students, and users who have already produced a significant record of struggles over the past few years, most prominently the struggle against institutionalization and for a new social work conducted in communities of social workers and users rather than within state institutions (Flaker 2006).[23] These activities have now been folded into Occupy Slovenia, often taking place, quite literally, in its "big tent." Like the Workshop on Precarity and Common Welfare, Direct Social Work intervenes in the increasingly intense struggle over who is to have control of social reproduction—states, financial markets, or those whose lives are directly affected.[24] While I met activists associated with Direct Social Work at assemblies and other Occupy actions, I had not been to one of their workshop meetings until we gathered inside the large military-grade tent.

Ten of us sit around a table opposite the kitchen and push stacks of books from the library against the side of the tent to make room. We are not far from the smoky kerosene heater that has drawn most assemblies inside now that the temperature has dropped below freezing.

At first I am confused about the close collective reading of the Law on the Exercise of Rights to Public Resources (*Zakon o uveljavljanju pravic iz javnih sredstev*) that we are carrying out. Vito, a professor of social work in his midfifties, seems to have the most comprehensive understanding of the law and many questions are directed to him. Marta, a student of social work in her midtwenties who is facilitating the workshop, is, nonetheless, careful when multiple hands are raised to select participants other than Vito to speak first, especially, it seems to me, the three participants who would be officially designated "users" of social services. There are four other students around the table as well as Gregor, formerly a junkie, now an activist on issues surrounding drug policy. Another workshop he participates in, the Workshop to End Prohibition, recently held a "smoke-in" at the Ministry of Health to protest the lack of access to medical marijuana. Gregor clearly has a sophisticated understanding of the rules—and the loopholes—of Slovenia's social safety net. He discusses his strategy of using a community organization with which he is associated to register the homeless as residents of Ljubljana. Legal registration of one's address is a constant challenge for those who are homeless, and legal residence is the font of all social rights, including access to the national health care system.

Despite constant interruptions—especially a steady trickle of homeless who enter and exit the tent, usually greeting members of the workshop with great familiarity[25]—we continue to a do a fine-grained reading of the statute. Why is it so complicated to assess what constitutes an "adequate and appropriate apartment" for children? Why does individual social assistance often max out at 230€ ($290) when the legal maximum is 450€ ($570) per month? (We are occasionally forced to raise our voices because activists from Anonymous are having an animated debate at the other side of the tent about technical issues with our live-stream feed, which broadcasts video of our direct actions and assemblies.) How is your assistance level adjusted if you have a small pension? How does someone access housing assistance from the municipality? Users explain their struggles in navigating these questions, especially in the face of administrative obfuscation at various offices. Slowly, from this morass of bureaucratic minutia, from numerous wandering accounts of personal experiences with social workers, the logic of our inquiry emerges. These direct social workers, i.e., all those gathered here, are amassing the costs—institutional, financial, and personal—of the current system of state controls associated with each kind of transfer payment.

The argument that is slowly cohering is that the current regulations serve to prevent many from accessing the funds to which they are entitled. The controls in place often cost more than they save. Because of this bureaucracy the social assistance that is given is therefore significantly smaller than it could be. Humiliations abound for those seeking to exercise the social rights defined in the law. Moreover, because social workers are compelled to police users' compliance with a complex array of regulations, their relationship—as both social workers and users in the workshop testify from their distinct perspectives—has become charged with discipline and stigmatization rather than collaboration. This fraught relationship is further deteriorating in the face of the sovereign debt crisis and consequent austerity policies. That is, despite public debt and deficits that are relatively small by EU standards, Slovenia is being forced to follow the dictates of the financial markets and implement policies similar to those states designated as PIGS (originally, Portugal, Italy, Greece, and Spain, but now often expanded to include others).[26] Those present argue that the austerity policies being implemented affect social workers and users more than perhaps any others in society. "Social workers are always in offices," says one young social worker, "we're always filling out paperwork. We are not meeting with users in the daily conditions in which they struggle."

Marta proposes, and others quickly embrace, a demand for a complete overhaul of state policies: a basic welfare package of 550€ ($698) that would be guaranteed to all instead of the current regime of interlocking programs for those deemed needy within a complex range of rubrics. Perhaps there should be means testing at the very upper end of income brackets, perhaps not; this remains unresolved. By the end of the meeting, activists draw up plans for direct action against the Ministry of Work, Family, and Social Affairs; the Center for Social Work; and the Ljubljana Public Housing Fund. The actions must be grounded, Marta reminds us, in the personal experience of social workers and users, not in abstractions of social critique.

Several qualities of Direct Social Work stand out and help to make more concrete what is involved in the "politics of becoming" that proponents claim is facilitated by the democracy of direct action. Most importantly, the meetings of Direct Social Work were clearly spaces of encounter. Within the broader context of the intense antagonism that characterizes social worker–user relations—which one Direct Social Work activist described hyperbolically as akin to that between "an occupying army and local inhabitants"—the spaces for communication and cooperation described above were highly unusual. Through the process of dialogue, common study, and reflection—as well as weekly direct actions—those who participated built new intersubjective understandings and consensus, especially in the original sense of consensus as "common sentiment" or "feeling" (*Oxford English Dictionary* 2010). The workshops thus serve as spaces for encounter grounded in common struggle, spaces in which differences come together and are transformed in the process.

Although I found the dynamics I saw within Direct Social Work workshops remarkable, especially their capacity to create settings for collaboration across significant social divisions, I was, nonetheless, left with the nagging sense that they were also a particularly striking example of a central tension implicit in the workings of the democracy of direct action, a tension that was not being acknowledged by participants but which would have leapt out at my anarchist informants in Zagreb. After another Direct Social Work workshop, I asked Marta whether there is a contradiction in the Occupy Slovenia movement between, on the one hand, the declared rupture with representative democracy—the effort to start rebuilding society through practices of direct democracy that encourage encounters between differences and therefore becomings—and, on the other hand, the continued use of terms such as *welfare* and *rights* or the development of demands for policy changes addressed to the state and its representatives? She responded,

> Well, you have to understand the specific practices of becoming we're developing here. It's not just about bringing people together and hoping they change. Direct Social Work struggles to transform social relations in dialogue with the concrete conditions in which people find themselves. That's why participants, whether social workers or users, have to speak from their own experience. That's why I complain, for example, about the way the new laws have a disastrous effect on my ability, as a social worker, to speak with users. So, sure, at some level there are contradictions. How could there not be? These are the contradictions of the lives we live today. We need to start from within these contradictions, not some other place we wish we lived.

What Marta was laying out, in other words, was a belief that the process of changing one's circumstances begins with a critical description of the limits and frustrations of one's current predicament and continues with the struggle to change this predicament.[27] Through this critical yet empirical analysis—carried out collectively, in a time and place of their own choosing—Direct Social Work participants have in essence already embarked on the transformation of these conditions and their social relations. "Anyway, [beginning from the actual circumstances we find ourselves] isn't just some philosophical point," Marta added later,

> It's a very pragmatic one. If you want to work with a homeless person whose only income, besides what he manages to beg or steal, is a small welfare payment, how can you not address the actual consequences of this welfare and its relationship to state institutions? Are you going to criticize [the homeless] for addressing their concerns to the state? Good luck with that one.

I later discussed Marta's comments with Andrej, asking him to grapple with the same questions about demands addressed to the state and, in particular, his own frequent references to rights. "Doesn't this inevitably lead," I asked, "to the alienation characteristic of representative politics that you so vehemently reject?" In asking about alienation, I had in mind a specifically political form of alienation I had heard activists discuss as the "outsourcing" of control over one's own life to political representatives. "The anarchists I've worked with in the past," I added, "would never have engaged in such a language of rights, such direct engagement with the state." "Well, Marta is right, I think, to acknowledge the contradictions we find ourselves lodged within," Andrej responded, thinking for a moment before continuing,

> There is, after all, no position outside of power relations from which we might act. It is possible, however, to use a discourse of rights without falling into state-centered politics. There is no necessary contradiction, in fact, between claiming rights while trying to construct stateless sociabilities and communities. Direct democracy for us means that we reject the transfer of rights and powers to any sovereign. So we have to find new ways to produce rights—by defining them such that we simultaneously build our power to realize them. This is a politics of small steps that accumulate new forms of alternative power that can be used in the war being waged globally by financial institutions, markets, and the institutions of representative democracy against our generation.
>
> In this sense, becoming in Occupy Slovenia is not understood as originating in some imaginary point of perfect freedom. It is more related to the Foucauldian notion of freedom as an expansive threshold . . . The goal of action is not freedom itself but processes of liberation, the struggle to resist the actual conditions in which we find ourselves today. In this sense, the process of producing together new claims, new rights like those that Direct Social Work articulates, is as important as the content of the rights.

What Andrej is describing is a radically different understanding of rights (Kurnik 2011) than one encounters within classical liberal theory. What he envisions are not natural rights, God given or otherwise, which we have by belonging to the human race (human rights), or legal rights, which we have as citizens of a state, democratic or otherwise, that has guaranteed these rights constitutionally (civil rights). Instead, these are rights that are produced collectively, that we possess only insofar as we have the capacity to assert them socially, i.e., only insofar as we build together with others the collective capacities to exercise them. They derive, Andrej claims, from the Spinozan right of aggregated people to claim nothing less than the right of God, which is absolutely free (Spinoza 2002:683; cf. Speed 2008).[28] More prosaically, as Speed has asserted, these are human rights that exist only insofar as they are exercised, as they are enacted. They are granted not by the state (Speed 2008:169). Maybe this understanding of rights sounds nebulous, Andrej is quick to concede, when pressed. "What would the right to housing look like concretely in our terms? Well, we've begun to challenge the banks' authority to evict, as have the movements in the U.S. We should move on to squat vacant bank-owned properties and distribute them to those most in need. We will govern this resource in common together, assuring that empty homes don't go unused. Hey, we love the Boj za encampment, but it should not be the best we have to offer the homeless."

The practices of Direct Social Work offer one example of the kinds of spaces of encounter for those with quite distinct, even antagonistic perspectives. These spaces, perhaps more than the general assemblies, made it possible for participants to enter into sustained dialogue, even a process of becoming-other-than-one-now-is. We also see what I described earlier—in relation to Zagreb anarchists' efforts to change their own political desires, to create new individual and collective subjects—as a "subjective turn," from a different vantage point. One does not simply set out to become what one wishes, as sometimes seemed to be the starting point of some of my anarchist informants. One begins the difficult process in dialogue with others, from the concrete conditions of one's own subjective predicament, striving to develop intersubjective understandings and articulate common demands and political hopes.

Whereas most activist movements would, of course, define themselves as seeking social change, Occupy Slovenia is one of those very rare social forms that is engaged in self-conscious processes of becoming-other-than-one-now-is in an open-ended manner, both in terms of encounters with difference and collective struggles against existing conditions.

Comparative Direct Democracy

When he addressed OWS, Žižek declared that direct democracy is not a "universal solution."[29] In fact, as we see in this chapter, far from being a universal template, direct democracy takes on quite different textures in the historically specific settings where it is emerging as a response to a broad crisis of liberal democracy. My purpose in comparing the democracy of direct action to the consensus decision making of OWS is not to promote one model over another but to make clear the distinct political practices and democratic imagination emerging in Ljubljana. The practices of OWS have been remarkable on a number of levels, far exceeding the expectations of those who contributed to their organization (Graeber 2011). Indeed, it may be in this moment of a global effervescence of direct action and direct democracy—as, to give only U.S. examples, *Time* declares "the protester" 2011 person of the year, direct-democracy hand signals are used without requiring explication on network TV, and encampments have arisen (and been violently dismantled) throughout U.S. cities[30]—that it becomes possible and necessary to begin to ask more critical and nuanced empirical and comparative questions about the range of direct democratic practices that are emerging.

With humility and openness to collaboration, anthropology can contribute to what should be a rich public discussion of the varied practices and divergent political implications of direct democracy.[31] The need for further ethnographic research is particularly urgent and appropriate because direct democratic practice extends across the fabric of daily life and is inseparable from lived experience; it is, therefore, best studied with participatory and collaborative methods. After all, although I am admittedly more ebullient in my assessment of direct democracy than Žižek, this is not the reason I dispute his dismissal of the decision-making process adopted by Occupy Slovenia or OWS. His dismissal of direct democracy's historical prospects may or may not be proven correct by subsequent events. His position, however, is articulated from an epistemological perch that simply cannot grasp the actual texture and significance of direct democracy—at least, not after a single visit to OWS. These practices come to be known by attending daily assemblies, listening to the accounts of others, channeling those accounts with your own voice via the people's mic, asking how one's own predicament is linked to the crisis, comparing those links with others, and jostling among others during direct action, in short, by inserting oneself into the reflexive and transformative practices of direct democracy.

The research that is beginning to emerge on this new wave of directly democratic innovations has been done rapidly—that is, in the midst of ongoing events, though usually also drawing on earlier fieldwork—and therefore refusing one of the key ways anthropologists distance themselves from both their subjects and political relevance: temporally (Graeber 2012; Juris and Razsa 2012; Razsa and Kurnik 2012; Maeckelbergh 2012). Furthermore, when encountering collaborators whose practices are themselves already paraethnographic (Holmes and Marcus 2008)—i.e., they already exhibit developed forms of reflexive and empirically grounded understandings that are analogous to our own—anthropologists must be prepared to share ethnographic authority and question institutionally defined roles as fieldworkers by deferring to collaborators' knowledge practices, as I have done with Andrej's insights throughout this chapter. Whereas I often felt there was critical insight in Rimi, Pero, and Jadranka's anarchist practices, the ways they put their politics into action, it was Andrej's theoretical and political insights that deeply impacted my own thinking, coming to color my analysis, even my view of the world. Both relationships indicate that we anthropologists may need to open ourselves to a process of becoming-other-than-we-now-are as ethnographers.[32] Drawing on my collaboration with Andrej, I turn now, in conclusion, to some preliminary political and theoretical reflections. I focus on the implications of the shift toward a minoritarian politics and the embrace of becoming as examples of the kinds of political and theoretical insights that I hope a broader ethnography of direct democracy will generate.

Occupy Slovenia has emphasized the decentralized and minoritarian empowerment of workshops and a more restricted role for the assembly as a space of encounter. The general assembly of OWS, by contrast, has functioned as a central organ of collective decision making. One account of these differences, one I have emphasized, runs through the experiences of Slovene activists—including those from stigmatized minority and migrant groups—who, having worked together in previous struggles against exclusionary democracy, crafted democratic practices that are affirmatively minoritarian. This means in essence that they displace any notion of a popular majority, which is the nominal source of political authority, legitimacy, and sovereignty within a liberal democratic framework. Although I trace these specific practices to activists' encounters with the particularly stark violence of state formation and subsequent ethnonationalist majoritarian rule in the former Yugoslavia, they have broader significance. First, the exclusionary dangers of majoritarian democracy are not limited to newly formed postsocialist states; they have been evident, for example, in California's (directly) democratic denial of rights to sexual minorities and noncitizens through ballot initiatives. Indeed even where they do not wholly exclude, such practices render those affected as second-class participants in social life, a process that some activists called "hierarchical inclusion" rather than "exclusion" (Razsa and Kurnik 2014). Second, in its affirmative minoritarian ethics and practices, Occupy Slovenia gives us a glimpse of the contours of a living antiessentialist and antisovereign democratic imagination—giving substance to theoretical elaborations of potential nonstate and nonidentitarian political forms, such as the one Hardt and Negri (2005) have described as "the multitude."

Viewed in this light, my ethnography of the democracy of direct action allows us to extend the ways that anthropologists (Graeber 2002, 2004, 2009, 2011; Juris 2008, 2012; Maeckelbergh 2009) and others (Day 2004; Paris 2003; Shantz 2003) have theorized direct democracy over the past decade—and indeed as I have earlier in this book. A vein running through this scholarship, much of it informed by the practices and concepts of anarchism, has been an emphasis on the prefigurative. David Graeber, for example, defines direct action as a rejection of a politics "which appeals to governments to modify their behavior, in favour of physical intervention against state power in a form that itself *prefigures* an alternative" (2002:62, emphasis added). This literature illuminates why my interlocutors in Zagreb emphasized how they were organized and how they made decisions in the present, as much as they articulated what they hoped to achieve in the future. Such a shift toward means rather than ends also opened up a critical analytical space one desperately needed in a Croatian postsocialist context in which any criticism of capitalism was immediately associated with the discredited communist legacy of using repressive means to pursue nominally utopian ends (Razsa 2008; Razsa and Velez 2010). Croatian anarchists themselves understood their interventions in the urban landscape as embodying their political and ethical ideals; understood them, for example, to be modeling different social relationships than the acquisitive and competitive ones that were becoming dominant in neoliberal Zagreb.

To be sure, many actions of Occupy Slovenia could, and indeed were, understood as prefigurative of other political futures as well. Danijela, twenty-four, for example, insisted that the creativity and diversity of initiatives on display at the assembly modeled the kind of collectively directed energies—to collaborate, to communicate, to share—that capitalism not only cannot animate but often actively blocks. Similarly, Andrej spoke of the assembly as a concrete example of "our collective capacity to manage our own lives and reconstruct society from below." To further complicate any rigid distinction between a politics of being and a politics of becoming, when my anarchist interlocutors engaged in direct action, they inevitably engaged in a process of becoming. As I have argued above, one cannot fight neo-Nazi youth, squat a community center, and face off against the police at protests without being transformed by the experience. Indeed, I have made clear that my collaborators' activism centered on cultivating themselves as different kinds of subjects, as much as it was directed toward macropolitical change (Razsa 2013).

As these articulations of being and becoming are, therefore, inextricably entangled, what I want to highlight are the political and theoretical limitations of theorizing direct action and direct democracy as *primarily* prefigurative—especially the ways that an emphasis on prefiguration limits our ability to analyze and even valorize the process of becoming. The shift in Ljubljana toward an emphasis on becoming highlights some of these implications. First, activists have explicitly tried to ground their critique, and the articulation of the possibilities of change in their current circumstances, from within the contradictory predicaments in which they now find themselves lodged. Rather than seeing direct action, as Graeber has described it, as the "defiant insistence on acting as if one is already free" (2011) or expressing hope in an eventual telos of freedom, activists around Occupy Slovenia are engaging in a messy, already compromised, and, some activists stressed, *never-ending* liberation struggle. Second, the practices of Occupy Slovenia facilitate encounters with difference that allow for a becoming-other-than-one-now-is. In other words, the fruit of the democracy of direct action as political practice grows in unexpected ways from the soil of countless hours of dialogue, bickering, and common struggle—among social workers and users, precariously employed researchers and migrant laborers, students, professors, rent-striking construction workers, outsourced Bosnian dockworkers, and Erased waiters. Third, prefiguration implies that we know in advance what form struggles can take—which has echoes of a kind of utopian telos, no matter how near at hand. The innovative development of the democracy of direct action itself indicates that direct democracy must be conceived of as an open-ended process that will involve unexpected new forms. In this spirit, movement organization and decision making themselves must be submitted to critical reflection, must be opened to a process of becoming. To quote L. A. Kauffman, the Occupy Movement "has opened up for questioning so much that was previously taken as given. May it do the same with its own methods" (2011:48–49). By opening up direct democracy to becoming and by insisting that creative practice may rush ahead of theory, we can recognize the minor but important role that the ethnography of direct democracy can play in documenting, reflecting on, and contributing to a reimagined democracy.

CONCLUSION:
FROM CRITIQUE TO AFFIRMATION

All this was queer and moving. There was much I did not
understand, in some ways I did not even like it, but I recognized
it immediately as a state of affairs worth fighting for.
—GEORGE ORWELL, *HOMAGE TO CATALONIA*

"Rebel Peninsula"

My ongoing research, and its representation in this book, began to look
very different to me in the wake of the global financial crisis that began in
2008. During my first period of fieldwork with radical activists in ex-Yugoslavia, from mid-2001 to late 2003, I struggled to interest Croatian journalists and public intellectuals in the activists with whom I collaborated—just
as I struggled to arouse the concern of local human-rights organizations regarding the covert police surveillance and overt police repression my collaborators experienced. So it was with some trepidation that I returned to Zagreb
in 2010 for the premiere of *Bastards of Utopia* at ZagrebDox. I was unsure of
what response to expect at the film festival, which promised a very public air-
ing of my collaborators' activities—and my research with them. I was taken
aback when a stream of surprisingly sympathetic reporters invited me to do
a dozen print, radio, and television interviews. On the day of the screening,
hundreds had to be turned away after the five-hundred-seat theater filled beyond capacity. While in the early 2000s I had struggled to explain anarchist,
anticapitalist, and antinationalist ideas—or even the existence of an under-

ground activist scene that advocated such views—from 2010 onward, criticism of the commercialization of everyday life, the privatization of public services and public space, and the moral bankruptcy of the political elites who had dominated Croatia since independence were the assumed starting points for discussions with reporters, filmmakers, and intellectuals in Zagreb. These new political attitudes could not be attributed to the fact that each of the three main "characters" of the film had achieved a certain public renown while I was away. They reflected more fundamental shifts in Croatian and regional post-Yugoslav public culture.

Since 2009, a series of protests, strikes, occupations, and even, in some cases, open urban uprisings swept the former Yugoslavia, helping shape a very different social reality than Rimi, Pero, and Jadranka confronted in the early 2000s. In Zagreb, several movements exemplify these changes. The student occupation of the Philosophy Faculty of Zagreb University initially focused narrowly on opposition to tuition hikes, demanding instead fully government-funded education at all levels. Students declared a strike and disrupted scheduled classes, organizing instead an ambitious self-education program.[1] They adopted directly democratic organization, centering on *plenums* (general assemblies) and other antiauthoritarian practices, including rotating and anonymous spokespeople, which helped to prevent the emergence of internal hierarchies of expertise and press contacts (Studenti Filozofskog fakulteta u Zagrebu 2009). The approach was remarkably open: not only enrolled students but all present were given a voice in discussion and decision making in plenums that sometimes numbered more than one thousand (watch "Blokada").[2] In part, the student movement built on directly democratic political forms first developed within the alterglobalization movement because—like the Occupy protests in Slovenia—activists with extensive earlier movement experience (including Jadranka) were involved from the outset.[3] Continuities aside, a whole new generation was politicized in the course of a student movement that overcame some limitations of the alterglobalization movement in Croatia, with much wider participation, publicity, and popular support than anarchists had enjoyed. The movement spread to twenty campuses across Croatia (Studenti Filozofskog fakulteta u Zagrebu 2009)[4] and students began to ask more fundamental questions about what was still being called "transition"[5] some twenty years after the end of state socialism.

Pravo na grad (or, Right to the City) also stands out for its dynamism and its resonance with Rimi, Pero, and Jadranka's earlier urban interventions. By 2010, a concept I had initially used to theorize their actions, especially their squatting, "the right to city" (Mitchell 2003; Harvey 2008; Jeffrey et al. 2011) was familiar to a wide Croatian public and associated with a popular movement. This campaign was a joint initiative of Pravo na grad and *Zelena akcija* (Green Action), the organization which had launched most of the bicycle-rights actions in Zagreb since the early 1990s. Centered on resistance to a new shopping center and parking garage that were encroaching on an important pedestrian zone, Pravo na grad drew attention to SDP mayor Milan Bandić's suspect role in real-estate development schemes. Those associated with the campaign also questioned more elemental issues of democratic practice. Why was there no popular participation in decision making about urban space? What kind of city might inhabitants envision for themselves? In other words, as Paul Stubbs argues, the campaign was able to move successfully between particular problems and structural issues, "mobilizing broad, popular concerns over corruption, the links between political and economic elites, the failure of Ministerial regulation and control, the structural nature of 'conflicts of interest,' and the lack of public participation in planning" (2012:23). Despite strong support, and clear evidence of irregularities in the approval process, riot police forcibly dislodged the Pravo na grad protest-camp blockade in July 2010. Close ties—and corruption—among political and economic elites ignited even more spectacular social conflict in Slovenia.

In November 2012, Slovenia's widely perceived success, and self-satisfaction, already worn thin by the economic crisis and frayed by Occupy Slovenia, was torn asunder by a wave of urban unrest known locally as "the uprisings." The militancy of the protesters—and the brutality of police repression— went beyond anything seen during Occupy, shocking a society accustomed to relatively polite and consensual politics. Less surprising was that the strife started in the northeastern city of Maribor. While much of Slovenia prospered following independence—with accession to the EU, adoption of the Euro, and the attainment of the highest levels of per-capita GDP in postsocialist Europe—Maribor was decaying even before the financial crisis began. This one-time "Manchester of Yugoslavia" deindustrialized precipitously, becoming mired in deep and persistent unemployment (Kirn 2013). The spark for the unrest was a prototypically neoliberal arrangement, a private-public partnership to establish a system of stationary speed radars for the city's roads. After seventy thousand tickets were issued in the first few days of operation, nearly one for every registered vehicle in the city, it emerged that the private partner received 92 percent of all fines—and had close business ties to the mayor (*Večer*, December 5, 2012). Protests were organized on Facebook and the slogan "He's Finished!" (*Gotof je!*) was soon heard throughout the city. After several conflagrations—including a crowd of twenty thousand surrounding and then ransacking city hall while a police helicopter rained tear gas down from above—the protests spread to more than fifty Slovene towns. The slogan was extended to "They're finished." The resignation of Maribor's mayor in December 2012 was followed, a month later, by the fall of the government as the prime minister was swept up in a corruption scandal of his own (Kurnik 2014).

Surveying the ex-Yugoslav movements of this period, and there were many,[6] along with uprisings in Bulgaria, Greece, and Turkey, inspired some critical local intellectuals to christen the Balkans the "rebel peninsula" (Horvat and Štiks forthcoming 2014:2). Of course, the Balkans are not alone in this insurrectionary spirit; the years since the financial crisis began have been a time of remarkable European organizing and outrage, and of broader "global uprisings" (Juris and Razsa 2012). While ex-Yugoslav activists are certainly responding to specific local circumstances, protest movements have also erupted across Southern Europe, North Africa, Latin America, and even North America on a scale not seen since 1968. Such movements demand that we rethink the categories we use to explain the social, political, and economic situation in the Balkans and elsewhere (cf. Horvat and Štiks forthcoming 2014:8). As a student of, and participant in, social movements, I have been inspired politically by the wave of global uprisings. My sense of transnational movements' importance after the relative "quiet period" that followed the peak of alterglobalization organizing in the early 2000s has also been reinvigorated. But this moment posed unexpected challenges to the way I initially conceptualized radical activism, especially with regards to neoliberalism as a focus of critique.

Neoliberalism Is Dead! Long Live Austerity!

Anthropologists have been among the most sophisticated scholarly critics of neoliberalization (Comaroff and Comaroff 2000; Ferguson 2006, Ong 2006), perhaps in part because many of us have conducted research among those directly affected by privatization, trade liberalization, and precarization. I understood myself to be working in this critical tradition when I began my fieldwork in the former Yugoslav republics of Croatia and Slovenia. Accordingly, I organized much of this research around a critique of neoliberalism, drawing on the ways that activists' interventions offered an empirically grounded and critical vantage point—at once local and transnational—from which to understand "transition" in the neoliberal era. This is most evident in my attention to the former Yugoslavia's triple transition: to independent national statehood, to liberal democracy, and to a market economy. The financial crisis that began in 2008 has unsettled the self-evidence of neoliberalism across much of Europe and the world, however. Anthropologists' skepticism is now widespread. This skepticism extends far beyond those who directly participated in the recent wave of initiatives, protests, and uprisings. As the contours of the crisis came into sharper focus, figures from center-right French president Nicolas Sarkozy to Marxist historian Eric Hobsbawm declared the end of neoliberalism itself and compared the fall of Wall Street to the fall of the Berlin Wall (Jamie Peck et al. 2009). What are the consequences of this wider re-evaluation, even delegitimation, of a key concept of anthropological analysis and critique? Should this be a moment of vindication for those of us who have long been dubious of neoliberal triumphalism in the wake of socialism's collapse? Ironically, as the swirling waters of the global financial crisis threatened to wash away the foundations of the postsocialist European order, eroding the consensus around neoliberalism as a model of development, the limited political efficacy of critical scholarship on neoliberalism was brought into stark relief.

The Slovenian and Croatian economic booms of the mid-2000s—funded in large part by cheap international credit to households and the construction sector—came to a grinding halt in late 2008 as panic ricocheted through the global financial system and credit dried up for the suddenly risky European periphery. Slovenia, and then Croatia as well when it joined the EU in July of 2013, found themselves in the shadow of the EU-IMF bailouts to the so-called PIGS (Portugal, Ireland, or sometimes Italy, Greece, and Spain). After the Cypriot crisis and rescue from 2012–2013, they were frequently mentioned as likely to fall next. While as of this writing neither has sought a bailout, both are under intense pressure from international markets (Brown 2014; Kuzmanović 2013; Steen 2013). The mere possibility of a bailout and accompanying "haircut" for creditors, i.e., default, drove up borrowing costs for both states. On several occasions, the yields on long-term Croatian and Slovenian bonds have approached or surpassed the 7 percent rate that triggered earlier European bailouts (Brown 2014:1; Kuzmanović 2013). Despite the lack of a formal bailout and the presence of externally imposed conditionalities, and despite the campaign promises of right and left parties to the contrary, both states have pursued austerity policies to reassure international financial markets that they can continue to meet their debt obligations.

In practical terms, all this has meant an intensification of the neoliberal transformation of the early 2000s: accelerated privatization of state-owned firms; liberalization of the labor market to increase competitiveness; and slashing of pensions, unemployment, and other social benefits (Brown 2013; Horvat and Štiks 2012; Prug 2011; Živković forthcoming 2014). Budgets for education and healthcare have been cut deeply. Of course, the gutting of the remaining welfare protections is happening during a period when an increasingly impoverished populace is most dependent on those protections. Official unemployment in Croatia, for example, has risen to 17.6 percent overall and 52.4 percent among youth (EuroStat 2013).[7] In other words, the wave of protests—focused on increased school fees, redundancies, lowered wages, industrial and public service privatization schemes, and the selling off of public spaces—point to the persistence, even escalation, of neoliberalism in the guise of austerity.[8]

The Limits of a Critical Anthropology of Neoliberalism

Put another way, political elites across Southern Europe responded to a sovereign debt crisis precipitated by neoliberal policies with further neoliberalization. "All this," said Andrej, the Occupy Slovenia activist, "even though the public has never been more opposed to such policies—or more open to movement attacks on market rule." Many factors contribute to such policy continuities despite the confidence-shaking crisis—not least neoliberal institutional arrangements and the unchallenged power of the financial sector. These policy continuities make clear that "Wall Street," whether as a metonym for a specific set of firms based in New York City or for financial capitalism generally, has not fallen in any way comparable to the Berlin Wall.[9] The zombie life of neoliberalism highlights one of the crucial difference between 1989 and 2008: in 1989 there was an "aggressively expansive strain of free-market capitalism" waiting on the other side of the Berlin Wall, while today there is no such self-evident successor to neoliberalism (Peck et al. 2010:101).[10] Margaret Thatcher would finally seem to be right, descriptively if not proscriptively: "there is no alternative."

For those scholars who want to contribute to fundamental political change, further critique in this context may only confirm neoliberalism as the primary frame of reference. The responses of varied audiences to *Bastards of Utopia* expose another facet of the same general crisis, the crisis of political imagination that began with the fall of state socialism as capitalism's primary rival. Many viewers asked, in one form or another, "Okay, I see all the things they are against—nationalism, corporations, the police, private property. But what are they *for*?" I had initially mistaken this to be a necessarily hostile question because, after all the years I had spent with them, the political, social, and economic alternatives implicit in their initiatives were obvious to me. Slowly I came to understand, however, especially as the financial crisis deepened, that the question highlighted genuine frustration with the limits of purely oppositional politics—and the ways I represented my collaborators' political interventions in the film. It is necessary to be much more explicit about what I see as the implicit alternatives embedded in my informants' lives and actions than I was in the lightly narrated and largely observational film. There is a need to move beyond what James Ferguson has called a politics of "the antis" (2010:166), a politics which only denounces. There is a need to move beyond a politics that, as Petra Rethmann describes it, can "only imagine itself in terms of antagonism and opposition—as, for example, in anti-imperialism, anti-neoliberalism, anti-privatization, and antiglobalization—and not in terms of building, invention and creation" (2013:228). If anthropology is to be relevant during these crises—this economic crisis, as well as this crisis of the political imaginary—it must be prepared to make an ethnographic contribution to the reimagining of politics. And to be clear, while I speak of anthropology, the scholarly tradition I know best, much of what I argue applies to critical intellectual activity more generally. In order to contribute politically, one cannot only rail against dominant political arrangements. What is needed is an affirmation of other social and political possibilities. In some sense, such an affirmative turn would be a return to anthropology at its best: the exploration of ways of being human that are at odds with what appears natural and inevitable from the vantage point of the present (cf. Hage 2012), from the point of view of our own contemporary "common sense" (Herzfeld 2001:1).

In response to this need for affirmative ethnography—as well as my own desire to bridge the gap between militant research and scholarly publishing— I develop several lines of affirmative anthropology through this book, developing new strategies of ethnographic representation to bring my collaborators' political alternatives into sharper relief.

Toward an Affirmative Anthropology of Political Possibilities

Affirmative Writing

Those in the critical tradition will be quick to object that scholarship on social movements—especially if avowedly affirmative—risks romanticizing its object of study (Ortner 1995; cf. Abu-Lughod 1990; Reed-Danahay 1993). Sherry Ortner, for example, has warned against "ethnographic refusal," by which she means the refusal to acknowledge that "individual acts of resistance, as well as large-scale resistance movements, are often themselves conflicted, internally contradictory, and effectively ambivalent, in large part due to internal political complexities" (1995:179). By embracing the affirmative, however, anthropologists are not rendered suddenly and helplessly uncritical. An affirmative anthropology does not require that we sanitize political resistance, accepting self-imposed analytic blindness to the shortcomings, double standards, internal divisions, and contradictions of radical activism. The internal political complexities, especially the divisions that crosscut the movement of movements, are evident throughout this ethnography. There are the gendered tensions between Jadranka and Rimi, freighted with questions of nominally masculine and feminine styles of political expression and action. There are the inequalities of national citizenship, which, for example, prohibited those with Serbian or Bosnian passports from traveling to Thessaloniki, validating the internal movement critique of "summit hopping." There are the generational divisions, between those like Vjera, who reached a point in her life when she needed a more stable income—and the structure and legitimacy of NGOs—and the younger generation, willing to scrape by with scavenging, petty theft, and squatting. There are the divisions between "local" (Croatian) activists and "internationals" (Dutch, Germans, British, and, yes, American), evident in the fraught decision to give up the Free Store. The internationals are, as Pero described them, "always more ready for action," not least because of their relative privilege. There are other contradictions, including the ex-Yugoslav activist predicament of being pulled between the political desire to resuscitate local traditions of resistance and a realization that those traditions had been discredited by their association with the socialist regime.

So when activists opted for "franchising from below," it was with some ambivalence. The negative aspects of franchising from below, including its relatively shallow roots in the Croatian context, reinforced the isolating effects of activists' commitment to antinationalism, cutting them off from the

possibility of a broader, more inclusive, and more politically influential movement. Furthermore, the volatility of these movements—from day to day, and
over the larger cycles of the dozen years that I have studied and participated
in them—meant they were dynamic and militant one moment, nearly non-
existent another. Other contradictions are also on display. At those moments
when the movement was experienced as very tangible, potent, and coherent,
as it was during countersummits such as Thessaloniki—when activists experienced themselves to be locked in a Manichean struggle with a fundamentally hostile state—they also, ironically, put at risk the most remarkable qualities of the alterglobalization movement. When there was an armed enemy
hunting you through the streets—with chemical weapons, armored vehicles,
helicopters, and batons—it felt like your survival depended on being with a
group of like-minded activists prepared to defend itself rather than opening yourself to cooperation with other political traditions converging in the
movement of movements. When activists did manage to build innovative political forms like Occupy Slovenia's democracy of direct action—which facilitated a sense of collectivity yet also enabled meaningful encounters with
those quite different from one another—there was the constant risk of centrifugal forces splintering the common struggle into factions.

Analytically, these fundamental contradictions, limitations, divisions,
and ironies cannot be ignored, nor should they be. It is worth stressing that
activists never asked me to ignore these divisions. Antiauthoritarian movements have, as Maeckelbergh (2008) documents, absorbed the critical insights
of feminist and racial justice movements; sophisticated and penetrating critiques of internal inequalities are a part of everyday movement discourse. In
short, it is unnecessary, and undesirable, to romanticize the resistance of the
movement of movements. Activists themselves believe only robust critique
will allow the movement to reckon with its own contradictions.

If we hope to approach social movements, radical politics, and collective struggle ethnographically—and affirmatively—we must also do justice
to the romance. Powerful feelings of camaraderie, commonality, loyalty, solidarity—even love for one another and the collective—are a critical part of
radical political experience, born of shared struggle. In some cases, these experiences are at the very emotional center of individual motivation and inspiration. If scholars cannot convey these emotional stakes, critical reflection will be only cynicism, and blinkered cynicism at that. We must find
ways to represent the powerful emotional charge generated when activists

transcend social divisions of gender, class, and national belonging, no matter how fleetingly. Successfully representing "love at the barricades"—as well as the quiet solidarity of a shared meal—requires finding ways to communicate, for example, those experiences that make palpable one's belonging to a global movement, the sense that one is fighting not only beside those standing shoulder to shoulder at the burning barricade, but also alongside people from what seem to be remote corners of the world.

In this book, I have drawn on a number of strategies to represent these experiences and their political implications. I have drawn extensively on video, both the description of recorded footage, as well as links to actual edited scenes on video, so as to better engage the bodily, sensory, and affective dimension of politics. Video enabled me to position the reader/viewer in relation to activist experiences; positioning them, for example, within the Free Store as tension mounts and riot police gather outside. Ethnographic filmmaker and theorist David MacDougall, in arguing for a more productive role for cinematic ethnography within anthropology, stresses precisely this capacity of film to enable corporeal identification with others as it envelops viewers in film's mimetic qualities such that they respond physically and emotionally to images on screen (2006:20). In light of the contributions of video to this ethnography, I believe that the continuing marginal place of images within anthropology must be reconsidered, especially if we aspire to represent the visual and affective dimensions of politics rather than perpetuate the disciplinary preference for the discursive (cf. Taylor 1996). Additionally—and here militant research methods and scholarly publishing are partially reconciled—I have drawn on my own experiences, my own subjective accounts of what it feels like to find oneself in these struggles, especially at moments of crisis.

In order to affirm the distinctive contributions of antiauthoritarian activism, I have also found it necessary to move beyond the dominant social-movement paradigms, which, as Juris and Khasnabish highlight, have tended "to narrowly define what counts as movement success by focusing on the impact of movements in the formal spheres of governance and policy" (2013: 19). This is not to say that larger political impact does not matter—or has not been made. The alterglobalization movement contributed mightily to the discrediting of the Washington Consensus. Occupy returned questions of inequality to the center of American political life. However, a narrow focus on dominant political and policy spheres obscures movements like those I have described in Croatia and Slovenia, which "aim to radically unsettle existing power structures while bringing new sociopolitical relationships, subjectivities and imaginations into being" (Juris and Khasnabish 2013:6). What is needed instead is an affirmative ethnography in the spirit that Graeber describes, in which,

> one observes what people do, and then tries to tease out the hidden symbolic, moral, or pragmatic logics that underlie their actions; one tries to get at the way people's habits and actions makes sense in ways that they are not themselves completely aware of. One obvious role for a radical intellectual is to do precisely that: to look at those who are creating viable alternatives, try to figure out what might be the larger implications of what they are (already) doing, and then offer those ideas back, not as prescriptions, but as contributions, possibilities—as gifts (Graeber 2004:11–12).

Activists themselves may not need such a gift. This book certainly contains little that will surprise experienced activists. What I hope it does is tease out the implicit alternatives embedded in my collaborators' politics, especially relevant to those who ask, with heartfelt urgency, "But what are they *for*?"

Affirmative Politics

To be clear, the notion of an affirmative politics is not something I impose on my collaborators' politics from outside, the byproduct of my own intellectual preoccupations. The central place of direct action in anarchist politics always involves not only interventions against the existing system but the enactment of alternatives, the prefiguration of other possibilities. It is in the description of the alternatives implicit in their actions—of other collective subjects, other transnational collaborations, other forms of organization, other property relations, other practices of democratic decision making, nothing less than other ways of being human—that my ethnography is affirmative. Again, it is worth recalling that the most common slogan of the alterglobalization movement, including in Zagreb, was "Another World is Possible." This was not just a politics of reaction, a politics of "the antis."

The antinationalist subculture activists developed was not only a rejection of the political violence of Croatian state formation—including their experience of it within their own families and childhoods—or a refusal of the nationalist culture that predominated for years after the war. Those around Antifascist Action, and other strands of radical activism, not only rejected nationalist symbolism, language, and urban toponyms. They not only resisted incorporation into the national body politic. Instead, they actively participated in the production of an alternative transnational community through a whole web of collaborations that transcended national frontiers. They worked with activists across the ex-Yugoslav region, Europe, and beyond on initiatives related to online and print publishing, music distribution and touring, trainings, countersummits, and protest, as well as video production, circulation, and consumption. They took up and used, in their specific social circumstances, tactics developed elsewhere—including Food Not Bombs, Noborder Camps, Critical Mass, Antifascist Action, and Anti-McDonalds Day—which gave them a lived experience of sharing in the global commons of the alterglobalization movement. This meant that globalization was not some geographic scale above Zagreb and Croatia; it was woven throughout activists' lives. In all of this, they rejected the nationalist concept of culture as internally unified, unchanging, and bounded from that which is "outside" national borders. In so doing, they affirmed culture as a participatory field of struggle, as a place to make meaning—and new people—together with others.

Similarly, my collaborators in Croatia and Slovenia rejected the forms of representative democracy and civil society that were so often promoted by bureaucrats of transition as the vital tissue of a democratic society. Instead, activists struggled in many different settings to enact other, more direct, forms of democracy. They joined affinity groups, trying to reach consensus on a common course of militant direct action. They convened spokescouncils to manage the coordination of varied political initiatives from disparate political traditions at transnational countersummits. They assembled in encampments to debate endlessly with fellow residents of their city—sometimes only to agree to disagree and support one another despite these differences—so that they could create a movement that would be inclusive of "minorities," inclusive of those who had experienced marginalization in majoritarian democracy. The commitment to direct democracy was often the glue among activists with divergent political visions, among activists who could not agree on much else. More recently, the commitment to varied experiments in directly democratic self-rule was the common denominator in the Casbah in Tunis, Tahrir Square in Cairo, Syntagma Square in Athens, Puerta del Sol in Madrid, Tel Aviv's tent city, the Wisconsin statehouse, and the hundreds of encampments associated with the Occupy Movement (Juris and Razsa 2012).

Direct democracy was also integral to activist efforts to model an alternative to dominant forms of property. In addition to becoming part of a democratic collective management project, the former printing press Knowledge was transformed in ways that transcended the public-private property binary, and the specific forms of exclusion and control each property regime entails. Knowledge became, for however brief a time, "a common." It was repurposed to serve a social good, reorganized around exchange based on mutual aid rather that profit, reoriented away from legal title and toward the support of the wider neighborhood and city for its defense, and opened to all who saw its mission as an important one for Zagreb. This assertion of a right to the city was important to activists because they understood that specific configurations of urban space could enable particular social relationships and political desires. And activists felt that if they did not assert their rights, urban arrangements were going to be imposed on their lives without their say-so. Knowledge Press was therefore more than simply a space; it was a means of producing the kinds of individual and collective subjects activists were struggling to become. The Boj Za (Struggle For) encampment of Occupy Slovenia shared much of this agenda—and held out under enormous pressure for more than seven months.

This struggle for autonomy—a struggle for autonomy of self-fashioning that I have described as constituting a subjective turn—ran through much of what activists did. They strove to develop an antinationalist sentiment, beliefs, and everyday sensibilities in the most inhospitable of settings, even interpreting encounters with nationalist violence as one of the sources of their antinationalist orientation. They refused the polite and proper forms of political expression encouraged by "civil society," cultivating themselves instead as unruly subjects, not least through their repeated viewing of riot porn and subsequent re-enactment of images of confrontation with the state. Some militants even went so far as to co-opt state violence to write these lessons "onto their own skin," and in the process changed their own political desires, to create new individual and collective subjects.

Those in Occupy Slovenia perhaps took this subjective turn furthest (Razsa and Kurnik 2012; Razsa 2012a). With the practices of minoritarian democracy and encounters with others quite different themselves—the democracy of direct action—they did not simply set out to become what they already knew they wanted to become, as was the impetus for some anarchist collaborators. They initiated the difficult process of "becoming-other-than-one-now-is" in dialogue with people quite different from themselves. They began from the concrete conditions of the subjective predicament in which they found themselves, struggling to develop intersubjective understandings and articulate common demands and political hopes, and never quite knowing where this might take them.

Individual and Collective Becomings

In a rousing article on anthropology's potential contribution to "Imagining Political Possibility in an Age of Late Liberalism and Cynical Reason," Petra Rethmann (2013) compares various forms of resistance—and finds direct action lacking. She argues that, on the one hand, there are urgent forms of politics, and she specifically has in mind David Graeber's (2009) work on direct action—especially his emphasis on taking immediate and unmediated action against hierarchical institutions. On the other hand, there are traditions of refusal "that constitute not simply 'resistance' but a particular kind of endurance—an endurance that in and of itself resists to keep open possibilities and avoid the pitfalls of failure" (Rethmann 2013:229).[11] Given my long-term research and close personal relationships with direct-action activists, I initially bristled at the implication that my collaborators' politics were fleeting and unsustainable. I soon recognized, however, the wariness with which I return to the region after each longer absence. To be sure, I worry each time that I will find my collaborators in jail or in the midst of some other crisis. I also worry, more prosaically, that I will find them simply burned out, exhausted from the draining effort of fighting on so many fronts at once, fighting in conditions that seem to undermine their efforts at every turn. Graeber has described the common trajectory of those drawn into antiauthoritarian movements. They tend to react,

> first with a sense of wonder, of almost infinite horizons, on discovering that radically egalitarian forms of organization are possible, then, a growing exhaustion in the face of state repression, and a growing sense of exasperation as they discover the endless petty troubles, subtle forms of domination, and dilemmas of privilege that still endure (2009:533).

Mindful of such forces, and my worries about how long my collaborators can sustain their radical oppositionality, it is worth returning to the individual life trajectories of my closest informants and the ways they did or did not continue to struggle for their politics in recent years. This is what I know of Rimi, Pero, Jadranka, and Andrej's lives as this book goes to press.

Rimi

Of the four, Rimi felt most acutely the constraints of material survival impinging on his life. During research trips in 2008, 2010, and 2013, I found that he was working longer and longer hours in the Kraš warehouse. The three-month revolving contracts they offer mean "no security," as Rimi noted, because, "You can't speak up without risking not being rehired." Following up, I asked him if he found time for activism when he was working such long hours. He answered, "Things build up [on the job]. So I work through those frustrations with the band, and with activism" (watch "No Security"). In this response, you could sense the degree to which activism had become more of an outlet rather than the exclusive focus of his energies, as it had been when I first spent time with him in 2001–2003. That said, I conducted this interview in the midst of the Balkan Anarchist Book Fair, which Rimi had had a hand in organizing, and at which he was tabling with his distro. He expressed the same radical anarchist antagonism to the dominant strains of Croatian social life that he always had. He continued to organize anarchist punk shows, sometimes in Jadranka's former squat, Vila Viktorija. Additionally, he still managed to find time to tour. For several years, he fronted a new band, Ljubiša Samardžić, named for a Serbian actor famous for his roles in Partisan films. The band enjoyed more popular success than AK47, but by 2013, Rimi was back to his original AK47 lineup. When I saw him briefly in May of 2013, just after the close of the Tenth Balkan Anarchist Book Fair (watch "Anarchist Book Fair"), he ended our conversation on an ambiguous note:

> In the changing outlooks of the very ordinary Croats I work with day in and day out, I've seen an opening I didn't expect a few years ago. They believe less and less in the promises that this system has made to them over the past twenty years. They are slowly realizing they will need to take action for themselves. The question remains, of course, will this coming explosion be directed positively, against the elite that has abused them? Will it lead toward self-organized alternatives? Or [will it be] again channeled into fascist shit, you know, against false "national enemies"?

This indeed is the question posed by the expansion of global uprisings beyond those with longstanding antiauthoritarian, antinationalist, and directly democratic commitments. Rimi asked it with hopefulness, leavened with dread.

Pero

Pero continues to live in the Zagreb apartment he inherited from his grandmother, dedicating a good deal of time to the Zen Buddhist meditation practice of Zazen, traveling to study with resident masters in Budapest and Bu-
charest. He has by no means renounced politics for personal enlightenment,
however. In 2009, he was again arrested. This time during a Pravo na grad action. Nor is Pero finished with film. He had a supporting role in *Old-School
Capitalism* (*Stara škola kapitalizma* 2009), a hybrid documentary-fictionial
film produced by the legendary Serbian experimental filmmaker Želimir
Žilnik. Together with Belgrade anarchists from the Anarcho-Syndicalist Initiative (ASI)—the activists we had stayed with on our way to and from Thessaloniki—Pero played a supporting role as a member of an anarchist collective
that kidnapped corrupt and abusive Serbian factory owners. When I returned
for the premier of *Bastards* in 2010, however, Pero was in much more serious
trouble, facing precisely the kind of emergency I feared as I prepared for each
visit. Shortly after the release of the *Old-School Capitalism,* six members of
ASI were arrested for allegedly throwing Molotov cocktails at the Greek Embassy in Belgrade in solidarity with a Greek anarchist, Thodoris Iliopoulos.
Iliopoulos was the last political prisoner of the December 2008 uprising—and
was in the midst of a forty-day hunger strike (*Jutarnji list* November 9, 2009).
Learning that his comrades faced potential fifteen-year sentences, Pero traveled to Belgrade "to show solidarity." As his friends were in the dock to face
indictments for international terrorism, Pero held up a sign at the rear of the
courtroom that read "Anarchism isn't Terrorism." He was promptly arrested.
Though he was released from jail after thirty hours, his passport was seized by
the Serbian Ministry of Internal Affairs. This left him unable to return to Croatia, homeless, and without means to support himself. He got by with the assistance of anarchist networks in Belgrade, moving from apartment to apartment. A collection was even taken up at the *Bastards* premier in Zagreb to
fund his living expenses. After more than seven months, his passport was returned and he traveled home to Zagreb to tell tales of his adventures.

Andrej

Andrej continues to collaborate extensively within transnational social-
movement networks from his home base in Slovenia. He meets regularly with
organizers from the Arab Spring and European antiausterity protests. He
traveled again to Chiapas for a "political school" in the summer of 2013. Not

surprisingly, he was swept up in the Maribor and All-Slovenian Uprisings. A key turning point in the uprisings came when the government succeeded in dividing the demonstrations into "good" and "bad" protesters. Prosecutors singled out the "bad protesters"—those who had been celebrated earlier by supporters of the uprisings for their roles confronting the police—for criminal charges. Most of those arrested in Maribor belonged to what Andrej characterized as the "second precarious generation," the children of those who lost their jobs during the rapid deindustrialization that accelerated after Slovenia's independence. Many faced prison sentences of one to five years despite contradictory and unreliable evidence from the police. Andrej became one of the only public intellectuals involved in their defense, often working closely with the mothers of those arrested. He recently moved to Maribor to participate in the political and legal struggle there, and to initiate a new militant research project on the daily conditions and outlooks of these youth. He helped participants in the uprising develop a statement in which they articulated the legitimacy of their collective actions while avoiding acknowledging individual actions during the uprisings that might incriminate them (Skupina "Svoboda vstajnikom!" 2014). He is still commuting to Ljubljana and has held his position at the university. I joined Andrej in Maribor in the summer of 2014 to collaborate on this new militant research. I was particularly struck by Andrej's conclusion regarding the political outlook of the young Maribor residents with whom he is working. "Though they would never call themselves activists," Andrej observed,

> they pose a fundamental challenge to those of us who are activists. We always thought of ourselves as those who saw the limits of this political order most clearly and were most willing to challenge it. But these guys have no illusions that the political elite give a damn about them, or that this system will assist them in solving their existential problems. They are more hostile to this system than we are. They are also prepared to take more radical action than almost any self-described activist. This makes me almost think the figure of the activist, as such, should be abandoned.

When I returned to this question later, Andrej extended this critique to my own research and writing. "I see the importance of what you are calling an 'affirmative anthropology,'" he said, "but specifically affirming activists? Self-described activists have failed to seize the historical moment they find themselves in today. What should be studied and affirmed are the new forms of organization and subjectivity among those who are willing to confront this system on the streets." This conversation was cut short, however, because Andrej was preparing to travel to Bosnia, where a wave of urban unrest against corrupt privatization and postwar ethnic political elite had broken out, first in Bosnia's analogue to Maribor, the industrial city of Tuzla. As always, Andrej embraced with both arms these new opportunities for encounters with other life experiences.

Jadranka

More than any other single individual I have met, Jandranka's life follows the rhythms and traces the geography of the last dozen years of social and political protest in Europe, the Middle East, and North Africa. She lived in a rural squat and intentional community in the foothills above Genoa and in an urban squat in Turin during a period of intense Berlusconi-directed repression. She lived for a time with her Libyan boyfriend in London, learning Arabic, working without papers in home healthcare, often caring for Alzheimer's patients. She participated in the civil unrest in France during 2005—the furious riots in the largely migrant *banlieues*—and in the remarkable December 2008 uprisings following the police killing of Alexandros Grigoropoulos (see Schwartz et al. 2010). She traveled throughout Syria, Beirut, and Palestine. Not long after American activist Rachel Corrie was run down by an Israeli Defense Forces bulldozer, she volunteered with the International Solidarity Movement, participating in nonviolent blockades of Palestinian homes slated for bulldozing. In late 2008, Jadranka returned to Zagreb to finish her studies, transferring to a nursing program. She was soon closely involved with the student blockade. Unable to find a slot for her nursing specialization due to cuts to the public health budget, she volunteered to treat the injured in Benghazi, Libya, during the civil war that ousted Gaddafi from power. When I last heard from her, in 2014, she was en route to volunteer at the enormous Za'atari "camp," which houses the more than 80,000 of the Syrian refugees who fled to Jordan. The only regret I sensed in Jadranka was that she could not be in two places at once.

*   *   *

In their efforts "to become the people they wanted to be" in what Rimi once described as "impossible circumstances," these activists developed themselves as unruly political subjects. They cultivated within themselves desires that drove them constantly into conflict with the societies in which they lived. They insisted, each in his or her own way, but also in common struggle with others, that life could be different, and they modeled this possibility with their own choices, with the material realities of their everyday lives. They turned their individual lives into wrenches to be thrown into the works of the postsocialist order. This book and this film, if they are of any worth, bring readers and viewers closer to these activist experiences. Watching and rewatching, writing and rewriting their lives, has permanently marked me with their creativity and courage—and forced me to ask hard questions about my own choices. One of the ironies of this book is that even as it has etched their experience deeply into my own, it also represents a step further from my time of direct collaboration with them during fieldwork, toward a career in the academy, toward a secure life within hierarchical institutions. My time in the former Yugoslavia in general—and in collaboration with a new generation of radical activists in particular—have convinced me, however, that we do not know what the future holds. Each of us must reckon with the limits of our own imagination if we are to ask how life could be otherwise.

NOTES

Introduction

1. When I use the term "radical" in this political context, I have in mind activists whom Day describes as seeking "change at what they consider to be the 'root' level of one or more social antagonisms: radical feminists seeking to eradicate patriarchy, radical socialists seeking to eliminate capitalism, radical environmentalists seeking to end the domination of nature" 2004:732.

2. Historically known as Jagodina, the communists renamed the city for Svetozar Marković, founder of the Serbian Social-Democratic Party, when they came to power in 1945. In 1992 the city again became Jagodina.

3. I had a number of opportunities to witness such far-right nationalist gatherings during my years in the former Yugoslavia. In 2002, for example, early in my fieldwork with radical activists, I went to a concert by the far-right rock star Thompson (watch "A Real Croatian Public"). Though the war had ended seven years earlier, the rage and hatred of the mid-1990s were still palpable.

4. Arguably by 1990, most of the progressive features of the Yugoslav system had already been stripped by the federal 1989 enterprise law, which effectively ended self-management. By 1990, Yugoslavia had been subjected to nearly a decade of structural adjustment, bankruptcy, and the growth of private-sector restructuring. Furthermore, Yugoslavia's (semi)peripheral position and its insertion into the global economy through increasing trade liberalization with Europe, increasing Western FDI, and the financialization of links with the outside world (contributing to a growing foreign debt) had been reshaping the Yugoslav economy since at least the early 1970s in radical ways that were accentuated internal regional disparities.

5. This loss and concomitant disorientation was felt in many places around the world in the 1990s; see Castañeda 1993; Holloway 2002; Jakoby 1999.

6. With *Partisan*, I engaged the contemporary politics of remembering the World War II antifascist resistance movement in Yugoslavia. Filmed in Bosnia, Croatia, and Slo-

venia during the summer of 2000, the film draws on interviews, archival footage, Yugo-slav-era feature films, popular music, and original observational footage. At the heart of the film is the response of aging antifascist veterans to the nationalists' return to power and the rehabilitation of the region's fascist past.

7. Activists in Zagreb closely identified with the killed activist Carlo Giuliani (watch "Fallen Soldier"), as was clear in the many conversations that referenced his fate.

8. Interestingly, these terms were echoed in scholarly analysis—in Brecher et al. 2000, Appadurai 2000, and Maeckelbergh 2009, respectively—and, in fact, any clear line be-tween native and analytical concepts is thoroughly blurred. As Cunningham 1999 notes, there has been extensive terminological exchange between the spheres of activism and scholarship for some time.

9. There were varying levels of self-consciousness about this subjective turn. Anar-chists, like Rimi, stressed individual and collective "autonomy" in creating the "way of life (način života) we want." Slovene Noborder organizers, on the other hand, who were in the midst of translating into Slovene Hardt and Negri's *Empire*—a book that helped make accessible the ideas of Operaismo for an English-language-reading public—spoke explic-itly of "creating a biopolitical union," so as to "struggle together to create the social condi-tions in which we create new forms of life collectively and are ourselves transformed into new kinds of people."

10. For a more formal use of this method, see Cowan 1990:137–138 and Herzfeld 2004:92–93. Herzfeld developed a visual questionnaire, which he used to elicit the inter-pretation of recorded interactions from a wide range of people. In my own experience, the editing process—I would often work with activists to edit material I had shot—can be a time when many issues that are otherwise implicit are made explicit. Questions arise about how the movement should be represented, who should be included, what should be concealed from non-participants, what are the most important political messages to con-vey, and how to imagine broader public reactions to these images. These questions are often the subjects of intense debate.

11. Activists even used my footage as evidence of police abuses, distributing some footage to the media, who, based on that material, published sympathetic accounts of Pe-ro's treatment by the police. Later, Rimi and Pero used some scenes of Pero's arrest in a music video for their band AK47.

12. For example, how should I have responded when Pero invited me to go on a "graf-fiti expedition" one evening (watch "Honk For Police")? What relationship, if any, is there between anthropological ethics and legality?

13. There is, however, a growing body of literature that productively engages the re-surgence of anarchism within anthropology; see Graeber 2002; 2004; 2009; Juris 2008; Maeckelbergh 2008; Razsa 2008; and other disciplines White and Sproule 2002; Paris 2003; Shantz 2003; Day 2004. Not surprisingly, there is a growing literature by those in law-enforcement and security studies on how to contain the threat of anarchism such as Borum and Tilby 2005 "Anarchist Direct Actions: A Challenge for Law Enforcement" in Studies in Conflict and Terrorism.

14. In fact, it is very difficult to offer any kind of numerical estimate. The network form is notoriously difficult to assess, at times bringing together a large number of participants, such as during the protests against the war in Iraq, organized largely by anarchist methods, and at other times seeming to almost disappear completely.

15. The relationship with more formal institutions of "civil society" is complicated. Many declared anarchists are actively involved in nongovernmental organizations. I address these issues in more detail in my discussion of the Croatian movement against the U.S.-led invasion of Iraq.

16. This does not mean that they are not interested in the history, literature, culture, and ideology of anarchism. Many read classic works of anarchist literature (Pierre-Joseph Proudhon, Emma Goldman, and Peter Kropotkin) as well as contemporary writers (Noam Chomsky, Bob Black, and Jason McQuinn). On more than one occasion, I witnessed heated debates that made reference to classic anarchist polemics, like that between Karl Marx and Mikhail Bakunin during the First International. In addition, many read from the history of the anarchist struggles of the Spanish Civil War. Indeed, you could buy a pamphlet on Spanish Civil War hero Buenaventura Durruti and his Durruti Column at most punk concerts in Zagreb. Some identified with the cultural legacy of anarchism, the red-and-black flag, the anarchy symbol, or anarchist punk dress, hairstyles, music, etc. This shared cultural legacy was evident when contributors to *Abolishing the Borders From Below,* an Eastern European anarchist courier with regular reports on anarchist activities throughout the region, including Croatia, gathered in Prague for protests against the expansion of NATO. They all knew the lyrics to the anarchist hymn, "A las barricadas," and sang them late into the night. But like any aspect of anarchist life, this heritage is the subject of extensive debate. Some were also critical of visible markers of anarchist identity—especially those markers of anarchist youth subculture—that they feared might isolate them from a broader public.

17. The critical discussion of riot porn did not include all the positions developed in the protracted scholarly and feminist debates surrounding pornography, such as sex-positive positions that recuperate pornography. The notion of porn remained largely one of opprobrium. Thus we find Warcry 2006, a prominent activist commentator, making a feminist critique of riot porn as a concept that inappropriately conjoins porn, which is problematic, with riots, which are viewed as resistance.

1. Grassroots Globalization in National Soil

1. For more on the rich trope of Balkan shit, see "The Balkan's Cesspool" Bjelić 2006.

2. These attacks were ordered in retaliation for "Operation Flash," which recaptured Serbian-held territory in the Western Slavonian region of Croatia. These actions became the grounds for ICTY indictments against Milan Martić, the president of RSK, and Momčilo Perišić, a JNA army chief.

3. While there was little conflict initially, a later series of conflicts, including those in Nagorno-Karabakh; South Ossetia; Abkhazia; Tajikistan; and Chechnya, produced a comparable record of human destruction.

4. Alliez and Negri 2003 argue that war is the ultimate means of turning the multitude into the people.

5. Public polling data confirmed the rise in intolerance and nationalist sentiment; see Ilišin 2002.

6. For a sustained analysis of the varieties of post-Yugoslav resistance to both Serbian and Croatian nationalism, see Jansen 2000. For more on antiwar organizing, see the groundbreaking work of Bilić 2012, which covers such phenomena as ARKzin and the Antiwar Campaign in Croatia and Women in Black in Serbia.

7. For more on the gendered dynamics around the anarchist scene in Zagreb, see Razsa 2014. Among anarchists, men who espouse anarchism but nonetheless reproduce gender inequality or homophobia are often termed "manarchists."

8. Following a prolonged accession process, Croatia finally joined the EU in the summer of 2013.

9. Even after eight months of participating in anarchist life in Zagreb, I sometimes struggled to adjust to its meandering rhythms. I left for the field following an intensive period of involvement in the Harvard Living Wage Campaign, which, though also conducted according to anarchist principles of consensus decision-making and antiauthoritarian organization, epitomized the Harvard work(aholic) ethic, which my Croatian collaborators would surely have viewed, with its preoccupation with goals, achievement, and efficiency, as obsessive.

10. This pavilion itself epitomizes the violent transformations that the twentieth century has visited on Croatia. Designed by sculptor Ivan Meštrović, the building has served in turns as an art gallery, a mosque, and a museum of the socialist revolution, before being restored to an art gallery. For a comprehensive history of the political and symbolic struggles over this square as a site of memory, see Pavlaković 2013.

11. Graffiti were often written one over the other, with commentaries, criticisms, and interventions against earlier ones; so much so that an entire book was dedicated to graffiti on the square; see Botica 2000.

12. Some graffiti were more sarcastic: "I don't need anything, everything has already been promised to me"; "Sport against social change"; "Catechism on public transportation!" "Catechism on public transportation!" was a satire of the ongoing public debate surrounding the return of Catholic education to the public school curriculum in Croatia.

13. The militia, among the most "ambitious" of the Croatian paramilitaries formed in this turbulent period, was known as HOS, an acronym it shared with the armed forces of the Independent State of Croatia (NDH), Croatia's World War II fascist puppet state.

14. Rumors even circulated that it was NDH gold from Argentina—secreted away in the days before Tito's antifascist partisans seized Zagreb—that funded the HSP; see Hockenos 2003. Most of the funding for Croatian paramilitary units was probably generated, however, in much more mundane ways, by the likes of Ottawa pizza baron turned Minister of Defense Gojko Šušak, church picnics in Frankfurt, and folk-dance ensembles from Australia; see Hockenos 2003. Šušak was pivotal in gathering (and even more pivotal in spending) the funds to build the Croatian military while the territory of the for-

mer Yugoslavia was under international arms embargo. During this period, Croatia was left facing the JNA without substantial weapons of its own.

15. The HSP paramilitary's black uniforms and black flags displayed the slogan "*Za dom spremni!*" (the Ustaša salute, "For the Homeland—Ready!"); even the "U" symbol of the Ustaša was prominent. Party President Paraga spoke warmly of the Ustaša regime—as did President Tuđman on occasion—as an expression of the oft-proclaimed Croatian thousand-year dream for a national state. The HSP went so far in its enthusiasm for the NDH that it organized a commemoration in Zagreb in 1992 of the fifty-first anniversary of the establishment of the NDH; see Senjković 2002:27.

16. Many of these trips were nothing more than organized raiding expeditions, including some within Zagreb itself. Pero said the HSP and HOS were responsible for some of the worst atrocities against civilians in Croatia. Indeed, about six weeks earlier I had seen a film in the Human Rights Film Festival in Zagreb called *Paviljon 22* by the production house FACTUM directed by Nenad Puhovski. Paid for but never screened by Croatian national television (HRT), the documentary discussed the history of those associated with HOS who were responsible for the kidnapping of Serbian civilians from their Zagreb apartments, followed by their interrogation and torture at a hall of the Zagreb Fairgrounds, Pavilion 22, and their execution at Pakračka poljana, some fifty kilometers from Zagreb.

17. The neofascist symbolism and rhetoric of the HSP—as well as the right wing of President Tuđman's own HDZ—made it easy for Serbian president Milošević and his representatives among the Serbian minority in Croatia to paint the Croatian drive for independence as a rehabilitation of the WWII NDH regime. Divisions between Tuđman and the HSP eventually became untenable, however. Paradžik, the HSP vice president and HOS leader, was machine-gunned to death in suspicious circumstances only twelve hours after publicly declaring Tuđman a "traitor" in a news conference; see *Toronto Globe and Mail,* September 25, 1991. Tuđman then dissolved HOS, either disarming or incorporating its units into the Croatian Army.

18. All three of the main "characters" eventually agreed the scene should be included in the international version of the film but not the one for Croatian film festivals.

19. In fact, there is a tradition of stealing and desecrating national flags by members of the "opposing" nation. In the first months after Croatia adopted its new republican flag—with the traditional checkerboard coat of arms that many Serbs saw as tainted by its presence on the NDH flag—there was a political war of flags in Croatia; see Senjković 2002. But flags were only one front. Perhaps most contentious was the destruction of the monuments commemorating the WWII Partisan struggle, as well as the rehabilitation of symbols that had been adopted by the NDH. Rebel Serbs, including in their eventual trials at the ICTY, regularly cited these symbolic issues as motivating their rebellion because they were convinced that, once again, they were in mortal danger from the majority Croats.

20. To be clear, AFA was not unique to Croatia, indeed AFA initiatives in Northern Europe had inspired Croatian activists to adopt and organize their own actions. The form took on a particular political urgency—and risk—however, in a territory with a history

of fascist statehood, rehabilitated by prominent figures in leading political parties, and which, only a few years earlier, witnessed armed operations against civilian populations.

21.   Changes in Croatia have included the recasting of urban topography, the social rhythms of life as entailed by holidays and commemorations, and the symbolic geography of national belonging, especially the definition of Croatia as European rather than Balkan; see Dunja Rihtman-Auguštin 2000. National, religious, and state symbols have been invented or resuscitated (Senjković 2002), and women's role in society has been redefined with traditionalist discourse; see Jambrešić-Kirin 2002; Škokić and Jambrešić-Kirin 2004. Of particular relevance, given the anarchist orientation of my closest collaborators, Croatian nationalist ideology was particularly preoccupied with statehood, and many trace some form of continuity from the medieval "Croatian" state of King Tomislav in the tenth century.

22.   Many activists complain that the club has become primarily a concert hall rather than the political and social center originally intended.

23.   For more on the sometimes jarring mix of urban and rural development, as well as the permanent state of transition Zagreb experienced in the twentieth century, see Blau and Rupnik's *Project Zagreb: Transition as Condition, Strategy, Practice* 2007.

24.   Rimi met members of Miss Helium six months earlier during AK47's own tour in Basque country.

25.   An infoshop is an anarchist bookstore and reading library that also usually serves as an activist meeting space. Ironically, one of the few nonanarchist usages of the term "infoshop" that I have encountered is the World Bank's Washington, D.C. reading room.

26.   The club was closed ten months later, in 2004, when city health inspectors discovered it had been operating for six years without toilets or public access to running water. In 2009, Attack would again secure space in the empty industrial complex Medika; see Janković and Strpić 2013.

27.   Rimi and Marin were talking about some antifascists who had been imprisoned in Poland for fighting skinheads and who were now perceived as martyrs of a sort among activists. Rimi joked that the anarchist curse should be: "May you end up on a T-shirt!" Indeed on the wall in the adjoining room, where T-shirts were printed and punk albums assembled for distribution, above a large black banner with a picture of a masked protestor with a slingshot above the words "support your local black bloc," was a photo of Carlo Giuliani, the Genoa martyr. There was a traditional black ribbon of mourning over the right-hand corner.

28.   The videos turned out to be far flung in origin and varied in content. A few are archival recordings from 1940s German denazification. Large swastikas explode into concrete dust. Others appear to have been recorded from television and then digitized in the universal digital video codec, mpeg1, which is usually used to ensure that videos will work in any program and any operating system. The first is an action by the Biotic Baking Brigade. No fewer than three big white sticky pies strike Bill Gates square in the face in the eight-second video. The second is even simpler in its narrative. Entitled "Free the Animals," the video, still bearing the watermark of Fox Television, shows a man brand-

ing a horse through a clapboard fence. In a movement that is only really discernable when you go back through the video in frame-by-frame slow motion, the horse leans a little forward and swings its leg up and between the boards. The horse kicks the man square in the stomach with such force that he simply disappears from the frame.

29. For a thorough and ethnographically informed overview of Croatia's youth subcultures, see Perasović 2001.

30. In this live version of "On the Backs of the People," the ritual burning of the HSP flag replaces the audio sample that opens the studio version. The sample features Tudman speaking to Croatian troops just after the military has recaptured Knin and expelled 150,000 Serbs from Croatian territory to end the "Homeland War."

31. Given that AK47 plays "crust," a genre of hardcore punk alternatively known grindcore or stenchcore, I could not actually make out the lyrics as Rimi belted them out. Fortunately, Rimi published his lyrics in his zine, *Borba* (The Struggle).

32. See also Baker 2010.

33. For fuller analysis of Thompson, see Baker 2010.

34. Interestingly, Rimi echoes Althusser 2001 on the importance of the "ideological state apparatuses" in producing subjectivities loyal to the state.

35. Arguably some feminist groups also maintained links throughout the war, though there were some clashes along national lines among feminists; see Bilić 2013. In any case, these links have not remained robust in the years since the war.

36. Experiments with user-generated media were, in fact, developed initially for activist needs, especially with IndyMedia, and only later commercialized in the form of YouTube and Twitter.

37. The path of this tape is itself a telling example of the tenuous yet persistent linkages that exist globally among far-flung activists. After being produced in Argentina, a box of the videocassettes was carried to the European Social Forum in Florence by French sympathizers. At the Social Forum, it was purchased by a Croatian activist and carried back to Zagreb on a bus of activists attending the forum from the former Yugoslavia originating in Niš, Serbia.

38. In this basic format, Subverzije has analogs in other radical activist scenes with which I am familiar: Kamera Revolta and VHS Guerila, held in the historic Metelkova squat in Ljubljana, or the Radical Movie Night series at Boston's Lucy Parsons Center.

39. DSM (Another World is Possible) email list posting, June 21, 2003.

40. The past decade has seen a rapid growth in European social movements' preoccupation with immigrants of all kinds. To some degree, this concern is a reaction to the central place given to immigrants by right-wing parties over the past decade. But it reflects, I believe, a theoretical and political commitment to the subversion of the biopolitics of the new "borderless Europe," which are intimately connected with the policing of the body politic, especially borders and migration.

Some have gone so far as to see migrants as the new revolutionary class. Hardt and Negri, echoing Marx on communism, write that a "specter is haunting the world and it is the specter of migration" 2000:213. In early articulations of their revolutionary subject—

the multitude—the migrant's search for a better life through movement takes a privileged place. But it is not clear if their observation responds to what movements are doing or inspires the activities of movements. The Slovene organizers of the Noborder Camp, for example, were in the process of translating *Empire* into Slovene when they organized the camp. This is one of the interesting complexities of doing research with these movements, the issue Giddens termed "the double hermeneutic." The very terms that social scientists would use to analyze the social world are the terms that are structuring that world. That is, they are the terms that social actors themselves use to make sense of their actions; see Razsa and Kurnik 2012.

41. These similarities are ironic, given that Boas developed his notion of culture with an agenda of opposing racism and intolerance.

42. This understanding of the nation was of a "natural community possessing of itself an identity . . . which transcends individuals and social conditions"; see Balibar 1991:96.

2. Uncivil Society

1. On its website, ZaMir describes itself as "a citizen association (not-for-profit organization) dedicated toward civil society development, promoting the culture of peace and the idea of sustainable development in Croatia and the region" (www.zamirnet.hr).

2. In fact, Nina and Ante are not NGO professionals. Ante teaches ethics in the Philosophy Department at the Faculty of Humanities and Social Sciences, and Nina works for INA, the national oil company. This indicates the degree to which, at least for Rimi, being an NGOnik was as much a matter of political orientation and style as employment status.

3. This does not mean, however, that there are not significant tensions, especially around the relatively opaque decision making of the WSF and the prominent role that leftist "superstars" played. So while Jadranka has attended both ESF and WSF gatherings, she is quite critical of these tendencies.

4. While the leading parties of the ruling coalition, the Social Democratic Party (SDP) and the Croatian National Party (HNS), were eventually forced to take contradictory positions on the war, distancing themselves from the invasion in some statements for a domestic public, they did not ask to have the Croatian signature removed from the Vilnius Declaration and did not restrict the coalition's access to Croatia's infrastructure and army facilities.

5. Though the scholarly literature on "transition to democracy" began with the unexpected Portuguese revolution in 1974, it was after 1989 that the subdiscipline bloomed. See Schmitter and Karl 1994 for an early critique of the universalism of this literature.

6. Gramsci wrote that totalitarian political systems aim to destroy all other organizations or incorporate them into a system of which the state is the sole regulator (1972:265). More generally, "civil society" was not, of course, only positive for Gramsci. It was, rather, one of the major obstacles to revolutionary change, a "bulwark" of liberal democracy.

7. Hearn writes, for example, that more politically right notions of civil society tend to stress private property rights and delimit the concept less clearly from the market (2001:342).

8. The case of Vojislav Šešelj exhibits perhaps an even more dramatic reversal than Tuđman's. A professor of sociology and Yugoslav political dissident in the republic of Bosnia-Herzegovina, Šešelj was arrested and charged with "counterrevolutionary activity" for his writings. His arrest and sentencing led to a domestic and international human-rights campaign for his release (Dragović-Soso 2002:57). Later, Šešelj became an infamous advocate and perpetrator of ethnic violence, on trial at the ICTY in the Hague for crimes against humanity at the time of writing.

9. And as Bilić 2012 has documented, many of the anarchists of ARK were socialized in *Svarun,* a Zagreb-based anarchist initiative of the late 1980s.

10. For more on this campaign, see Stubbs 2001.

11. For another reading of activist generations or "waves" in Croatia, see Stubbs 2012.

12. Critical journalist Srećko Pulig summed up the ideological contraints of these two variants of mainstream Croatian political rightism in a Facebook post: "The Right: Croatia for Croatians. The Left: Croatia for Those Who Can Afford Her!"

13. Again, these included anarchist punk concerts and tours, DIY publishing, alternative circuits of distribution, email listservs, trainings, reciprocal visits, planning meetings, speaking tours, and, especially, modular tactics like Food Not Bombs, Critical Mass, and the Black Bloc.

14. In part, I understand this to be a matter of people "crawling out of the woodwork," as Pero put it. In other words, people who were no longer socially, culturally, or politically active were drawn back to the streets on this occasion. I was, for example, introduced to numerous figures who were familiar names from accounts of Zagreb's anarchist punk scene in the past.

15. *Jutarnji List,* February 16, 2003:1.

16. These dynamics mimic, in miniature, the question of diversity of tactics during transnational mobilizations.

17. For a fuller analysis of the Radio 101 protests, see Kalapoš 1998.

18. *Jutarnji List,* February 16, 2003:1.

19. "Millions join anti-war protests worldwide," *BBC News Online,* 17 February 2003; or, "The Anti-War Movements—Waging Peace on the Brink of War," Karin Simonson, paper prepared for the Programme on NGOs and Civil Society of the Centre for Applied Studies in International Negotiation, March 2003.

20. There was a personal dimension to Pilsel's attacks. Activists interpreted his desire to find fault with the organization of the event as stemming from the fact that he had been spurned as a speaker for the DJR gathering.

21. Jadranka's description of these "elites" or "patriarchs" echoes Chatterjee's argument from the Indian context, in which "the new domain of civil society will long remain an exclusive domain of the elite, that the actual 'public' will not match up to the standards required by civil society, and that the function of civil-social institutions in relation to the public at large will be one of pedagogy rather than free association" (Chatterjee 2000: 44). In Zagreb, it was the 1971 generation, those who came of age politically during the student political mobilizations of this period, who were particularly patronizing in their attitudes toward both the peace activists of the 1990s and the radical activists of the 2000s.

Figures like Ivan Zvonomir Čičak and Žarko Puhovski became active in the explicitly hierarchical Croatian Helsinki Committee (HHO), adopting an air of intellectual, social, and political superiority toward activists (Stubbs 2012).

22. During the meeting, I suggested that the anarchists who participated in the flag burning should not be viewed as "anti-Americans." After all, I added, they would be just as likely to burn a Croatian flag—as I had seen them do at anarcho-punk concerts. They were, I tried to explain, critical of all states, not only the U.S. Branimir scoffed that they would never dare burn a Croatian flag in such a public setting, and he was probably right.

23. At the press conference, however, one spokesperson did go so far as to say the police should have prevented the flag burning since burning a national flag is a criminal offense in Croatia.

24. See Chapter 3 for more on these debates in the alterglobalization movement. More recently, exchanges between Chris Hedges 2012 and David Graeber 2012 about Black Bloc tactics in Occupy Oakland have demonstrated the persistence of these debates within activist circles.

25. Previously the director of Center for Civic Cooperation and an expert in training "civil society," Primorac was hired as an expert on nongovernmental organizations only weeks after he penned his attack on DJR by the Coalition Provisional Authority, which ruled Iraq after the U.S. invasion.

26. Croatian attitudes toward the U.S. are of course multivalent. As Vjera pointed out, for many in her generation, those born in the late sixties and early seventies, American popular culture, including film, literature, and music, was a great countercultural inspiration. At the same time, there were strains of hostility toward the U.S. that predated the shifts in U.S. foreign policy that occurred during the period of my fieldwork. For example, ambivalence about the liberal "Anglo-Saxon" political and economic model was sometimes also associated with the U.S. as a whole.

27. And though the Multimedia Institute was an NGO with a history of significant funding from major international as well as Croatian state sources, they openly stated their identification with the struggle against economic globalization, but expressed that they were for alternate forms of social and political globalization (Multimedia Institute 2003).

28. There were earlier calls for a boycott of U.S. grants by organizations such as the Slavonian regional environmental organization Osijek Greens (Osječki zeleni) and Stepping Out/Forward (Iskorak), a gay- and lesbian-rights organization. However, these organizations' declarations did not have the same impact as the Multimedia Institute's. Neither had received U.S. funding and, given their politics, neither seemed likely to in the near future.

29. The Multimedia Institute's statement went on to say that the Iraq war was incompatible with their mission to support the public sphere and democratic deliberation processes (Multimedia Institute 2003).

30. From what I learned of the difficult internal deliberation among the Multimedia Institute's principals, these theories do a disservice to the political commitment of the

Multimedia Institute's decision and the financial hardship it caused. It is telling, however, that these were the ways the action was interpreted by many activist observers. Rimi seemed to have almost welcomed the news, saying it confirmed what he already suspected: these NGOs were part of a global professional class for hire by the highest bidder.

31. When confronted directly about U.S.AID funding, a spokesman for B.a.B.e.—a women's organization that had been openly affiliated with Enough Wars!—replied defensively, arguing that their programs had nothing to the with questions of war, and therefore should not be tainted by their funding from the U.S. (*Večernji list,* March 2, 2003).

32. In the case of Soros funding, many of these right-wing attacks seemed to imply the lurking presence of a Jewish lobby opposed to Croatian independence.

33. While Jadranka saw these arguments as examples of the kind of self-serving "professionalism" she resented among the civil society elites, she said what particularly irritated her was the way in which Puhovski smeared activists with what she saw as a typical tactic of the right, alleging activists were antiglobalist Luddites of a sort. She was particularly shocked that he used such rhetoric against the MAMA, as those around the Multimedia Institute were in close communication with some of the most sophisticated circles of new-media critics, open-source software developers, peer-to-peer media, and tactical media activists in the world, regularly hosting them as guest lecturers and researchers at their media laboratory in Zagreb.

34. Several said that, though a figure like Primorac was clearly a "lunatic" *(luđak),* they agreed with his characterization of U.S. policy as one of cooptation.

35. This tendency is not limited to activists themselves—who are perhaps more susceptible to such polarized conceptions of politics because they are frequently targets of state repression. As Tania Li 2008 points out in her critique of *Seeing Like a State,* James Scott, one of the most eminent scholars to openly embrace anarchism, tends to see state power as "up there," looking down on ordinary life, imposing itself on an otherwise autonomous sphere.

3. "Feeling the State on Your Own Skin"

1. A new member country takes over the rotating EU presidency every six months.

2. Though the protest agenda in Thessaloniki was remote from the more routine political concerns of Zagreb's anarchists, the protests in Greece sparked a series of mobilizing tactics—like this discussion and planning meeting—that reflected existing networks, reanimated dormant links, and offered an opportunity to make new connections locally, regionally, and beyond. Indeed, as Juris 2008 points out, the period prior to summit protests is always one of intense networking activity.

3. Invitations to mass mobilizations seemed to be relatively random, dependent on chance encounters. One of the Greeks who visited from AM had a girlfriend who had spent a few nights in Vila Viktorija on her way to Italy. A Macedonian traveling with the Bicycle Caravan had found a fanzine from some Zagreb anarchists at the Swiss squat where he lived and had contacted them to alert them that the caravan was coming. Czolgolsz had their tour of Basque country coordinated by the same promoter who had orga-

nized AK47's tour. Despite the apparently coincidental character of such encounters, they happened with great consistency.

4. The Antiauthoritarian Movement describes itself not as a federation but rather an open organization that can accept many organizational forms without being committed to any one, as long as they are in accordance with its three minimum core values, namely that they are antiauthoritarian in character, adopt direct democracy, and oppose occupation by force. http://www.resistance2003.gr/en/texts/text.php?id=40

5. The protests in Seattle alone have spawned dozens of titles, e.g., Thomas 2000; Yuen et al. 2001; Rikowski 2001; Danaher 2001; Reed 2005; Paris 2003.

6. For an extensive and thoughtful analysis of the ethnography of transnational activism, see Juris and Khasnabish 2013.

7. Such critiques were disseminated widely on activist listservs and appeared in a variety of activist fora online. Most significant were assertions that protest participation requires a significant degree of privilege. One widely distributed critique was written by a Dutch activist associated with the EuroDusnie squat in Leiden, famous for its strong community organizing; see Juris 2008:221–226. He argued that it is difficult for activists from poorer countries to take part in summit protests, and this is one of the reasons that the protests are predominantly white, even though "Westerners are hit least by capitalism." Traveling across the globe from summit to summit may be very exciting, but only activists with financial means can be so mobile; see Marco 2005. A Canadian activist writing about North American radical politics perceived a similar dynamic, pointing out that women with children, people without legal citizenship, refugees, poor people, etc., face barriers to involvement in large actions away from home that younger white males with middle-class privilege do not; see Dirks 2002. In the context of transnational mobilizations, but also in smaller transnational actions like the visit of the Bicycle Caravan, or the Free Store, discussed below, the differential privilege of activists' respective citizenships was often of concern for activists.

8. Jadranka said the shared costs of gas and tolls, some seventy dollars each, represented a month's disposable income. Her small scholarship for the study of sociology was her primary source of cash along with occasional part-time work paid under the table.

9. Rimi wrote warmly of the hospitality we enjoyed in Macedonia after the grueling drive. Rimi also described the hard work of feeding hungry activists at the kitchen wagon of the Bicycle Caravan in Thessaloniki in glowing terms. He wrote with pride of the sharing of food "collectivized" from stores around the occupied university campus where we all camped. There was, in fact, a rather strict ethic of collectivism among activists. Eating, drinking, or smoking something without offering it to others present—already subject to social sanction in Croatia, Serbia, and Macedonia generally—was especially scorned among anarchists. In many respects this politicized commensality was one with deep roots in the Balkans. See, for example, Papataxiarchis 1991; Herzfeld 1987.

10. Rimi, for example, found himself cooking for the Serbs from ASI in Zagreb a few months later. Six months after that he drove the Macedonians' band on a tour of Spain in a borrowed van.

11.   Administrators, in moving through a fixed set of positions in fulfilling their colonial duties, began to discern a national pattern to this movement and mutual identification with other administrators traveling similar paths. Much more open and networked forms of subjectivity are produced by these seemingly random but nonetheless cohering webs, which are quite at odds with the ideology and practice of the nation-state container.

12.   Dupuis-Déri writes that in the context of the end of the 1990s and the beginning of the twenty-first century, it is especially antiauthoritarian militants—whether they describe themselves as "anarchists" or not—who will use it. The diffusion of this mode of organization has enlarged the influence of anarchism (2005).

13.   In a set of conclusions about what he learned in Greece, Rimi reflected critically on the decision of Croats and Slovenes to stay together as an affinity group during the protests, arguing that the passport one holds is the wrong criteria for forming an affinity group: there must be tactical agreement so that you can move as a collective through the terrain of struggle.

14.   While the affinity group was the basic building block of anarchist action, there were experiments with a number of other organizational forms in protests of this period. A cluster, for example, is an intermediate grouping of affinity groups that come together to work on a certain task, often part of a larger action. Thus, a cluster might be responsible for blockading an area, organizing one day of a multiday action, or putting together and performing a mass street theater performance. Clusters, like affinity groups, can be organized around where groups are from, an issue, or an action.

15.   Hurl 2005 describes the functioning of this model of decentralized organization in the mass direct actions against the WTO meetings in Seattle. Groups were networked together on various levels, building from affinity groups up through affiliated clusters. These were then distributed like wedges of a pie to surround the conference center. Decisions could then be made in a direct, decentralized, and flexible fashion, effectively communicating to other groups and enabling the adaptation plans as circumstances changed.

16.   These portable forms provided a global reservoir—or commons—of tactics, terms, and social knowledge, but also frequently effaced local possibilities and traditions of struggle.

17.   Besides the migration policies of "fortress Europe," activists from a variety of groups objected to the EU on other grounds. They were upset about EU participation in wars in Iraq and Afghanistan, implementation of policies on genetically modified organisms, declines in social rights and privacy, and especially the perceived pro-trade, pro-business orientation of the economic union; see Vrencev 2003; Greek Social Forum 2003; Antiauthoritarian Movement 2003.

18.   Activist Chris Hurl describes the variety of agreements reached to practically implement diversity tactics at various summits. Activists sought to ensure the coexistence of multiple strategic and tactical standpoints through the segmentation of the space-time of the event. For example, different "blocs" were exhibited in Prague, different zones or territories of protest in Quebec City, and different days of action in Genoa; see Hurl 2005. In Quebec, Prague, and Genoa, this took the form of various constituencies negotiating

in advance, often through spokescouncils, about the area of the city where each would protest.

19. The reality was, as always, far more plural and chaotic than any organizational chart, even an anarchist one, could approximate. There were always countless affinity groups (not to mention individuals) that chose to act outside the contexts of consensus decisions reached in spokescouncils. There were also other constituencies, such as small Marxist-Leninist parties or even local youth, who joined actions spontaneously who were never party to spokescouncil decisions. Even blocs that opted for nonviolent action are sometimes so outraged by the actions of the police that they become involved in more physical confrontations with the police than they had planned, as happened around the five-kilometer perimeter fence that enclosed the Free Trade Area of the Americas meetings in Quebec. To make matters more confusing, the anarchists and antiauthoritarians participating in Thessaloniki represented only one constituency in a network of networks that included various coalitions of Marxist parties, the international ATTAC network, and the European Social Forum, among others. Finally there were groups that came to play samba, block intersections, rappel down buildings and drop banners, dance in the streets, plant trees in the middle of the road, and juggle.

20. The Black Bloc, it must be recalled, is a tactic of militant protest rather than an organization with any continuity beyond the event for which it is planned. While individuals of various political persuasions might choose to participate in a Black Bloc, it was, in my experience, most popular among militant anarchists.

21. When I saw the Black Bloc in action for the first time, in Genoa, I was struck by the strange calm of the six of them when they appeared beside us, and it was immediately clear to me that I had the wrong impression about the Black Bloc. I had expected mindless hordes, the radical leftist equivalent of how I viewed football hooligans.

Two of them took up positions as lookouts for the other four. One gave another a boost up to the security camera, three meters above the ground, just to the right of the entrance. The other two set about shattering the large plate-glass window of Banca Carige with a two-meter piece of scaffolding. Five minutes later they tossed piles of paper, file cabinets, and office furniture into the street. Before making their way down a side street, they spray-painted over the façade: "Bank On This!" As an anthropologist of anarchism, I was reminded of Maddox's 2005 description of the anarchists who efficiently sacked the centuries-old churches of Aracena, burning the paintings, crucifixes, and pews.

22. Graeber 2012 has highlighted, for example, the ways that dominant representations render only activist actions as violence, while the police are simply perceived as using force, which is always already justified.

23. The question of the actual reception of these protests by observers, outside these militant direct actions, is beyond the scope of this book. Nonetheless it is important to note that participants conceived of them as forms of communication.

24. In particular, Jadranka and others were angered by the disavowal of radical activists, especially those committed to antiauthoritarianism, by relatively powerful figures who had positioned themselves as responsible representatives of the movements. She felt they had seized these roles by publicly criticizing militants. Activist anger and a sense of

betrayal at powerful "representatives" was undermining the understanding that this was a movement of movements with any commonality at all. Radicals were beginning to believe that there was an ethical core of the movement that would be sold out at first opportunity and that they had to be ready to fight.

25. The photo's very existence indicates that we were not only interested in capturing images but also aware of our own place in potential images. After all, we were primarily videotaping in Thessaloniki (when this was possible). We did not take many photos. But we had the presence of mind to have our photo taken by another activist on the roof, one of only a dozen photos we have from Thessaloniki. Another shows Pacho trying on his Soviet gas mask. We too were influenced in part by romantic images of ourselves in the midst of this struggle.

26. This is quite different from the moving image production of, say, anticolonial-period Third Cinema (Solanas & Getino 1976) or the Newsreel of the 1960s New Left, which required specialized 16mm film skills and great expense for production equipment, film processing, and editing; see Nichols 1980.

27. The iconic example of this was the Tutte Bianche (White Overalls), who developed a kind of offensive-yet-absurdist approach to the police. Wrapping themselves in Styrofoam, padding, and inflatable tires, they would attempt to bounce their way through police lines—as they did quite successfully in Prague.

28. In Greece, to a degree I had not witnessed at other transnational movement gatherings, stereotypes were central to the relationships between "international" activists and their Greek hosts. Greeks themselves, such as Kostas, an activist with IndyMedia Thessaloniki, were quick to take up these stereotypes. Kostas stated that he was worried about protests the next day because a Greek cannot hold a Molotov cocktail in his hand for more than five minutes without throwing it. As the protests developed, it seemed that many Greeks found in these stereotypes a template, even perhaps a way of managing their relationship vis-à-vis internationals. Playing the role to the maximum may have been perceived as a way of maintaining the dominant position of being the most militant activists present. Ironically, for activists with such declared antinationalist positions, they adopted a performance that, at least on the surface, owed a great deal to the imagery of the national liberation struggle of the *kleftes,* patriotic guerillas who raided against the Turks; see Herzfeld 1985. In valorizing their own outlaw status and opposition to the state, they may have been drawing on these nationalist traditions more than they realized; see Herzfeld 2004. However, these international stereotypes and their local adoption were not always accepted in this antinational setting. Rimi, for example, rejected Greek stereotypes as an excuse for any breakdown of anarchist principles, indicating that, though frequently proffered, stereotypes were not necessarily accepted. Indeed, Rimi's rejection of "Greek temperament" mirrors contemporary anthropological skepticism toward the notion of "mentality" and "national character." For activists from the former Yugoslavia, the rejection of national categories of analysis was a litmus test for being an anarchist.

29. Jadranka said that she fell in love that day and, as it turned out, not only with the feeling of teamwork, not only with insurrection. She fell in love with a Libyan communist in her affinity group. When I returned to Europe four years later to see what had be-

come of Croatian activists, Jadranka and Omar were living together in a squatted London council flat, though she would eventually return to Croatia to complete a degree in nursing.

30. Jadranka would say that such encounters allowed her to understand better how the state often appears to others who are violently marginalized, especially migrants who feel in constant danger from the state.

31. Despite the skepticism I expressed only a few days earlier, I was not immune to this experience in Genoa. When our march dissolved under police assaults, I fled the Carabinieri and found myself wedged at the base of a hill—in the very square where Carlo Giuliani would be killed an hour later. I felt the rush of emotion immediately as fellow protesters began erecting barricades—the very feelings of attachment that Holmes describes. Before I had fully considered what was happening, I was pushing a large, overturned recycling bin down the street toward the barricades, trying to erect a defensive structure with a half-dozen others.

32. Even years later, for example, when I watch the images from the Arab Spring, especially protesters struggling for control of Tahrir Square in Cairo, I feel a sense of proximity and emotional solidarity that I doubt I would have had had I not had my own glimpses of state repression of public gatherings.

33. Besides questions of gendered viewing, which I return to, these images call to mind other common associations with pornography: they have low production values, glamorize action over exegesis and narrative, and are inattentive to context.

34. For a more extensive analysis of militant engagements with video, see "Beyond 'Riot Porn:' Protest Video and the Production of Unruly Political Subjects," Razsa 2014.

35. One activist commentator made a feminist critique of riot porn, writing that,

> It's also true that most porno is made by men for men, and have (sic) a predictable and dominating view of women. Porno is a fitting representation of the intersection between Capitalism and Patriarchy. Porno may be so popular because it is a sexual outlet in the repressed and alienating modern civilization where technology 'satisfies our desires.' Riots on the other hand are the liberation of desire, and not a Capitalist product (Warcry 2006).

36. On this score, it is worth noting that, first, activists never referred to militant video as "riot melodrama" or "riot horror" and, second, what distinguishes porn from other body genres is its focus on pleasure and desire as the primary vehicles for meaning; see Williams 1991.

37. The universally shared human experience of embodiment, and the powerful affective charge carried by images of bodies, should not be ignored in and of themselves. After all, they offer one explanation for the transcultural mobility of many activist videos and, by extenstion, for the relative promiscuity of images as compared to texts.

38. While in Goričko for the camp, activists conducted impromptu inspections at several centers in the growing archipelago of immigrant detention—funded in large part by the EU. Activists had seen the desperation in the eyes of the men, women, and children

gathered in these detention centers. There were Cubans, Iraqis, Chinese, Afghanis, Roma, and Serbs, the latter of whom had been, until recently, fellow citizens of Yugoslavia for the Croatian and Slovenian activists present. Earlier in the week, six migrants had used an activist visit to their detention center as a diversion, pulling up a section of chain-link fence and escaping.

39. The direct action staged by the Noborder Campers in Slovenia cannot therefore be understood without reference to video's mimesis, to its indexicality, that is, to the direct physical link between the image recorded and the historically existing world. Far, however, from any direct or simple mimicry, the reenactment of the Woomera assault on the detention center is suspended in a web of mimetic practices clustered around, and threaded through, video's mimesis. The indexicality of the image allows us to perceive the image, and our perception is itself an active apprehension and mimesis of the world beyond us. As Taussig describes it, perception itself is mimetic, creating a "palpable, sensuous connection between the very body of the perceiver and perceived" (1992:16).

40. Alternately, other activist critics of "riot porn" have seen the genre as potentially masturbatory rather than action oriented; see Anonymous 2011.

4. "Struggling for What Is Not Yet"

1. The Give-Away Shop was operated in the Eurodusnie Squat in Leiden, the Netherlands. For more Eurodusnie and Dutch DIY politics, see Poldervaart 2001.

2. Jadranka made this statement in an episode of the documentary series, Direkt, in which she was featured ("Sapuni od magaraćeg mlijeka" 2002).

3. Marilyn Strathern has argued for a fundamental connection between modern subjects and concepts of private property. Western notions of property, she argues, necessitate the severing of a great number of pre-existing social relations and claims so that a boundary can be formed. Only then can a singular identity be effected (Strathern 1996).

4. As Vuković argues, earlier Zagreb squatting was not by and large in response to commercialization, or land speculation, like it often was in the West, but because activists felt there were no spaces for alternative culture. Indeed, in the year before Kuglana was squatted, the ruling HDZ had closed the *Dom omladine* (Youth Club), a relatively autonomous youth cultural center, and converted it to a Hard Rock Café (Vuković 2005).

5. Police tried on numerous occasions to evict the young squatters, but the complex was so large, with so many access points, that it was impossible to keep them from returning. When Pero recalled the repeated street fights against skinheads around the complex, he insisted that they worked in coordination with the police to do their "dirty work."

6. For more on the European squatting tradition, see Squatting Europe Kollective 2013.

7. For a more complete history of Zagreb squatting, see Vuković 2005.

8. When the banner was initially mounted, Gotovina was an international fugitive. Below the massive photo of the general in combat fatigues, the text read: "A Hero, Not A Criminal." Gotovina would later be captured in the Canary Islands and convicted by the International Criminal Tribunal for the Former Yugoslavia of the murder of 324 Ser-

bian civilians during Operation Storm, the final offensive of the Croatian War of Independence. In 2012, however, in a controversial decision that sent shock waves through the region, Gotovina was acquitted of all charges and released from custody (watch "Heroes and Criminals" to see a banner similar to Zadar's in front of a Veterans Association in Zagreb).

9. The staples we collect tonight are going to tomorrow's Food Not Bombs (*Hrana a ne oružje*) (watch "Food Not Bombs")—a collectively prepared vegetarian stew of scavenged foodstuffs that is served on the street. Earlier today others collected discarded produce from several of Zagreb's open-air farmers markets.

10. The "200 families programme" was Tuđman's plan to create a "HDZ nobility" that would henceforth be the motor of development; see *Christian Science Monitor* January 26, 2000.

11. Anarchists were in fact rarely alone as they picked through the bruised, wormy, and wilted vegetables left behind by Zagreb's produce vendors. Such scavenging was dominated by Zagreb's most economically marginalized, such as Roma or pensioners without family networks to supplement their meager retirement checks.

12. If anarchists' activities help bring the changed urban landscape into view, they also reveal a changed terrain of struggle. Activists appear to be meeting post-Fordism on its own terrain—the terrain of flexible labor and consumerism.

13. One could also question what motivated the strong desire on the part of viewers to identify the contradictions, even hypocrisy, of activists. Was this a strategy that allowed viewers to hold the critical force of activism at arm's length, a strategy that relieved them from having to confront their own lived contradictions? I ask because I was certainly not immune to such sentiments in my own relationship to my collaborators. My close collaboration with these activists nonetheless drove home to me just how much more willing they were than I to reorganize their way of life on the basis of their ethics—and to take personal risk to promote those ethics.

14. I heard numerous references to variants of this phrase among European activists; see Francesca Polletta's *Freedom is an Endless Meeting: Democracy in American Social Movements* (2002).

15. For a more complete discussion, see Graeber 2009. Pero, for his part, insisted that direct democracy is an end in itself. It both assumes that people are capable of running their own lives and helps them develop the skills to actually run their own lives.

16. A much more successful history of squatting overshadowed leftist or small-scale Roma squats around Zagreb: countless apartments were unofficially seized from ethnic Serbs during the 1990s. In some cases, these were the retirement apartments of JNA officers. In other cases, the seizures followed unofficial accusations of treason—including charges that one was a "weekend Četnik," in other words, that one was going to the war zone to fight with Serb irregulars. In many cases, Croatian veterans of the "Homeland War" moved into the apartments of those evicted. Like the paramilitary-led ethnic cleansing of the rural areas of Croatia—by both Serbs and Croats—this form of seizing property was treated with much more leniency and even tacit official approval.

17. The relatively well-distributed radical publication by the small Rijeka Anarchist Initiative, which I purchased at Rimi's distro, summed up the reorganization of the urban landscape in this port city, indicating that the pattern emerging in Zagreb was common in other major Croatian cities; see Riječka anarhistička inicijativa 2002:6–7.

18. Socialist Yugoslavia, unlike those states that were part of the Warsaw Pact, had an economy that included a stronger role for markets, extensive private ownership rights, and more robust personal liberties, especially freedom of movement.

19. Interestingly, activists' own claim to use the property echoed earlier socialist property concepts, and depended in part on an argument that their labor, invested in the renewal of Knowledge, should not be alienated from them.

20. Geographers have been at the forefront of this development of a critical new conceptualization of the common and commoning; see Blomley 2008; Harvey 2008; Jeffrey et al. 2011; McCarthy 2005. Michael Hardt and Antonio Negri have also placed the common at the center of their political theorizing, especially in their third collaboration, Commonwealth 2009. They do not limit the definition of the common only to the common wealth of the material world—the air, the water, the fruits of the soil, and all of nature's bounty—which in classical European political theory is sometimes claimed to be the inheritance of humanity as a whole. More capaciously, and significantly, they understand the common to include those results of social production that are necessary for social interaction and further production, such as knowledge, languages, codes, information, affects, and so forth. In the era of globalization, issues of the maintenance, production, and distribution of the common in both these senses, they argue, becomes increasingly central (2009:viii).

21. Henri Lefebvre argues not only for material access to urban space but also a renewed right to urban life (1996:158).

22. This is, it seems to me, not a right that will be guaranteed by the state, but asserted by people acting in common. Such a notion of rights is radically different than one encounters within classical liberal theory; see Razsa and Kurnik 2012; cf. Speed 2008.

23. Even their attacks on NATO, the EU, and to a degree the IMF, institutions to which many Croatians looked for an affirmation of Croatian national independence and international standing, were sometimes seen as treasonous, except among some nationalists who misunderstood these activists to be defending Croatian sovereignty. Similarly, when they had acted in solidarity with striking workers or the occasional factory occupations, they found that the nationalist orientation of many Croatian workers—or at least their appeals in this hegemonic language—rendered collaboration difficult if not impossible for these committed antinationalists.

24. Pacho and I quickly realized that this window might allow us to solve our dilemma as well. When the police arrived, Pacho discovered that he had six full DV tapes in his camera bag. We did not have time to review them all, but the oldest of these tapes, we feared, might contain the footage of the locks being changed. In any case, we worried that our footage might be seized as evidence of activist crimes. We smuggled our footage through the rear window to a friend.

5. The Occupy Movement

1. In his animated speech Žižek went so far as to declare the "holy spirit" present in the encampment, embodied in the "egalitarian community of believers who are linked by love for each other, and who have only their own freedom and responsibility" (2011) with which to pursue their goals.

2. There is a good deal of controversy around NLB, which is considered a financial pillar of the Slovene economy. The state-owned bank appeared to be on the verge of requiring recapitalization following the imposition of stricter ECB (European Central Bank) rules on cash reserves. Recapitalization with public funds was extremely unpopular in Slovenia, especially because of what are known as tycoon (*tajkun*) loans. Banks gave credit under "friendly" terms to Slovene oligarchs, which enabled these oligarchs to consolidate their ownership of important companies. With Europe's economic crisis, those loans went sour and the banks faced huge losses; see Damijan 2009. NLB, in its previous incarnation as Ljubljanska Banka, was also perceived by many in other former Yugoslav republics as having stolen deposits during the dissolution of Yugoslavia. It renamed itself Nova Ljubljanska Banka in the process; see Pirc 2006.

3. I have chosen to use the name Occupy Slovenia here because it is the one Slovenians used for their activism when comparing it with or linking it to the Occupy Everywhere Movement in the United States, which I do extensively in this chapter. Slovene activists more frequently used 15o, for the October 15 start of the encampment.

4. This quality was of particular importance for non-Slovene participants in Ljubljana. For accounts of the complicated relationship between the U.S. Occupy Movement and people of color, see Juris 2012 and Lim 2011.

5. Research, or "militant investigation," as it is often called among activists in Ljubljana, has been central to the Invisible Workers of the World, which began with collaborative research within workers dormitories in Slovenia and expanded to engagement with migrant workers in a whole variety of social settings; see Beznec 2009; Kurnik 2009; Mozetič 2009.

6. Both the Direct Social Work approach and the earlier teach-in at NLB were grounded in personal experience, which, Andrej argued, reinforced the democracy of direct action in three ways. It grounded the movement's demands in its own knowledge and experience; it ensured that it was empirical, that is, it corresponded to social reality. This, in turn, was the basis of its political authority—to speak and act on its own behalf, on what its participants knew. Finally, by speaking in terms of both personal experience and personal willingness to take action, activists avoided the abstractions of (often sectarian) analysis. For more on this distinct subjective turn among Occupy Slovenia activists, see Razsa 2012a.

7. Initially *Večer,* the third-largest Slovene daily, invited Andrej to write a personal diary of the first week of Occupy Slovenia. He proposed, instead, a collective diary, and activists who had been involved in organizing actions gathered at Social Center Rog to compose it. Activists broke into groups chronicling different days of the week. Sitting around the large central table, they then edited together and synthesized the varied voices

and emphases of the different constituencies present before publishing under the collective name of 15o. As many of the activists present had worked together previously with the Invisible Workers of the World and coauthored many collective political statements, the process of negotiating the relative weight of different perspectives and understandings was one that—though never easy—had been honed through years of common experience.

8. See the Occupy Slovenia website (http://www.15o.si/index.php/si [hereafter 15o. si]) for an extensive selection of the media coverage from this period.

9. Although networking and social-media tools were highly visible within Occupy Slovenia, few activists placed a very strong emphasis on them or saw them as playing a particularly influential role in movement dynamics; cf. Juris 2012. Most indicated that Twitter, for example, was useful primarily as a newsfeed, as a way to keep up-to-date on what was happening within movements elsewhere. Common Twitter hashtags include #Revolucija15o, #Boj_za, and #OccupyLjubljana. The Revolucija 15o Facebook group (revolucija15o@groups.facebook.com) was quite active in updating those who were already involved. Websites remained important, especially 15o.si, which hosted a wealth of photos, videos, workshop schedules, statements, press releases, media coverage, and so on. The website of the Invisible Workers of the World (http://www.njetwork.org) also hosted a great deal of content related to Occupy Slovenia.

10. The practice of deferring to those who have not yet spoken, like nominating those who have not yet done so to serve in the role of moderator, is part of a widely dispersed repertoire of antiauthoritarian procedures that help ensure that minority voices are not shunted aside and that the skills of participation are learned by all.

11. Winter in Ljubljana posed a serious challenge for the existence of Occupy Slovenia's camp. Activists managed to equip the camp somewhat for the cold by erecting large military tents with space heaters, enabling assemblies and workshops to be organized there. By the time the camp was closed in March of 2012, however, only a few people were still sleeping in the camp. The encampment, or *boj za* (the struggle for), was declared, Andrej pointed out, as a common public space whose existence depended on broader social support—not on a group of determined activist campers. The camp was therefore watched over with pickets, rotating night watches, and those attending daily workshop meetings and assemblies and not primarily through a residential presence. Andrej insisted, for example, that the camp was not meant to be a space in which activists suffer for society's ills—that is, "not to be the bad consciousness of society but to be the public hub of the movement's self-organization."

12. The financial crisis in Slovenia was felt most accutely in the construction industry. Since the crisis began, major construction firms like SCT and Vegrad had collapsed. The biggest social cost of the crisis was eventually paid by migrant workers, who made up 10 percent of the active working population and who were vastly overrepresented in construction. The massive unemployment and subsequent deportations of migrant workers from Slovenia during the crisis were the direct consequences of a migration regime that linked residency to a specific employer and therefore fostered the personal dependency of workers on employers.

13. Emil also pointed out that eviction would mean that workers would no longer be able to pursue their legal demands against the bankrupt firm. He implied that this might provide added incentive to evict them.

14. Parts of the movement in Greece, France, and Spain have embraced the notion of "indignation" in the face of the economic and political crisis, especially as a response to the calls for austerity. In some contexts—particularly France, where the popular book *Indignez-Vous!* (Hessel 2010) has been a common reference—the media has often referred to movements that started in Maghreb and came to Europe with the May 15 movement in Spain as fomented by "the indignant." As these movements erupted in large part outside of civil-society organizations and existing political organizations, the notion of "indignation" as "the raw material of revolt and rebellion" (Hardt and Negri 2009:236) seems a quite appropriate appelation.

15. Some may decide for consensus decision making, as did anarchists active in the workshop Why Go to the Elections?

16. A spokescouncil system was later organized to streamline OWS decision making about "operations," that is, the life of the encampment, and was empowered to make some decisions without seeking consensus in the general assembly, though this move was quite controversial; see Gessen et al. 2011.

17. See Kaufman 2011 for a history of consensus decision making and critical reflection on its limits.

18. Transnational networking in Europe has been persistent yet nonetheless highly volatile. Since the first cycle of alterglobalization struggles, such transnational networking has been important to Slovene activists. The activism of the late 1990s and early 2000s led to the development of the EuroMayDay, No Border, and Frassanito networks. During the campaign for migrant workers' rights that started in the framework of Invisible Workers of the World in 2007, activists based in Social Center Rog also established cooperation with a network of activists and researchers from Bosnia and Hercegovina. In the period since 2007, networking among the so-called "new generation of social centers" connected Slovenian, Italian, and Spanish social centers. The meetings in Tunisia and in Barcelona were the product of networking around university struggles in the framework of the Knowledge Liberation Front and gave birth to a new network spanning the Mediterranean called *Reseau des Luttes* (Network of Struggles). Additionally, collaboration across the border between Slovenia and Italy was reanimated in early January 2011 by common actions of Occupy Ljubljana and Occupy Trieste in the form of a playfully serious march of the "Clown Army." For more on Clown Armies, see Routledge 2012.

19. Until the recent crisis shook bond market confidence in Slovenia's capacity to repay debts, it was almost universally represented as a success story, whether in scholarship (Ramet 1998), the media (Wood 2005), or offical reports (U.S. Department of State 2011).

20. The ethnic definition of the Slovene state was initially contested by center-left members of parliament, who promoted a more civic vision of political community in which Slovenia was the state of its citizens, not the state of the Slovene nation *(narod)*. The ethnic definition of the state, as seen in the preamble of the 1990 Constitution, came to be increasingly dominant in legal and political life through the 1990s: "Proceeding

from . . . the basic and lasting right of the Slovene nation to self-determination and from the historical fact that Slovenes have, over centuries of struggle for national liberation, formed their national identity and established their own statehood, the Parliament of the Republic of Slovenia enacts the Constitution of the Republic of Slovenia"; see Hayden 1996:791. For a more complete account of the ways that initial civic articulations of Slovenian statehood were displaced by more ethnonationalist ones, as well as the ways that citizenship came to be defined in an ethnically exclusionary manner, see Zorn 2005.

21.   See Juris et al. 2012 for a fuller analysis of internal debates within the U.S. Occupy Movement about the dangers of majoritarian populism within the movement.

22.   The minoritarian as a "universal figure," as articulated by Gilles Deleuze and Félix Guattari, describes quite closely the practices of the democracy of direct action (1987:106).

23.   This strain of radical social work is linked to a tradition that stretches back to the 1980s and even 1970s, complicating the generational story we told above; see Maglajlić and Stubbs 2012:12.

24.   For a discussion of the ways that financial expropriation and the politics of austerity have led to a turn toward community-based unionism in Wisconsin, including struggles over the terms of social reproduction, see Collins 2012.

25.   There was some debate, as in occupations elsewhere, about the inevitable presence of a great number of homeless and those labeled "mentally ill" in the encampment, where shelter, heat, food, and companionship were nearly always available.

26.   See Woodward 1995 for an extensive description of the role of the debt crisis and structural adjustment in the unmaking of socialist Yugoslavia.

27.   I have described this elsewhere as the "subjective turn" in Slovene activism (Razsa 2012a). While, like Zagreb anarchists, Occupy Slovenia activists can be seen as intervening in individual and collective processes of subjectivation, they are also drawing extensively on their understandings of their own subjective positions within society through militant research.

28.   As Spinoza wrote,

> So from the fact that the power of natural things by which they exist and act is the very power of God, we can readily understand what is the right of Nature. Since God has right over all things, and God's right is nothing other than God's power insofar as that is considered as absolutely free, it follows that every natural thing has as much right from Nature as it has power to exist and to act. For the power of every natural thing by which it exists and acts is nothing other than the power of God, which is absolutely free (2002:683).

29.   Indeed, when he was asked about the future of OWS, Žižek told those assembled in New York, who had become a symbol of consensus-based direct democracy, that "participatory democracy is not the universal answer," arguing that such political forms are impotent in the face of large-scale social problems. "The left," he continued, "should also drop certain taboos: discipline, hard work, following orders on things on which we agree can be positive and important" (Žižek 2011).

30.   See Juris 2012 for more on the posteviction politics of U.S. occupations.

31. For more on the complexities of collaboration with social movements, see Edelman 2009.

32. Many would surely object that this is what good anthropology has always done—and I would not disagree. But there is a shift of degree here that is worth pausing to examine. Andrej is not particularly interested in the scholarly (and, even less, the anthropological) significance of the movements in which he is participating. He would describe himself first and foremost as an activist—even as a committed revolutionary—and his thinking about this material is, therefore, primarily political. By entering into collaboration with him and the broader Occupy Slovenia movement—and cotheorizing or co-conceptualizing this movement (Rappaport 2008:4–5) with him—I break with the ethnographer's traditional engagement with interlocutors. Andrej's analytical and theoretical voice is fully present in this text, at times entangled with and at others eclipsing mine. Traces of this ethnographic becoming are evident throughout this text, not least in the moments of instability when the ethnographer's analysis does not merge in unity but at least intermingles with Andrej's analysis and that of other movement interlocutors.

Conclusion

1. Jadranka, for example, always interested in the transnational dimension of movements, gave a workshop on student struggles in Greece and California.

2. The collectively authored *Blokada kuharica*, Studenti Filozofskog fakulteta u Zagrebu 2009, was published by the Centar za anarističke studije (Center for Anarchist Studies) and intended as a how-to guide for activists elsewhere, initially in the region, and later, in English translation as the *Occupation Cookbook*, for use elsewhere; see Markisa 2011. Additionally, the protests are documented in a feature-length film, *Blokada*, Restart 2012.

3. For a critical review of the less than fully decentralized and minoritarian structure of the plenum model promoted by Zagreb students, see Pope 2011.

4. There were several phases of student actions, but the most significant was the occupation that lasted thirty-four days in the spring of 2009 and managed to forge links with other sectors of society, including workers and even peasants, Restart 2009, that had long evaded alterglobalization activists. When students learned of peasant protests against changes to agricultural subsidies, they hosted the first peasant plenum on campus; see Horvat and Štiks forthcoming 2014. The relationship between students and peasants, especially the representatives of the dairy union, was fraught; see Restart 2009. Significantly, while making the relatively narrow—yet ambitious—single demand of free education, the Blockade helped to launch a much broader critical analysis of the contemporary Croatian social predicament. For more on the analysis of the student blockade as a social movement, see Mesić 2009.

5. For more on the ways that a continued insistence on postsocialist states' "transition" status infantilizes them vis-à-vis those Western states that ultimately are arbiters of this status, see Buden forthcoming 2014.

6. These other initiatives included worker occupations and strikes, such as the struggle for worker control of the firm Petrokemija; see Kraft forthcoming 2014; a popular

campaign against the privatization of a vast public area above Dubrovnik as a private golf resort (*Srđ je naš!*); and the so called Anti-Government Protests (*Antivladin protesti*), Facebook-organized demonstrations across Croatia demanding the resignation of the HDZ government in 2011 (Janković n.d.). Additionally, there were a number of new and ongoing self-education and theoretical efforts to develop alternative research and learning. These included the Center for Peace Studies (Centar za mirovne studije), Balkan Anarchist Bookfair, Center for Anarchist Studies (Centar za anarhističke studije), Center for Workers' Studies (Centar za radničke studije), Center for Women's Studies (Centar za ženske studije), Subversive Festival, and Balkan Forum.

7. The corresponding numbers in Slovenia are 10.1 percent and 23.8 percent (Euro-Stat 2013).

8. The neoliberal shift in development policy of the 1980s made austerity a cornerstone of the Washington Consensus; see Blyth 2013. Previously imposed on the third world by the IMF in the form of structural adjustment, these policies were brought to bear on Western Europe with the sovereign debt crisis. Yugoslavia had, of course, already been subjected to IMF-imposed structural adjustment during the 1980s; see Woodward 1995. In this regard, the recent debt crisis is a matter of continuity rather than discontinuity for ex-Yugoslavia, as Andreja Živković argues in "From the Market . . . to the Market: The Debt Economy after Yugoslavia," forthcoming 2014.

9. As for Wall Street in the more specific sense, the U.S. pressured Germany to guarantee the full debts of those states requiring bailouts, rather than allow any to default, to ensure that the chains of debt stretching back to U.S. investment firms were not broken; see Watkins 2013. More generally, financial institutions, including an array of European banks, were bailed out such that their losses became public debts and were accompanied by imposed austerity policies that meant these financial market losses were, essentially, taken from public expenditures, not least from healthcare, education, and transfer payments.

10. See also John Quiggin's *Zombie Economics: How Dead Ideas Still Walk Among Us,* 2010.

11. Rethmann has Elizabeth Povinelli 2011 and Hirokazu Miyazaki 2004 in mind as ethnographic representations of this more sustainable resistance.

#OccupyWallStreet New York City General Assembly
  2011 Declaration of the Occupation of New York City. Adopted September 29. Electronic document, http:// http://www.nycga.net/resources/declaration, accessed November 12, 2011.
Abu-Lughod, Lila
  1990 The Romance of Resistance: Tracing Transformations of Power through Bedouin Women. American Ethnologist 17(1):41–55.
Allen, Lori
  2009 Martyr Bodies in the Media: Human Rights, Aesthetics, and the Politics of Immediation in the Palestinian Intifada. American Ethnologist 36(1):161–180.
Alliez, Éric, and Antonio Negri
  2003 Peace and War. Theory, Culture & Society 20(2):109–118.
Almond, Gabriel A., and Sidney Verba
  1989 The Civic Culture: Political Attitudes and Democracy in Five Nations. Newbury Park, CA: Sage Publications.
Althusser, Louis
  2001 Lenin and Philosophy, and Other Essays. New York: Monthly Review Press.
Anderson, Benedict
  1991 Imagined Communities: Reflections on the Origin and Spread of Nationalism. London: Verso.
Anonymous
  2011 What is "Riot Porn?" Electronic document, http://www.reddit.com/r/Anarchism/help/faqs/Anarchism#WhatisRiotPorn, accessed November 12, 2012.
Appadurai, Arjun
  2000 Grassroots Globalization and the Research Imagination. Public Culture 12(1):1–19.
Arato, Andrew
  1981 Learning from Poland. Praxis International 1(2):206–211.

Aretxaga, Begoña
1997 Shattering Silence: Women, Nationalism, and Political Subjectivity in Northern Ireland. Princeton, NJ: Princeton University Press.

Baker, Catherine
2010 Sounds of the Borderland: Popular Music, War and Nationalism in Croatia since 1991. Farnham, England: Ashgate Publishing.

Balibar, Etienne
2004 We, the People of Europe?: Reflections on Transnational Citizenship. Princeton, NJ: Princeton University Press.

Balibar, Etienne, and Immanuel Maurice Wallerstein
1991 Race, Nation, Class: Ambiguous Identities. London: Verso.

Banac, Ivo
1984 The National Question in Yugoslavia: Origins, History, Politics. Ithaca, NY: Cornell University Press.

Barilar, Vesna
2000 Aktivistkinje: Kako "opismeniti" teoriju. Zagreb: Centar za ženske studije.

Bellamy, Alex J.
2003 The Formation of Croatian National Identity: A Centuries-Old Dream. Manchester, England: Manchester University Press.

Benjamin, Walter
1968 Illuminations. New York: Harcourt.

Bezinović, Igor
2012 Blokada. Factum. DVcam.

Bezinović, Igor
2009 Susret. DVD.

Beznec, Barbara
2009 Migracije in lateralni prostori državljanstva [Migration and the Lateral Spaces of Citizenship]. Časopis za kritiko znanosti 37(238):13–28.

Beznec, Barbara
2008 Once upon a Struggle. In Once upon an Erasure. Jelka Zorn and Uršula Lipovec Čebron, eds. Pp. 15–17. Ljubljana, Slovenia: Študentska založba.

Bežovan, Gojko
2001 Croatian Civil Society: On the Path to Becoming a Legitimate Public Actor. Civicus Index on Civil Society Occasional Paper Series 1(4):1–21.

Bićanić, Ivo
2001 Croatia. Southeast European and Black Sea Studies 1(1):158–173.

Biehl, João, and Peter Locke
2010 Deleuze and the Anthropology of Becoming. Current Anthropology 50(3):317–351.

Bilić, Bojan
2012 We were Gasping for Air: (Post-)Yugoslav Anti-War Activism and its Legacy. Berlin: Nomos.

Biondich, Mark
    2004 "We were Defending the State": Nationalism, Myth, and Memory in
    Twentieth-Century Croatia. *In* Ideologies and National Identities: The Case of
    Twentieth-Century Southeastern Europe. John Lampe and Mark Mazower, eds. Pp.
    54–81. Budapest: Central European University Press.
Bjelić, Dušan
    2006 The Balkans: Europe's Cesspool. Cultural Critique 62(1):33–66.
Bjelić, Dušan, and Obrad Savić
    2002 Balkan as Metaphor: Between Globalization and Fragmentation. Cambridge,
    MA: MIT Press.
Blau, Eve, and Ivan Rupnik, eds.
    2007 Project Zagreb: Transition as Condition, Strategy, Practice. Barcelona: Actar.
Blitz, Brad
    2006 Statelessness and the Social (De)Construction of Citizenship: Political Restruc-
    turing and Ethnic Discrimination in Slovenia. Journal of Human Rights 5(4):453–
    479.
Blomley, Nicholas
    2008 Enclosure, Common Right and the Property of the Poor. Social and Legal Stud-
    ies 17(3):311–331.
Blyth, Mark
    2013 Austerity: The History of a Dangerous Idea. Oxford: Oxford University Press.
Boas, Franz
    1911 The Mind of Primitive Man. New York: Macmillan.
Borum, Randy, and Chuck Tilby
    2005 Anarchist Direct Actions: A Challenge for Law Enforcement. Studies in Con-
    flict & Terrorism (28):201–223.
Bošković, Aleksandar
    2013 Yugonostalgia and Yugoslav Cultural Memory. Slavic Review 72(1):54–78.
Botica, Stipe
    2000 Suvremeni hrvatski grafiti. Zagreb: P.I.P. Naklada Pavičić.
Boyer, Dominic
    2006 Turner's Anthropology of Media and its Legacies. Critique of Anthropology
    26(1):47–60.
Brandtstädter, Susanne
    2007 Transitional Spaces: Postsocialism as a Cultural Process. Critique of Anthro-
    pology 27(2):131–145.
Brecher, Jeremy, Tim Costello, and Brendan Smith
    2000 Globalization from Below: The Power of Solidarity. Cambridge, MA: South End
    Press.
Brenan, Gerald
    1950 The Spanish Labyrinth: An Account of the Social and Political Background of
    the Civil War. Cambridge, England: Cambridge University Press.

Brentin, Dario
   2013 "A Lofty Battle for the Nation": The Social Roles of Sport in Tudjman's Croatia. Sport in Society (ahead of print):1–16.
Bringa, Tone
   2005 Haunted by the Imagination of the Past: Robert Kaplan's Balkan Ghosts. *In* Why America's Top Pundits are Wrong: Anthropologists Talk Back. Catherine Besteman and Hugh Gusterson, eds. Pp. 60–82. Berkeley: University of California Press.
Brown, David
   2014 Slovenia's stress test and whom to stress? Electronic document, http://www .pecob.eu/Slovenia-stress-test-whom-stress, accessed January 27, 2014.
Buden, Boris
   2015 (forthcoming) Children of Postcommunism. *In* Welcome to the Desert of Postsocialism: Radical Politics After Yugoslavia. Srečko Horvat and Igor Štiks, eds. Pp. 72–81. London: Verso.
Burawoy, Michael, and Katherine Verdery
   1999 Uncertain Transition: Ethnographies of Change in the Postsocialist World. Lanham, MD: Rowman & Littlefield.
Butler, Judith
   2011 Bodies in Public. *In* Occupy!: Scenes from Occupied America. Keith Gessen et al., eds. Pp. 192–195. London: Verso.
Caldwell, Melissa L.
   2012 Placing Faith in Development. Slavic Review 71(2):261–287.
Castañeda, Jorge G.
   1993 Utopia Unarmed: The Latin American Left After the Cold War. New York: Knopf.
Chatterjee, Partha
   2000 Two Poets and Death: On Civil and Political Society in the Non-Christian World. *In* Questions of Modernity. Timothy Mitchell, ed. Pp. 35–48. Minneapolis: University of Minnesota Press.
Cole, Juan
   2006 Of Crowds and Empires: Afro-Asian Riots and European Expansion. *In* States of Violence. Fernando Coronil and Julie Skurski, eds. Pp. 269–470. Ann Arbor: University of Michigan Press.
Colectivos Situaciones
   On the Researcher-Militant. Electronic document, http://transform.eipcp.net /transversal/0406/colectivosituaciones/en, accessed November 4, 2009.
Collins, Jane
   2012 Theorizing Wisconsin's 2011 Protests: Community-Based Unionism Confronts Accumulation by Dispossession. American Ethnologist 39(1):6–20.

Comaroff, Jean, and John L. Comaroff
2000 Millennial Capitalism: First Thoughts on a Second Coming. Public Culture 12(2):291–343.

Comaroff, John L., and Jean Comaroff
1999 Civil Society and the Political Imagination in Africa: Critical Perspectives. Chicago: University of Chicago Press.

Connell, Raewyn
2005 Masculinities. Berkeley, CA: University of California Press.

Coronil, Fernando, and Julie Skurski
2006 States of Violence. Ann Arbor: University of Michigan Press.

Costa-Gavras
1982 Missing. Universal Pictures. 35mm.

Cowan, Jane K.
1990 Dance and the Body Politic in Northern Greece. Princeton, NJ: Princeton University Press.

Cowan, Jane K.
2001 Ambiguities of an Emancipatory Discourse: The Making of a Macedonian Minority in Greece. In Culture and Rights: Anthropological Perspectives. Jane K. Cowan, Marie-Bénédicte Dembour, and Richard A. Wilson, eds. Pp. 152–176. Cambridge, England: Cambridge University Press.

Cowan, Jane K., Marie-Bénédicte Dembour, and Richard A. Wilson, eds.
2001 Culture and Rights: Anthropological Perspectives. Cambridge, England: Cambridge University Press.

CrimethInc. Ex-Workers' Collective
2007 No Gods, No Masters Degrees. *In* Constituent Imagination: Militant Investigations, Collective Theorization. Stephen Shukaitis, David Graeber and Erika Biddle, eds. Pp. 301–313. Oakland, CA: AK Press.

CrimethInc. Ex-Workers' Collective
2005 Recipes for Disaster: An Anarchist Cookbook. Salem, OR: CrimethInc. Collective.

Cunningham, Hilary
1999 The Ethnography of Transnational Social Activism: Understanding the Global as Local Practice. American Ethnologist 26(3):583–604.

Cunningham, Hilary
1995 God and Caesar at the Rio Grande: Sanctuary and the Politics of Religion. Minneapolis: University of Minnesota Press.

Damijan, Jože
2009 Zakaj so "tajkunski krediti" problematični? [What is Problematic about "Tycoon Loans?"]. Dnevnik.

Danaher, Kevin
2001 Democratizing the Global Economy: The Battle Against the World Bank and the International Monetary Fund. Monroe, ME: Common Courage Press.

Day, Richard J. F.
2004 From Hegemony to Affinity. Cultural Studies 18(5):716–748.
Deleuze, Gilles, and Félix Guattari
1987 A Thousand Plateaus: Capitalism and Schizophrenia. Minneapolis: University of Minnesota Press.
Della Porta, Donatella, and Herbert Reiter
2004 The Policing of Global Protest: The G8 at Genoa and its Aftermath. International Conference on Protesting and Globalization, Gothenburg.
Denich, Bette
1994 Dismembering Yugoslavia: Nationalist Ideologies and the Symbolic Revival of Genocide. American Ethnologist 21(2):376–390.
Dirks, Yutaka
2002 Doing Things Differently This Time: Kananaskis G8 Meeting And Movement Building. Electronic document, http://www.zmag.org/content/VisionStrategy/durks_kananaskis.cfm, accessed December 3, 2004.
Douglas, Mary
1966 Purity and Danger: An Analysis of Concepts of Pollution and Taboo. London: Routledge & K. Paul.
Doupona Horvat, Marjeta, Jef Verschueren, and Igor Žagar
2001 Retorika begunske politike v Sloveniji: pragmatika legitimizacije [the Rhetoric of Refugee Politics in Slovenia: Pragmatics of Legitimation]. Ljubljana: Mirovni inštitut.
Dragović-Soso, Jasna
2002 Saviours of the Nation?: Serbia's Intellectual Opposition and the Revival of Nationalism. London: Hurst & Co.
Drive-by Shooting
2002 Holiday Camp: How is Your Liberation Bound Up with Mine? tall storeez productionz. Video.
Dupuis-Déri
2005 L'altermondialisation à l'ombre Du Drapeau Noir: L'Anarchie En Heritage. *In* L'altermondialisme En France: La Longue Histoire d'une Nouvelle Cause. O. Fillieule E. Agrikoliansky N.Mayer, ed. Paris: Flammarion.
Edelman, Marc
2009 Synergies and Tensions between Rural Social Movements and Professional Researchers. Journal of Peasant Studies 36(1):245–265.
Epstein, Barbara
2001 Anarchism and the Anti-Globalization Movement. Monthly Review 53(4):1.
Eriksen, Thomas Hylland
2010 Ethnicity and Nationalism: Anthropological Perspectives. London: Pluto Press.
EuroStat
October 2013 Unemployment News Release. Electronic document, http://epp.eurostat.ec.europa.eu/cache/ITY_PUBLIC/3-29112013-AP/EN/3-29112013-AP-EN.PDF, accessed February 2, 2014.

Eyal, Gil
2003 The Origins of Postcommunist Elites: From Prague Spring to the Breakup of Czechoslovakia. Minneapolis: University of Minnesota Press.

Fabian, Johannes
1983 Time and the Other: How Anthropology Makes its Object. New York: Columbia University Press.

Ferguson, James
2010 The Uses of Neoliberalism. Antipode 41(1):166–184.

Ferguson, James
2006 Global Shadows: Africa in the Neoliberal World Order. Durham, NC: Duke University Press.

Flaker, Vito
2006 Social Work as a Science of Doing: In the Praise of a Minor Profession *In Von Der Idee Zur Forschungsarbeit: Forschen in Sozialarbeit Und Sozialwissenschaft.* Vito Flaker and Tom Schmid, eds. Wien: Böhlau Verlag.

Foucault, Michel
1977 Discipline and Punish: The Birth of the Prison. New York: Pantheon Books.

Friedberg, Jill, and Rick Rowley
2000 This is what Democracy Looks Like. Big Noise Films. Video.

Friedman, Thomas L.
1999 The Lexus and the Olive Tree. New York: Farrar, Straus & Giroux.

Fukuyama, Francis
1992 The End of History and the Last Man. New York: Maxwell Macmillan International.

Gagnon, V. P.
2006 The Myth of Ethnic War: Serbia and Croatia in the 1990s. Ithaca, NY: Cornell University Press.

Gaines, Jane
1999 Political Mimesis. *In* Collecting Visible Evidence. Jane Gaines and Michael Renov, eds. Pp. 84–102. Minneapolis: University of Minnesota Press.

Gantar, Pavel, and Tomaž Mastnak
1988 Pregled rasprava o civilnom društvu u Sloveniji. Pogledi 18(1):141–162.

Garces, Chris
2011 Preamble to an Ethnography of the People's Mic. Electronic document, http://somatosphere.net/2011/10/preamble-to-an-ethnography-of-the -people%E2%80%99s-mic.html, accessed January 12, 2012.

Gard, Sndor
2010 Focus on European Economic Integration(3):6–37.

Gessen, Keith, Carla Blumenkranz, Mark Greif, Sarah Leonard, Sarah Resnick, Nikil Saval, Astra Taylor, and Eli Schmitt
2012 Occupy!: Scenes from Occupied America. London: Verso.

Gibson, Nigel C.
   2006 Challenging Hegemony: Social Movements and the Quest for a New Human-
   ism in Post-Apartheid South Africa. Trenton, NJ: Africa World Press.
Ginsburg, Faye D., Lila Abu-Lughod, and Brian Larkin
   2002 Media Worlds: Anthropology on New Terrain. Berkeley: University of California Press.
Giordano, Cristiana
   2008 Practices of Translation and the Making of Migrant Subjectivities in Contemporary Italy. American Ethnologist 35(4):588–606.
Giovanopoulos, Christos, and Dimitris Dalakoglou
   2011 From Ruptures to Eruption: A Genealogy of Post-Dictatorial Revolts in Greece.
   In Revolt and Crisis in Greece. Antonis Vradis and Dimitris Dalakoglou, eds. Pp. 91–
   114. Oakland, CA: AK Press.
Goldstein, Daniel M.
   2012 Outlawed: Between Security and Rights in a Bolivian City. Durham, NC: Duke
   University Press.
Graeber, David
   2012 Concerning the Violent Peace-Police: An Open Letter to Chris Hedges. Electronic document, https://nplusonemag.com/online-only/online-only/concerning
   -the-violent-peace-police, accessed March 2, 2019.
Graeber, David
   2011 Occupy Wall Street rediscovers the radical imagination. Electronic document,
   http://www.guardian.co.uk/commentisfree/cifamerica/2011/sep/25/occupy-wall
   -street-protest, accessed September 26, 2011.
Graeber, David
   2009 Direct Action: An Ethnography. Oakland, CA: AK Press.
Graeber, David
   2004 The Globalization Movement and the New New Left. *In* Implicating Empire:
   Globalization and Resistance in the 21st Century World Order. Stanley Aronowitz
   and Heather Gautney, eds. New York: Basic Books.
Graeber, David
   2002 The New Anarchists. New Left Review 13(January-February):61–73.
Gramsci, Antonio
   1972 Selections from the Prison Notebooks of Antonio Gramsci. New York: Interna-
   tional Publishers.
Gray, Ros
   2012 Cinema on the Cultural Front: Film-Making and the Mozambican Revolution.
   Journal of African Cinemas 3(2):139–160.
Greek Social Forum
   2003 Vol. 2003.
Gregory, Sam
   2006 Transnational Storytelling: Human Rights, WITNESS, and Video Advocacy.
   American Anthropologist 108(1):195–204.

Gupta, Akhil, and James Ferguson
1997 Culture, Power, Place: Explorations in Critical Anthropology. Durham, NC: Duke University Press.

Hage, Ghassan
2012 Critical Anthropological Thought and the Radical Political Imaginary Today. Critique of Anthropology 32(3):285–308.

Hale, Charles R.
2006 Activist Research v. Cultural Critique: Indigenous Land Rights and the Contradictions of Politically Engaged Anthropology. Cultural Anthropology 21(1):96–120.

Hann, Chris
1996 Introduction: Political Society and Civil Anthropology. In Civil Society: Challenging Western Models. Chris Hann and Elizabeth Dunn, eds. London: Routledge.

Hardt, Michael, and Antonio Negri
2009 Commonwealth. Cambridge, MA: Harvard University Press.

Hardt, Michael, and Antonio Negri
2005 Multitude: War and Democracy in the Age of Empire. New York: Penguin.

Hardt, Michael, and Antonio Negri
2000 Empire. Cambridge, MA: Harvard University Press.

Harvey, David
2012 Rebel Cities: From the Right to the City to the Urban Revolution. London: Verso Books.

Hayden, Robert M.
2013 From Yugoslavia to the Western Balkans: Studies of a European Disunion, 1991–2011. Leiden: Brill.

Hayden, Robert M.
2000 Blueprints for a House Divided: The Constitutional Logic of the Yugoslav Conflicts. Ann Arbor: University of Michigan Press.

Hayden, Robert M.
1996 Imagined Communities and Real Victims: Self-Determination and Ethnic Cleansing in Yugoslavia. American Ethnologist 23(4):783–801.

Hearn, Jonathan
2001 Taking Liberties: Contesting Visions of the Civil Society Project. Critique of Anthropology 21(4):339–360.

Hedges, Chris
The Cancer in Occupy. Electronic document, http://www.truthdig.com/report/item/the_cancer_of_occupy_20120206, accessed June 6, 2013.

Hemment, Julie
2012 Nashi, Youth Voluntarism, and Potemkin NGOs. Slavic Review 71(2):234–260.

Hemment, Julie
2004 The Riddle of the Third Sector: Civil Society, International Aid, and NGOs in Russia. Anthropological Quarterly 77(2):215–241.

Herzfeld, Michael
  2004 The Body Impolitic: Artisans and Artifice in the Global Hierarchy of Value. Chicago: University of Chicago Press.
Herzfeld, Michael
  1993 The Social Production of Indifference: Exploring the Symbolic Roots of Western Bureaucracy. Chicago: University of Chicago Press.
Herzfeld, Michael
  1987 Anthropology through the Looking-Glass: Critical Ethnography in the Margins of Europe. Cambridge: Cambridge University Press.
Herzfeld, Michael
  1985 The Poetics of Manhood: Contest and Identity in a Cretan Mountain Village. Princeton, NJ: Princeton University Press.
Hessel, Stéphane
  2010 Indignez-Vous! Paris: Indigéne éditions.
Hirschkind, Charles
  2006 The Ethical Soundscape: Cassette Sermons and Islamic Counterpublics. New York: Columbia University Press.
Hirsi Ali, Ayaan
  2006 Europe's Immigration Quagmire. Los Angeles Times October 22:M1.
Hockenos, Paul
  2003 Homeland Calling: Exile Patriotism and the Balkan Wars. Ithaca, NY: Cornell University Press.
Holloway, John
  2002 Change the World without Taking Power. London: Pluto Press.
Holmes, Brian
  2003 Hieroglyphs of the Future. Zagreb, Croatia: Arkzin.
Holmes, Douglas, R., and George E. Marcus
  2008 Collaboration Today and the Re-Imagination of the Classic Scene of Fieldwork Encounter. Collaborative Anthropologies 1:81–101.
Holston, James
  2008 Insurgent Citizenship: Disjunctions of Democracy and Modernity in Brazil. Princeton, NJ: Princeton University Press.
Horvat, Srećko, and Igor Štiks
  2015 (forthcoming) Introduction. In Welcome to the Desert of Post-Socialism: Radical Politics After Yugoslavia. Srećko Horvat and Igor Štiks, eds. London: Verso.
Horvat, Srećko, and Igor Štiks
  2012 Welcome to the Desert of Transition! Post-Socialism, the European Union and a New Left in the Balkans. Monthly Review: An Independent Socialist Magazine 63(10):38–48.
Human Rights Watch
  1995 Croatia: The Croatian Army Offensive in Western Slavonia and Its Aftermath.

Huntington, Samuel P.
2004 Who are We?: The Challenges to America's National Identity. New York: Simon & Schuster.

Huntington, Samuel P.
1996 The Clash of Civilizations and the Remaking of World Order. New York: Simon & Schuster.

Hurl, Chris
2005 Diversity of Tactics: Coalescing as New Combinations. Ph.D. dissertation, University of Victoria.

Irvine, Jill
2007 From Civil Society to Civil Servants: Women's Organizations and Critical Elections in Croatia. Politics and Gender 3(1):7–32.

Jambrešić-Kirin, Renata
2002 Women Partisans as Willing Executioners in Croatian Popular Memory of the 1990s. In The Balkans in Focus: Cultural Boundaries in Europe. Sanimir Resić and Barbara Törnquist-Plewa, eds. Lund, Sweden: Nordic Academic Press.

Janković, Vesna
n.d. Virtual Networks and Protest in Croatia 2011.

Janković, Vesna, and Marko Strpić
2013 Mi gradimo Attack, Attack gradi nas! Zarez (353):26–27.

Jansen, Stef
2000 Anti-Nationalism: Post-Yugoslav Resistance and Narratives of Self and Society. Ph.D. dissertation, University of Hull.

Jeffrey, Alex, Colin McFarlane, and Alex Vasudevan
2012 Rethinking Enclosure: Space, Subjectivity and the Commons. Antipode 44(4):1247–1267.

Jileva, Elena
2003 Larger than the European Union: The Emerging EU Migration Regime and Enlargement. In Migration and the Externalities of European Integration. S. Lavenex and E. Ucarer, eds. Pp. 75–90. Oxford, England: Lexington Books.

Jordan, John
1998 The Art of Necessity: The Subversive Imagination of Anti-Road Protest and Reclaim the Streets. In DIY Culture: Party and Protest in Nineties Britain. George McKay, ed. London: Verso.

Junghans, Trenholme
2001 Marketing Selves: Constructing Civil Society and Selfhood in Post-Socialist Hungary. Critique of Anthropology 21(4):383–400.

Juris, Jeffrey
2012 Reflections on #Occupy Everywhere: Social Media, Public Space, and Emerging Logics of Aggregation. American Ethnologist 39(2):259–279.

Juris, Jeffrey
2005 The New Digital Media and Activist Networking within Anti–Corporate Glob-

alization Movements. The Annals of the American Academy of Political and Social Science 597(1):189–208.

Juris, Jeffrey S.
2008 Networking Futures: The Movements Against Corporate Globalization. Durham, NC: Duke University Press.

Juris, Jeffrey S., and Alex Khasnabish, eds.
2013 Insurgent Encounters: Transnational Activism, Ethnography, and the Political. Durham, NC: Duke University Press.

Juris, Jeffrey S., and Maple Razsa
Introduction: Occupy, Anthropology, and the 2011 Global Uprisings "Hot Spot." Electronic document, http://www.culanth.org/?q=node/641, accessed August 29, 2012.

Kahn, Hilary E., ed.
2014 Framing the Global: Entry Points for Research. Bloomington: Indiana University Press.

Kalapoš, Sanja
1998 The Young and a Society: An Example from Zagreb. Anthropology of East Europe Review 16(1):152–167.

Kapferer, Bruce
1988 Legends of People, Myths of State: Violence, Intolerance, and Political Culture in Sri Lanka and Australia. Washington, DC: Smithsonian Institution Press.

Kaplan, Robert D.
1993 Balkan Ghosts: A Journey through History. New York: St. Martin's Press.

Kauffman, L. A.
The Theology of Consensus. In Occupy!: Scenes from Occupied America. Keith Gessen et al., eds. Pp. 46–51. London: Verso.

Khasnabish, Alex
2013 Tracing the Zapatista Rhizome, or, the Ethnography of a Transnationalized Political Imagination. In Insurgent Encounters: Transnational Activism, Ethnography, and the Political. Jeffrey Juris and Alex Khasnabish, eds. Pp. 66–88. Durham, NC: Duke University Press.

Kirn, Gal
2013 Konture urbanih pobuna u Mariboru. Electronic document, http://lemonde diplomatique.hr/konture-urbanih-pobuna-u-mariboru/, accessed June 9, 2013.

Klein, Naomi
2011 Occupy Wall Street: Lessons from Anti-globalization Protests. Electronic document, http://rabble.ca/columnists/2011/10/occupy-wall-street-lessons-anti -globalization-protests, accessed November 11, 2011.

Kopecky, Petr, and Cas Mudde (eds.)
2003 Uncivil Society? Contentious Politics in Post-Communist Europe. London: Routledge.

Korten, David C.
2001 When Corporations Rule the World. Bloomfield, CT: Berrett-Koehler Publishers; Kumarian Press.

Kraft, Michael
2015 (forthcoming) Insurrections in the Balkans: From Workers and Students to New Political Subjectivities. *In* Welcome to the Desert of Postsocialism: Radical Politics After Socialism. Srečko Horvat and Igor Štiks, eds. Pp. 121–129. London: Verso.

Krohn-Hansen, Christian, and Knut G. Nustad
2005 State Formation: Anthropological Perspectives. London: Pluto Press.

Kropotkin, Peter A.
1902 Mutual Aid: A Factor of Evolution. New York: McClure, Phillips & Co.

Kršić, Dejan
2003 Kritika ciničkog humanizma. Zarez (102):20.

Kuper, Adam
1999 Among the Anthropologists: History and Context in Anthropology. London: Athlone Press.

Kurnik, Andrej
2014 Artikulacije potrebujejo neartikuliran bes. Časopis za kritiko znanosti (254):11–19.

Kurnik, Andrej
2011 Reševanje koncepta državljanstva na meji med gibanji in politično filozofijo [Resolving the Concept of Citizenship on the Border between Movement and Political Philosophy]. *In* Nov(o) Državljan (Stvo). Cirila Toplak and Žiga Vodovnik, eds. Pp. 165–187. Ljubljana: Založba Sophia.

Kurnik, Andrej
2009 Aktivistična raziskava, biosindikalizem in subjektiviteta migrantskih delavcev [Activist Research, Biosyndicalism and the Subjectivity of Migrant Workers]. Časopis za kritiko znanosti(238):53–65.

Kurnik, Andrej
2008 The Erased Go to Heaven. *In* Once upon an Erasure: From Citizens to Illegal Residents in the Republic of Slovenia. Jelka Zorn and Uršula Lipovec Čebron, eds. Pp. 133–144. Ljubljana: Časopis za kritiko znanosti.

Kuzmanović, Jasmina
September 23, 2013 Croatia May Sell Dollar Bond by Year-End Amid Rating Cut. Electronic document, http://www.bloomberg.com/news/2013-09-23/croatia-may-issue-dollar-bond-by-year-s-end-despite-rating-cut.html, accessed January 9, 2014.

Larkin, Brian
2008 Signal and Noise: Media, Infrastructure, and Urban Culture in Nigeria. Durham, NC: Duke University Press.

Li, Tania
    2005 Beyond "the State" and Failed Schemes. American Anthropologist 107(3):383–394.
Lim, Audrea
    2011 Chinatown is Nowhere. *In* Occupy!: Scenes from Occupied America. Keith Gessen et al., eds. Pp. 99–105.
Low, Setha M., and Sally Engle Merry
    2010 Engaged Anthropology: Diversity and Dilemmas. Current Anthropology 51(2):203–226.
MacDougall, David
    2006 The Corporeal Image: Film, Ethnography, and the Senses. Princeton, NJ: Princeton University Press.
Maddox, Richard
    1995 Revolutionary Anticlericalism and Hegemonic Processes in an Andalusian Town, August 1936. American Ethnologist 22(1):125–143.
Maeckelbergh, Marianne
    2012 Horizontal Democracy Now: From Alterglobalization to Occupation. Interface: A Journal for and about Social Movements 4(1):207–234.
Maeckelbergh, Marianne
    2009 The Will of the Many: How the Alterglobalisation Movement is Changing the Face of Democracy. London: Pluto Press.
Maglajlić, Rea, and Paul Stubbs
    2012 The Transnational Politics of Social Work in Post-Conflict and Transition Contexts: Experiences from South East Europe. British Journal of Social Work 41(6):1–28
Malkki, Lisa
    1992 National Geographic: The Rooting of Peoples and the Territorialization of National Identity among Scholars and Refugees. Cultural Anthropology 7(1):24–44.
Mansfield, Nick
    2000 Subjectivity: Theories of the Self from Freud to Haraway. New York: New York University Press.
Manoukian, Setrag
    2010 Where is this Place? Crowds, Audio-Vision, and Poetry in Postelection Iran. Public Culture 22(2):237–63.
Marco
    2005 What Moves Us? Electronic document, http://www.gipfelsoli.org/Home/Seattle_1999/4962.html, accessed June 11, 2008.
Marcuse, Herbert
    2007 The Essential Marcuse: Selected Writings of Philosopher and Social Critic Herbert Marcuse, Boston: Beacon Press.
Marker, Chris
    1978 Le Fond de l'Air est Rouge: Scènes de la Troisième Guerre Mondiale, 1967–1977. Paris: F. Maspero.

Markisa, Drago
2011 The Occupation Cookbook: Or the Model of the Occupation of the Faculty of Humanities and Social Sciences in Zagreb. London metropolitan basin of collective intelligence: Minor Compositions.

Mason, Paul
2013 Why It's Still Kicking Off Everywhere: The New Global Revolutions. London: Verso.

Massproduced video
2002 Argentina in Revolt. DVD.

Mastnak, Tomaž
1994 From Social Movements to National Sovereignty. *In* Independent Slovenia: Origins, Movements, Prospects. Jason Benderly and Evan Kraft, eds. New York: St. Martin's Press.

McCarthy, James
2005 Commons as Counterhegemonic Projects. Capitalism, Nature, Socialism 15(1):9–24.

McLagan, Meg
2005 Circuits of Suffering. PoLAR: Political and Legal Anthropology Review 28(2):223–239.

McLagan, Meg
2003 Principles, Publicity, and Politics: Notes on Human Rights Media. American Anthropologist 105(3):605–612.

Mesić, Milan
2009 Hrvatski studentski pokret: pokušaj teorijske analize. Politička misao 46(4):79–101.

Mesić, Milan
1991 Civilno društvo i postsocializam. Revija za sociologiju 22(2):307–314.

Mitchell, Don
2003 The Right to the City: Social Justice and the Fight for Public Space. New York: Guilford Press.

Miyazaki, Hirokazu
2004 The Method of Hope: Anthropology, Philosophy, and Fijian Knowledge. Stanford, CA: Stanford University Press.

Mozetič, Polona
2009 Kako su radnički domovi prošli kroz tranziciju? [how did the Workers' Dormitories Pass through Transition?]. Časopis za kritiko znanosti (238):77–92.

Multimedia Institute
2003 Statement on Refusal of U.S. Funding (press release, April 18)

Nagel, Joane
1998 Masculinity and Nationalism: Gender and Sexuality in the Making of Nations. Ethnic and Racial Studies 21(2):242–269.

Nash, June C.
2001 Mayan Visions: The Quest for Autonomy in an Age of Globalization. New York: Routledge.

Nichols, Bill
1991 Representing Reality: Issues and Concepts in Documentary. Bloomington: Indiana University Press.

Nichols, Bill
1980 Newsreel: Documentary Filmmaking on the American Left. New York: Arno Press.

Offe, Claus
1991 Capitalism by Democratic Design? Democratic Theory Facing the Triple Transition in East Central Europe. Social Research 58(4):865–881.

Ong, Aihwa
2006 Neoliberalism as Exception: Mutations in Citizenship and Sovereignty. Durham NC: Duke University Press.

Orgel, Mary Nothom
2001 Sueno Nuestro (our Dream): Anarchism and Anthropology in a Spanish Village. Ph.D. dissertation, University of Massachusetts, Amherst.

Ortner, Sherry B.
1995 Resistance and the Problem of Ethnographic Refusal. Comparative Studies in Society and History 37(1):173–193.

Papataxiarchis, Evthymios
1991 Friends of the Heart: Male Commensal Solidarity. *In* Contested Identities: Gender and Kinship in Modern Greece. Peter Loizos and Evthymios Papataxiarchēs, eds. Pp. 156–179. Princeton, NJ: Princeton University Press.

Paris, Jeffrey
2003 The Black Bloc's Ungovernable Protest. Peace Review 15(3):317–322.

Pavlaković, Vjeran
2012 Conflict, Commemorations, and Changing Meanings: The Meštrović Pavilion as a Contested Site of Memory. *In* Confronting the Past: European Experiences. Vjeran Pavlaković, Davor Pauković and Višeslav Raos, eds. Pp. 317–352.

Peck, Jamie, Nik Theodore, and Neil Brenner
2010 Postneoliberalism and its Malcontents. Antipode 41(s1):94–116.

Perasović, Benjamin
2001 Urbana plemena. Zagreb: Hrvatska sveučilišna naklada.

Perišić, Robert
2002 Užas i veliki troškovi. Zagreb: Ghetaldus optika.

Pilsel, Drago
2003 Šlamperaj i vandalizam. Novi list February 17:5.

Pirc, Vanja
2006 Pravna rešitev z neprecenljivo škodo [Legal Solution with Inestemable Dam-

age]. Electronic document, http://www.mladina.si/95165/pravna-resitev-z
-neprecenljivo-skodo/, accessed November 2, 2011.

Poldervaart, Saskia

2001 Utopian Aspects of Social Movements in Postmodern Times: Some Examples
of DIY Politics in the Netherlands. Utopian Studies 12(2):143–163.

Pope, Clara

2011 Review of the Occupation Cookbook, Or, the Model of the Occupation of the
Faculty of Humanities and Social Sciences in Zagreb. Radical Philosophy 169:84–85.

Povinelli, Elizabeth A.

2011 Economies of Abandonment: Social Belonging and Endurance in Late Liberalism. Durham NC: Duke University Press.

Prug, Toni

April 2, 2011 Croatia Protests Show Failure of Political Promise. The Guardian.

Putnam, Robert D., Robert Leonardi, and Raffaella Nanetti

1993 Making Democracy Work: Civic Traditions in Modern Italy. Princeton, NJ:
Princeton University Press.

Quiggin, John

2010 Zombie Economics: How Dead Ideas Still Walk among Us. Princeton, NJ:
Princeton University Press.

Rancière, Jacques

2006 The Politics of Aesthetics: The Distribution of the Sensible. New York: Con-
tinuum.

Rappaport, Joanne

2008 Beyond Participant Observation: Collaborative Ethnography as Theoretical Innovation. Collaborative Anthropologies 1:1–31.

Razsa, Maple

2014 Beyond "Riot Porn": Protest Video and the Production of Unruly Political Subjects. Ethnos: Journal of Anthropology 79(4):496–524.

Razsa, Maple

2012a Towards an Affirmative Ethnography. Anthropology News. September.

Razsa, Maple

2012b Images of Global Militancy: Reflections on Affect, Memory and Embodiment.
Audiovisual Thinking (4).

Razsa, Maple

2008 Mutual Aid, Anti-Authoritarianism, and Dumpster Diving: Anarchist Activism in Croatia since 2000. In Croatia since Independence: War, Politics, Society,
Foreign Relations. Sabrina P. Ramet, Konrad Clewing and Renéo Lukic, eds. Pp. 321–
342. München: Oldenbourg Verlag.

Razsa, Maple

2001 Partisan. DVD.

Razsa, Maple

1997 Balkan is Beautiful. Arkzin (87):18–19.

Razsa, Maple
1997 Crna (b)ruka na filozofskom: Balkan is Beautiful Part II. Arkzin 2 (92):24–25.
Razsa, Maple
1996 The Belgrade Circle: Intellectual Resistance to Radical Nationalism in Serbia. Bachelor's thesis, Vassar College.
Razsa, Maple, and Andrej Kurnik
2014 Occupy Slovenia: How Migrant Movements Contributed to New Forms of Direct Democracy. In Border Politics: Social Movements, Collective Identities, and Globalization. Nancy Naples and Jennifer Mendez, eds. New York: New York University Press. Pp. 206–229.
Razsa, Maple, and Andrej Kurnik
2012 The Occupy Movement in Žižek's Hometown: Direct Democracy and a Politics of Becoming. American Ethnologist 39(2):238–258.
Razsa, Maple, and Nicole Lindstrom
2004 Balkan in Beautiful: Balkanism in the Political Discourse of Tudman's Croatia. East European Politics & Societies 18(4):628–650.
Razsa, Maple, and Pacho Velez
2010 Bastards of Utopia. Documentary Educational Resources; Harvard Film Study Center Cambridge, MA. (54 min)
Razsa, Maple, and Pacho Velez
2002 Occupation: A Film about the Harvard Living Wage Sit-in. Filmmakers Library (44min) video.
Reed, T. V.
2005 The Art of Protest: Culture and Activism from the Civil Rights Movement to the Streets of Seattle. Minneapolis: University of Minnesota Press.
Reed-Danahay, Deborah
1993 Talking about Resistance: Ethnography and Theory in Rural France. Anthropological Quarterly 66(4):221–229.
Rethmann, Petra
2013 Imagining Political Possibility in an Age of Late Liberalism and Cynical Reason. Reviews in Anthropology 42(4):227–242.
Rihtman-Auguštin, Dunja
2000 Ulica moga grada: antropologija domaćeg terena. Belgrade: Biblioteka XX vek.
Riječka anarhistička inicijativa
2002 Riječki anarhistički manifesto 1:6–7.
Rikowski, Glenn
2001 The Battle in Seattle: Its Significance for Education. London: Tufnell Press.
Rivkin-Fish, Michelle
2008 "Change Yourself and the Whole World Will Become Kinder": Russian Activists for Reproductive Health and the Limits of Claims Making for Women. Medical Anthropology Quarterly 18(3):281–304.

Rivkin-Fish, Michelle
2004 Health Development Meets the End of State Socialism: Visions of Democratization, Women's Health, and Social Well-being for Contemporary Russia. Medical Anthropology Quarterly 18(3):281–304.

Robinson, Andrew, and Simon Tormey
2012 Beyond the State: Anthropology and "Actually-Existing-Anarchism." Critique of Anthropology 32(2):143–157.

Rosaldo, Renato
2009 Cultural Citizenship and Educational Democracy. Cultural Anthropology 9(3):402–411.

Routledge, Paul
2012 Sensuous Solidarities: Emotion, Politics and Performance in the Clandestine Insurgent Rebel Clown Army. Antipode 44(2):428–452.

Routledge, Paul
2003 Convergence Space: Process Geographies of Grassroots Globalization Networks. Transactions of the Institute of British Geographers 28(3):333–349.

Schmitter, Philippe C., and Terry Lynn Karl
1994 The Conceptual Travels of Transitologists and Consolidologists: How Far to the East Should They Attempt to Go? Slavic Review 53(1):173–185.

Schwarz, A. G. Tasos Sagris and Void Network, eds.
2010 We are an Image from the Future: The Greek Revolt of 2008. Oakland, CA: AK Press.

Senjković, Reana
2002 Lica društva, likovi države. Zagreb: Biblioteka etnografija.

Shantz, Jeff
2005 One Person's Garbage . . . another Person's Treasure: Dumpster Diving, Freeganism, and Anarchy. Verb 2005, 3, 1.

Shantz, Jeff
2003 Beyond the State: The Return of Anarchy. Disclosure: A Journal of Social Theory (12):87–103.

Shukaitis, Stephen, David Graeber, and Erika Biddle
2007 Constituent Imagination: Militant Investigations, Collective Theorization. Oakland, CA: AK Press.

Šimleša, Dražen
2006 Četvrti svjetski rat: globalni napad na život. Zagreb: Što čitas?.

Šimleša, Dražen
2005 Snaga utopije: anarhističke ideje i akcije u drugoj polovici dvadesetog stoljeća. Zagreb: Što čitas?

Sindbæk, Tea
2013 "A Croatian Champion with a Croatian Name": National Identity and Uses of History in Croatian Football culture–the Case of Dinamo Zagreb. Sport in Society (ahead of print):1–16.

Škokić, Tea, and Renata Jambrešić Kirin, eds.
2004 Između roda i naroda: etnološke i folklorističke studije. Zagreb: Institut za etnologiju i folkloristiku.

Smith, Jackie
2001 Cyber Subversion in the Information Economy. Dissent 48(2):48–52.

Solanas, Fernando, and Octavio Getino
1976 Towards a Third Cinema. Movies and Methods 1:44–64.

Speed, Shannon
2008 Rights in Rebellion: Indigenous Struggle and Human Rights in Chiapas. Stanford, CA: Stanford University Press.

Spinoza, Baruch
2002 Complete Works. Michael Morgan, ed. Indianapolis: Hackett Publishing Company.

Squatting Europe Kollective
2013 Squatting in Europe: Radical Spaces, Urban Struggles. London: Minor Compositions.

Steedly, Mary M.
1999 The state of culture theory in the anthropology of Southeast Asia. Annual Review of Anthropology 28:431–454.

Steen, Michael
April 26, 2013 Slovenia Struggles to Dismiss Bailout Talk: Balkan Jitters. Financial Times World News:3.

Strathern, Marilyn
1996 Potential Property: Intellectual Rights and Property in Persons. Social Anthropology 4(1):17–32.

Stubbs, Paul
2012 Networks, Organizations, Movements: Narratives and Shapes of Three Waves of Activism in Croatia. Polemos 15(30):11–32.

Studenti Filozofskog fakulteta u Zagrebu
2009 Blokadna kuharica. Zagreb: Centar za anarhističke studije.

Subcommandante Marcos, and Juan Ponce de Leon
2001 Our Word is our Weapon: Selected Writings. New York: Seven Stories Press.

Sullivan, Sian
2005 "Viva Nihilism!" on Militancy and Machismo in (Anti-)Globalisation Protest. Working Paper. University of Warwick. Centre for the Study of Globalisation and Regionalisation.

Sullivan, Sian
2004 "We are Heartbroken and Furious!" Engaging with Violence in the (Anti-)Globalisation Movement(s). Working Paper. University of Warwick. Centre for the Study of Globalisation and Regionalisation.

Tarrow, Sidney G.
2005 The New Transnational Activism. Cambridge, England: Cambridge University Press.

Taussig, Michael
   1992 Physiognomic Aspects of Visual Worlds. Visual Anthropology Review
   8(1):15–28.
Taylor, Lucien
   1996 Iconophobia. Transition (69):64–88.
Thomas, Janet
   2000 The Battle in Seattle: The Story Behind the WTO Demonstrations. Golden, CO:
   Fulcrum Pub.
Thompson, E. P.
   1971 The Moral Economy of the English Crowd in the Eighteenth Century. Past and
   Present 50:76–136.
Thrift, Nigel
   2000 Afterwords. Environment and Planning D: Society and Space 18(2):213–255.
Tocqueville, Alexis de
   1994 Democracy in America. New York: Knopf.
Todorova, Maria
   1997 Imagining the Balkans. Oxford, England: Oxford University Press.
Traynor, Ian
   2004 U.S. Campaign behind the Turmoil in Kiev. Electronic document, http://www
   .theguardian.com/world/2004/nov/26/ukraine.usa, accessed November 11, 2008.
Trouillot, Michel-Rolph
   2003 Global Transformations: Anthropology and the Modern World. New York: Pal-
   grave Macmillan.
Turner, Terry
   1997 Human Rights, Human Difference: Anthropology's Contribution to an Emancipatory Cultural Politics. Journal of Anthropological Research 53(3):273–291.
Turner, Terry
   1992 Defiant Images: The Kayapo Appropriation of Video. Anthropology Today
   8(6):5–16.
Velikonja, Mitja
   2009 Lost in Transition: Nostalgia for Socialism in Post-Socialist Countries. East European Politics & Societies 23(4):535–551.
Verdery, Katherine
   2003 The Vanishing Hectare: Property and Value in Postsocialist Transylvania.
   Ithaca, NY: Cornell University Press.
Verdery, Katherine, and Caroline Humphrey
   2004 Property in Question: Value Transformation in the Global Economy. Oxford,
   England: Berg.
Vertov, Dziga
   1929 Man with a Movie Camera.
Vrencev, Ljubiša
   2003 One World. Vol. 2003.

Vuković, Eugen
    2005 Skvotiranje u Zagrebu? 04 Megazin 2(10):21–25.
Warcry
    2005 The Linguistics of "Riot Porn." Electronic document, http://news.infoshop.org
    /article.php?story=200605291506131, accessed November 12, 2012.
Watkins, Susan
    2013 Vanity and Venality. London Review of Books 35(16):17–21.
Wedel, Janine R.
    1994 U.S. Aid to Central and Eastern Europe, 1990–1994: An Analysis of Aid Mod-
    els and Responses. *In* East-Central European Economies in Transition: Study Papers
    Submitted to Joint Economic Committee. Pp. 299–335. Washington, DC: Congress
    of the United States.
White, Robert, and Warren Sproule
    2002 Don't Mourn the Death of Theory, Organize! Globalization and the Rhizome of
    Anarcho-Syndicalism. Continuum Journal of Media & Cultural Studies 16(3):317–
    333.
Williams, Linda
    1991 Film Bodies: Gender, Genre, and Excess. Film Quarterly 44(4):2–13.
Williamson, J.
    1989 What Washington Means by Policy Reform: Institute for International Eco-
    nomics. Washington DC.
Wood, Nicholas
    2005, April 19 Ambitious Slovenia Plans for Prosperity. The International Herald
    Tribune News:5.
Woodward, Susan L.
    1995 Balkan Tragedy: Chaos and Dissolution After the Cold War. Washington, DC:
    Brookings Institution.
Ye'or, Bat
    2005 Eurabia: The Euro-Arab Axis. Madison, NJ: Fairleigh Dickinson University
    Press.
Yuen, Eddie, Daniel Burton-Rose, and George N. Katsiaficas
    2001 The Battle of Seattle: The New Challenge to Capitalist Globalization. New York:
    Soft Skull Press.
Žilnik, Želimir
    2009 Stara škola kapitalizma. video.
Živković, Andreja
    2014 (forthcoming) From the Market . . . to the Market: The Debt Economy after Yu-
    goslavia. *In* Welcome to the Dessert of Post-Socialism: Radical Politics after Yugosla-
    via. Srečko Horvat and Igor Štiks, eds. London: Verso.
Žižek, Slavoj
    2011 Occupy Wall Street. Electronic document, http://www.imposemagazine.com
    /bytes/slavoj-zizek-at-occupy-wall-street-transcript, accessed December 28, 2011.

Žižek, Slavoj
    2007 Resistance is Surrender. Electronic document, http://www.lrb.co.uk/v29/n22
    /slavoj-zizek/resistance-is-surrender, accessed January 12, 2012.
Žižek, Slavoj
    1994 The Metastases of Enjoyment: Six Essays on Woman and Causality. London:
    Verso.
Zorn, Jelka
    2005 Ethnic Citizenship in the Slovenian State. Citizenship Studies 9(2):135–152.
Zorn, Jelka, and Uršula Lipovec Čebron, eds.
    2008 Once upon an Erasure. Ljubljana, Slovenia: Študentska založba.

INDEX

MAPLE RAZSA

is Associate Professor of Global Studies at Colby College. A documentary filmmaker, his work includes *Bastards of Utopia* (2010) and *Occupation: A Film about the Harvard Living Wage Sit-In* (2002; both with Pacho Velez).